The Christians

For Karen

The Christians

An Illustrated History

TIM DOWLEY

LION

A Lion Book
an imprint of
Lion Hudson plc
Wilkinson House, Jordan Hill Road,
Oxford OX2 8DR, England
www.lionhudson.com
ISBN 978 0 7459 5225 3

First edition 2007
10 9 8 7 6 5 4 3 2 1 0

A catalogue record for this book is available
from the British Library

Typeset in 11/14pt Iowan Old Style
Printed and bound in Singapore

Contents

Introduction 7

1. The Jesus Movement 8
JESUS OF NAZARETH 9
Paul of Tarsus 11
APOSTLE TO THE GENTILES 13
Early growth 14
POLYCARP IS MARTYRED 15
Christianity's second century 16
THE CATACOMBS OF ROME 17
Constantine I 18

2. People of the Book 19
CHRISTIAN MUSIC 20
The making of the New Testament 22
Understanding the Bible 27
The Bible and the Reformation 30
Critical thinking 32
KARL BARTH 34

3. Defining Belief 36
Right teaching 37
A state religion 39
AUGUSTINE OF HIPPO 42

4. Rome and the Papacy 44
The Bishop of Rome 44
Gregory the Great 47
A YEAR IN THE LIFE:
THE CHURCH'S CALENDAR 48
Pope versus emperor 51
THE ANGELIC DOCTOR 53
The Great Papal Schism 55
Renaissance popes 56

5. Monks and Monasteries 58
Antony in the desert 59
SIMEON STYLITES 60
Western monks 62
Ireland 64
Monastic reform 67
New orders 70
New holiness 73
CHRISTIAN MYSTICS 74
Revolution 76
Monasticism today 76

6. The Eastern Church 78
Justinian I 78
Iconoclasm 79
The Great Schism 80
ORTHODOX ICONS 80
THE EASTERN ORTHODOX YEAR 81
What is truth? 82
FASTING AND PRAYER 83
Orthodoxy today 84
Russian Orthodoxy 84
The Third Rome 86
The October Revolution 88

7. Jihads and Crusades 91
The Prophet 91
The Caliphs 92
The Crusades begin 94
THE CALL TO CRUSADE 95
THE TEMPLE MOUNT, JERUSALEM:
JEWISH, CHRISTIAN, MUSLIM 97
The Turkish threat 100

8. Reformations 101

Corruption and decay   102

Humanism   103

Reform   104

Germany and the
Lutheran Reformation   105

MARTIN LUTHER   106

Calvin's Geneva   109

JOHN CALVIN   110

After Luther   111

The English Reformation   113

THE CHURCH OF ENGLAND   114

9. Catholic and Radical Reform 118

The Catholic Reformation   118

IGNATIUS LOYOLA   120

The Radical Reformation   121

THE JESUITS AND MISSION   122

SEPARATISTS AND BAPTISTS   124

THE QUAKERS   127

10. Heart and Soul 129

Pietism   129

THE AGE OF REASON   130

JOHN WESLEY   132

Methodism   134

HYMNS   134

The First Awakening   136

EVANGELICALISM   136

Methodism in America   137

THE SALVATION ARMY   139

Methodism worldwide   140

Pentecostalism   141

First Pentecostals   143

Pentecostalism worldwide   144

11. Post-Reformation Rome 148

The Council of Trent   148

The French Revolution   148

The American Revolution   149

THE INDUSTRIAL REVOLUTION   150

John XXIII   151

MOTHER TERESA   153

12. To the Ends of the Earth 155

Paul the missionary   155

The Jesuits   155

Protestant missions   156

A BAPTIST COBBLER   157

CHARLES DE FOUCAULD   160

Winning the world   161

A troubled century   162

A worldwide faith   164

BILLY GRAHAM   166

That they all may be one   169

Grassroots unity   170

Further Reading   171

Index   172

Picture acknowledgments   176

Introduction

Paradoxically, it is much more difficult to write a short book than a long one. A long book leaves room for lengthy narratives, for careful qualifications, for much detail and inclusiveness. A short text demands concision, difficult selections and dangerous generalizations, and inevitably leaves huge gaps.

It would be almost impossible to write a comprehensive chronological account of the development of Christianity in just 176 pages. And even if it were feasible, it would inevitably include topics or developments important to scholars but of little obvious relevance to the modern general reader. Instead, I have based this book around a topical outline – generally chronologically organized – of subjects that both illuminate and explain the genesis and growth of Christianity, but that also continue to influence or perturb the church and society today, whether they have longer or shorter 'roots' in Christian history.

I am painfully aware of omissions, overgeneralizations, and contentious areas that require several pages to untangle instead of a sentence or two to summarize. I have tried to be irenic without glossing over problems, to be objective without being uninvolved and, where possible, to allow the words of protagonists to speak for them.

Having previously edited several large popular histories of Christianity, it has been a challenging but exhilarating task to sketch some vital episodes in the story of the Christians. I am grateful to the publishers that this book is well illustrated, as in many instances a carefully selected painting, photograph or illustration can express powerfully what it might take pages of print to communicate.

My thanks to Morag Reeve for inviting me to write this book, and to Catherine Sinfield for her meticulous editing.

TIM DOWLEY

CHAPTER 1

The Jesus Movement

Sometime around the year AD 36, some uneducated peasants in Jerusalem, in the Roman frontier province of Judea, started shouting from the contemporary equivalent of soapboxes that their erstwhile leader, a former carpenter from the north named Jesus, who had recently been savagely executed – nailed to a wooden cross – had returned from the dead. These men and women seemed to be a tiny splinter-sect of Judaism, a religion the Romans generally considered barbaric and a nuisance disproportionate to their numbers.

Yet only three centuries later, the beliefs first voiced in such an inauspicious manner were pronounced a legal religion by the Roman emperor Constantine, and not long after became established as the official religion of the Roman empire.

Beginning with the extraordinary confidence of this tiny group of Jews that their leader, Jesus of Nazareth, was alive again, over the following centuries their faith spread far and wide and developed increasingly clearly defined belief systems and

patterns of worship, a distinctive set of morals and a collection of sacred writings. A sociologist would say it was in the process of developing from a group to a sect to an institution.

A scattering of Jews

From various sources, including Christian and a few secular writings as well as still-accumulating archaeological evidence, we have a relatively clear idea of how this 'Easter faith' first spread geographically. Since the initial believers were Jews, the fact that they were mainly based in the Jewish holy city of Jerusalem helped in the earliest transmission of their beliefs to others. The pilgrimages of first-century Jews to Jerusalem at the times of the great Jewish festivals might be compared with the pilgrimages of Muslims to Mecca today for the Hajj. At festival times, Jerusalem overflowed with Jews from far and near, the population possibly quadrupling in size.

With the coming of the Roman empire and the *Pax Romana* – the long-term absence of major conflict across the Mediterranean world imposed by Roman might and organization – the movement of peoples around that world had become much easier and safer. Most Jews were concentrated in Judea, Syria, western Asia Minor (modern Turkey) and Egypt, where Alexandria had become a major centre of Greco-Jewish culture. But Jews had also begun to move westwards, beyond Italy, and also eastwards, through the

Jesus of Nazareth

Around the year 4 BC a son was born to Mary, a young Jewish woman from Nazareth. He was named Jesus. Mary's husband, Joseph, a carpenter (or possibly mason), was an older man.

We know very little about Jesus' life over the next thirty years. But when he reached the age of thirty, he preached a controversial sermon in the Jewish synagogue in Nazareth, using the words of the Jewish prophet Isaiah:

The Spirit of the Lord is upon me,
For he has appointed me to preach Good News to the poor.
He has sent me to proclaim
That captives will be released,
That the blind will see,
That the downtrodden will be freed from their oppressors,
And that the time of the Lord's favour has come…

Then he said 'This Scripture has come true today before your very eyes!'

Not surprisingly, his words offended – even scandalized – his neighbours: this was the local carpenter's son, yet his words implied that he was ushering in a new age, and he might even be the longed-for Messiah.

After this landmark sermon, Jesus left his hometown for Capernaum, on Lake Galilee, where he gathered a group of twelve male followers. These 'disciples' were mostly ordinary people: fishermen, craftsmen, traders and a tax-collector. Together this group travelled the country, as Jesus demonstrated in words and actions what the new 'kingdom of God' he spoke about was to be like: not the liberation of Israel from Roman military oppression, but a new start for people – a new birth and a new creation, beginning now and coming to fruition in the future.

Many people followed Jesus for his vivid teaching – he used memorable stories about farming and everyday life to teach spiritual truths – and for his healing. Cripples were cured, the disturbed made whole, even the dead raised; and his followers recounted that Jesus also exhibited extraordinary power over nature, for instance by calming storms and walking on water.

Yet, paradoxically, Jesus shunned publicity. When his followers thought they had recognized who he really was, he told them to keep quiet. He did not want people to get the wrong idea and follow him from wrong motives.

But Jesus' radical teaching also made him many enemies. The Jewish 'zealots' – freedom-fighters dedicated to overthrowing the Romans – called for violence, not love. The Jewish religious leaders (particularly the Pharisees, criticized by Jesus for reducing God's law to a catalogue of petty and oppressive rules) attacked him for associating with social outcasts: tax-gatherers who collaborated with the occupying Roman authorities, prostitutes and the ritually 'unclean'.

By the third year of Jesus' mission, the Jewish religious hierarchy had had enough. When Jesus went up to Jerusalem to celebrate the Passover festival, his enemies seized the opportunity they had been awaiting. Jesus was arrested in a garden (Gethsemane) outside the city under cover of darkness, tried overnight for blasphemy by the religious court, and taken before the Roman prefect, Pontius Pilate, accused of sedition. After the Jerusalem mob had exerted their influence on Pilate, Jesus was condemned to Roman execution on a cross on the hill Golgotha, just outside the city walls of Jerusalem. There could hardly be a more humiliating and cruel form of judicial killing.

But for Jesus' disciples, the crucifixion and subsequent entombment of Jesus were not the end. The Gospels recount that his apostles and women followers found Jesus' tomb empty three days later, and describe their various encounters with a risen Lord. His disciples began to assert that Jesus is present with his people in all times and places. From such beginnings sprang a world-changing movement, and from such obscurity came one of the world's best known, most often portrayed and probably most misunderstood religious leaders.

Parthian empire, while for some time a sizeable migrant community had been established in Babylonia (in modern Iraq).

The Day of Pentecost

Many devout Jews 'of the dispersion' – those scattered throughout the Roman empire and beyond – considered it their religious duty when possible to travel to Jerusalem for one of the great annual festivals – *Seder* (Passover), *Yom Kippur* (the Day of Atonement) or Tabernacles (Harvest). (The Gospel of Luke tells the story of Joseph and Mary bringing the adolescent Jesus to Jerusalem from Nazareth in the north for the festival of Passover.) It was the festival of Pentecost that gave the first believers in the risen Jesus an opportunity to explain publicly their new faith and to proselytize not only fellow Jews resident in Jerusalem, but also the hordes of pilgrims visiting for the festival.

The book of Acts, Luke's narrative of Christian beginnings, written as a companion document to his Gospel, recounts an unforgettable story of a huge concourse of Jews – 'Parthians, Medes and Elamites; residents of Mesopotamia, Judea and Cappadocia, Pontus and Asia, Phrygia and Pamphylia, Egypt and the parts of Libya near Cyrene; visitors from Rome… Cretans and Arabs' – hearing the apostles inexplicably speaking in foreign languages – the foreigners' vernaculars. After listening to a stirring public speech by the ex-Galilean

fisherman Peter, more than three thousand people were evidently persuaded to adopt the fledgling faith and be baptized – possibly in the Jewish ritual baths known as *mikvaot*, some of the remains of which have been excavated in Jerusalem near the site of Herod's Temple, the focus of Jewish worship.

The pouring out of the Holy Spirit on the apostles, illustrated in a thirteenth-century manuscript of the psalms.

Presumably a proportion of these converts were drawn from the foreign pilgrims, who took back home with them their new-found beliefs, possibly discussing them with fellow pilgrims on the road and with fellow worshippers at their synagogues back home in Parthia, Media, Elam and the rest. So came about the first wave of proselytization, conversions and baptisms.

Opposition

The next major expansion of 'the Way', as it was sometimes called in the early years, came – not for the last time in the history of Christian growth – through the oppression, antagonism and persecution that the believers soon began to experience in and around Jerusalem, the centre of orthodox Judaism. The Pharisees and their allies thought they had seen off the threat of Jesus of Nazareth by having him judicially murdered by the Roman governor; they did not now intend to stand idly by while his disciples made preposterous and apparently blasphemous claims about his subsequent resurrection and claim to divinity. The Jewish authorities therefore began to arrest and execute some of the leaders of what they regarded as a new and heretical sect.

After the execution by ritual stoning outside a city gate of the Christian leader Stephen on a charge of blasphemy, many of the apostles fled Jerusalem and started to preach elsewhere. Philip, Peter and John all made numbers of conversions in Samaria, some fifty miles north of Jerusalem, and a prohibited area for 'strict' Jews. (Jesus once told a parable in which he used a Samaritan to illustrate the kind of person least likely to be regarded as a 'neighbour' by a Jew.) The coastal plain of Judea was also visited by Peter and Philip, who preached as far north as the Roman provincial capital and strategic port of Caesarea Maritima.

Philip even met on the road, and brought to the new faith, a court official from Ethiopia, whom we assume took his novel beliefs back with him to Africa.

Many other fleeing believers scattered to towns and villages throughout Judea and Galilee, and even as far north as Antioch – the third largest city in the Roman empire – and Damascus in Syria. Though spreading the faith may not have been their primary purpose in leaving Jerusalem, the 'followers of the Way' appear to have succeeded remarkably in communicating their beliefs and enthusiasm to neighbours, acquaintances and even strangers throughout Palestine, Syria and beyond.

PAUL OF TARSUS

Paul of Tarsus provides a significant example of persecution paradoxically helping the Christian movement to grow. After his dramatic conversion from ardent and active opposition to Jesus' followers, Paul became an equally fiery disciple for Jesus Christ. Having spent three years in Arabia, possibly preparing himself for his future mission, he re-emerged fervent with his new purpose. He was determined to preach not only to Jews but also to non-Jews – a project that was unacceptable to many of the Jewish believers in Christ in Jerusalem.

Paul first preached in Damascus, where he had previously intended to persecute believers, and then courageously in his hometown of Tarsus in Asia Minor. From the metropolis of Antioch, where believers were first – possibly mockingly – called 'Christians', Paul set out with a Cypriot named Barnabas and a young protégé named John Mark on his first major proselytizing expedition. The three travelled initially by sea to Cyprus, then to Asia Minor where, to Paul's enduring chagrin, Mark seems to have deserted.

Paul's strategy was normally to preach first in the local Jewish synagogue, but never to hide his purpose of converting non-Jews too. As they visited different towns, Paul and his companions encountered a mixed reception. When they performed miraculous cures, they were sometimes treated as Greco-Roman divinities; on the other hand, their preaching often caused such offence to traditional Jews that they were assaulted and thrown out for their pains.

Three expeditions

Paul and Barnabas' first, arduous, journey – presumably on foot – established a network of new churches in Asia Minor, and it was probably these communities that Paul addressed later in his important letter to the Christians of Galatia – 'Galatians' – today a section of the New Testament in the Bible. The journey completed, the two pioneering missionaries returned to Antioch, after which there followed an acrimonious council in Jerusalem, where the mission to non-Jews was debated fiercely, with Paul meeting stiff criticism from leaders of the Jerusalem believers.

Paul now set out on a second journey, re-visiting the towns and new believers of Asia Minor, and attempting to buttress the faith of these converts made on his previous tour. He was accompanied this time by a man named Silas (or Silvanus) as, despite Barnabas' wishes, he refused to give the errant John Mark a second chance.

At the town of Lystra Paul was joined by a young Greek named Timothy, who assisted him in his work in Galatia. At Troas – not far from the site of ancient Troy and the narrow channel of the Dardanelles, which divides Asia Minor from Macedonia – Paul responded to a vision in which a man pleaded with him to cross over to Macedonia, and for the first time entered Europe with the Christian message. He

proceeded to win followers of 'the Way' in Thessalonica, Philippi and Athens, the cultural capital of the Hellenistic Mediterranean world, where he also confronted sophisticated opposition and derision.

Paul seems often to have converted and baptized women. In Greek society, Jewish women had

A man small in size, with meeting eyebrows and a rather large nose, bald-headed, bow-legged, strongly built, full of grace.

SECOND-CENTURY DESCRIPTION OF PAUL

The dramatic conversion of Paul *en route* for Damascus, painted by Caravaggio (1573–1610).

I have been crucified with Christ: I myself no longer live, but Christ lives in me.

PAUL

greater freedom than in Judea and Galilee and were permitted to attend synagogue alongside the men, so enabling them to hear Paul's preaching firsthand. Hence Paul's notable success in finding women converts. It fulfilled his belief that the Jesus faith was for all – Jews and Gentiles, men and women.

Paul next settled for eighteen months in nearby Corinth, a city that seems to have been notorious for its sexual immorality. It was probably from here that Paul began to write and send out letters to the churches he knew, which now form a major segment of the New Testament. His letters were intended to encourage, teach, greet and sometimes correct the small believing groups he had gathered throughout Asia Minor and Achaia (Greece).

Paul then undertook a third lengthy proselytizing expedition, during which he also spent two years working at his trade of tent-making in the major cult-centre of Artemis, Ephesus, while helping to build up the significant Christian community there.

Apostle to the Gentiles

Vilified by some as a misogynistic kill-joy and perverter of the simple gospel of Jesus of Nazareth, others celebrate the spiritual vitality, breadth of vision and intellectual vigour of Paul of Tarsus. This one-time rigorous Jew set out to take the message of Christ to the whole of the ancient world, and he wrote a mini-library of long, sometimes challenging and often theologically complex letters to encourage and instruct the first Christians. Claiming that in Christ there was no distinction between Jew and Gentile, slave and freedman, man and woman, he helped break down barriers of prejudice.

Saul (his original name) was born a Roman citizen into a strict Jewish family in Tarsus (in modern south-east Turkey). He trained as a Pharisee and became a fanatical opponent of the new sect that sprang up to follow Jesus. In around AD 33, Saul set out from Jerusalem for Damascus with a commission to suppress the group of Christians that had sprung up there. *En route*, he was blinded by a vision, and claimed he heard a voice saying, 'I am Jesus, whom you are persecuting.' The humbled enthusiast made an about-turn and now threw all his energies into serving Christ.

After three eventful and dangerous missionary journeys, Paul returned to Jerusalem, where his Pharisee enemies provoked a riot in the courtyard of Herod's Temple that brought about his arrest and eventual trial before the Roman authorities. Paul finally appealed to Caesar, and was transported by merchant vessel to Rome for this appeal to be heard. Despite being shipwrecked off the island of Malta, Paul ultimately arrived in Rome, where Christianity had already taken root. He remained a prisoner there for two years, but may also have travelled to Spain with his Christian message. Paul was probably executed during the persecution of Christians instigated by the emperor Nero following the Great Fire of Rome in AD 64.

Although converted by a mystical vision of Christ, Paul believed the Christian faith to be rooted in the historic facts of the gospel – in Jesus' words and acts. Radically, Paul rejected the idea that non-Jewish followers of Jesus had to observe the law of Moses in such matters as male circumcision and the observance of feasts – a view which initially met fierce opposition, particularly from conservative Jewish believers in Jerusalem, who recognized that the logical consequence of Paul's position would be a split between the Jewish synagogue and the infant church. Nevertheless Paul believed fervently that Jewish and Gentile believers could unite in worship and fellowship.

Paul's teaching became formative for later Christian theology, particularly in the writings of such scholars as Augustine of Hippo and John Calvin.

Not by Paul alone...

It is important to emphasize that Paul was far from being the only pioneer missionary. Because we have such a full account of his exploits left by his travelling companion, the physician Luke, Paul's achievements have often erroneously become almost synonymous with early Christian growth.

Growth was also occurring in many other parts of the Roman empire – and outside its borders – the result in part of the proselytizing of Peter and other apostles, but also of unnamed believers passing on their new-found faith. It is almost certain that the apostle Peter preached the Christian message in Rome, and introduced Gentiles and Jews there to the faith. (We know that a Christian community already existed there when Paul wrote them a long and closely argued theological letter – the New Testament 'letter to the Romans' – before ever he visited the city.) Similarly, the apostle John preached and taught successfully over a long period in the province of Asia Minor. And a strong tradition has it that John Mark (the deserter from Paul's first journey) helped found the church in the major city of Alexandria, Egypt, and that Thomas, who had initially doubted Jesus' resurrection, took the Christian faith as far as India.

EARLY GROWTH

By the end of the first century, the church had already spread widely across the Mediterranean world. Asia Minor – modern Anatolia, or western Turkey – with its large, settled Jewish population, was the area of greatest early growth for the church, as Hellenistic Jews converted to Christianity. (When we use the word 'church' in this period we don't mean an ecclesiastical building of some description, but a local community of Christian believers. As we shall see, buildings came later, when Christianity became legal and official within the empire.)

John the Divine received his apocalyptic Revelation – recorded in the last book of the New Testament – while in penal exile on the Aegean island of Patmos, off the west coast of Asia Minor. In Revelation, 'seven churches' were sent messages of encouragement and/or criticism, and all were located in western Asia Minor. There were also important Christian communities in Italy – in Rome itself, in the port of Puteoli and around the Bay of Naples. Names of cities with

> *If the Tiber reaches the walls, if the Nile does not rise to the fields, if the sky does not move or the earth does... the cry is at once 'the Christians to the lion!'.*
>
> TERTULLIAN

Christian martyrs in the Circus Maximus, Rome, based on the painting *The Christian Martyrs' Last Prayer* (1883) by Jean-Leon Gerome.

Christian inhabitants are of course known to us from the New Testament, but also from contemporary correspondence. The Christian writer Ignatius tells of churches in Magnesia and Tralles, and other authors report a Christian presence in Alexandria, Egypt, the home of another of Paul's aides, Apollos.

An important church outside the borders of the Roman empire was located at Edessa (modern Urfa), capital of the little kingdom of Osrhoene, in northern Syria. Local legend has it that the little-talked-of apostle Thaddaeus (known in the local vernacular as 'Addai') brought Christianity to the city. Edessa was later incorporated into the Roman empire – but more importantly, it was a trading city situated on the great mercantile route to Persia and the Orient. Inevitably, Christian belief also travelled this road to the east, at least as far as Persia, which in this period was ruled by the Parthians. We know that Christianity was well established in Persia by the end of the second century.

Persecuted and misunderstood

As we have already noticed, a vital element in the early growth of Christianity was persecution and martyrdom. Initially, persecution was sporadic and local. The first concerted effort to eliminate Christians came after the razing of much of Rome by fire during the reign of the notorious emperor Nero in AD 64. Nero (reigned AD 54–68) scapegoated the Christians for the conflagration (which some believed he caused himself), and many believers were savagely tortured and burned, at least in and around Rome itself.

The emperor Domitian (reigned AD 81–96) also harshly persecuted both Christians and Jews. Christians were hated for a variety of reasons. They were dubbed 'atheists', since they would not take part in emperor-worship. They were accused of obscene practices – for example, the words 'eating Christ's flesh', used during the Eucharist (the Lord's Supper), were taken literally as evidence of cannibalism. And Christians were also held to be disloyal to the secular state, since they claimed a higher loyalty to God.

Even the emperor Marcus Aurelius (reigned AD 161–80), an educated Stoic, encouraged harsh measures against the Christians, whom he neither understood nor tolerated. Among those martyred during these various persecutions were important Christian leaders such as the apostles

Polycarp is martyred

Polycarp was Bishop of Smyrna (modern Izmir, Turkey) and a Christian leader in Asia Minor during the reign of the emperor Antoninus Pius. Around AD 155 he was arrested and taken to the local stadium to answer to the Proconsul:

'So [Polycarp] was brought before the Proconsul, who asked him if he was the man in question. He agreed, and the Proconsul tried to persuade him, urging him, "Have respect to your old age," and so on, in the customary way, "Swear by the genius of Caesar; repent; say, 'Away with the Atheists'."

[The Romans regarded the Christians as atheists as they did not acknowledge the pagan deities.]

'Then Polycarp turned a serious face on the crowd of lawless pagans gathered in the stadium, and, beckoning with his hand, said, "Away with the Atheists!"

'The Proconsul continued insisting and saying, "Swear, and I will release you; revile Christ."

'And Polycarp said, "Eighty-six years have I served him, and he has done me no wrong; how then can I blaspheme my King who saved me?"'

Polycarp continued to refuse all pressures to deny his faith or his Lord, and was eventually burnt at the stake in the stadium at Smyrna.

Paul (c. AD 64) and Peter (c. AD 68 – by improbable tradition, crucified upside-down), as well as Clement of Rome (AD 100), Justin Martyr (AD 165) and the venerable Polycarp of Smyrna (c. AD 156).

CHRISTIANITY'S SECOND CENTURY

In its second century, Christianity crossed the Mediterranean from Italy to the Roman province of North Africa and, later in the century, to Egypt. By the mid-second century, still only a little over a century after the death and resurrection of Jesus, flourishing churches existed in almost every Roman province between Syria in the east and Rome in the west. Such cities as Ephesus, Antioch and Corinth

continued to be particularly influential, and previous Christian gains were consolidated, as Christianity began to spread from its urban strongholds to the surrounding countryside.

The churches in the major cities of Alexandria and Carthage (in North Africa) grew, as did those beyond the eastern borders of the empire. The church in Gaul (modern France) also dates from this time, receiving the faith through Greek colonists who settled there. Early Gallic centres of Christianity included southern towns such as Vienne and Lyons.

The spread of Christianity by AD 300
By the end of the third century, the complexion of the Christian world had changed radically. In the aftermath of

> *They were in the habit of meeting on a certain fixed day before it was light, when they sang an anthem to Christ as God and bound themselves by a solemn oath not to commit any wicked deed...*
>
> PLINY ON THE
> EARLY CHRISTIANS

The early spread of
Christianity.

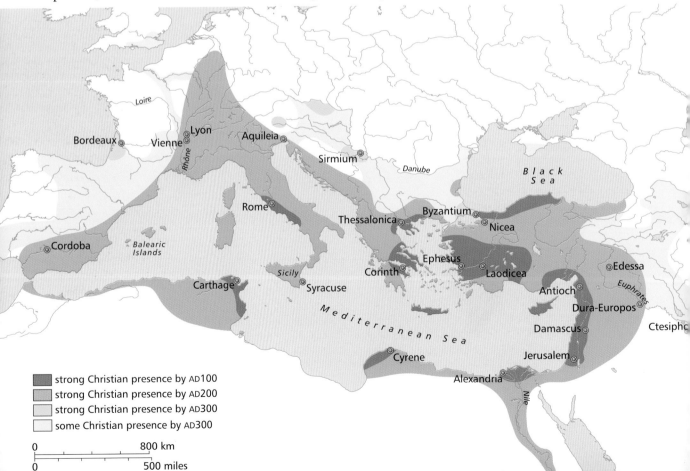

strong Christian presence by AD100
strong Christian presence by AD200
strong Christian presence by AD300
some Christian presence by AD300

0   800 km

0   500 miles

the failed Jewish revolts against Rome in AD 66–70 and AD 132–35, Christians and Jews had increasingly gone their separate ways, and Christianity had become more and more a religion of the Gentiles. By this time, Christians formed a majority of the population in the Roman provinces of Africa and Asia Minor, while there was also much Christian activity in Spain; and the church had continued its expansion westwards, now penetrating as far as Roman Britain.

Early in the fourth century, as a result of the preaching of Gregory the Illuminator, King Tiridates declared Christianity to be the religion of Armenia, making the country the first in the world to adopt Christianity officially. By the early fifth century, the Armenian monk and theologian, Mesrop Mashtots (AD 360–440), had created an Armenian alphabet and the translation of the Bible into the vernacular began.

The church at Rome, associated with Paul and Peter in New Testament times, was by now beginning to dominate, and to become the unacknowledged centre of Christianity – in place of Jerusalem – partly as a result of being the capital of the empire.

More persecution

Alongside the continuing expansion, empire-wide persecution of Christians recurred periodically during the third and early fourth centuries. Thousands of Christians died for their faith; relatively few recanted. Insecure emperors such as Decius (reigned AD 249–51) and Valerian (reigned AD 253–60) used persecution to divert attention from their own political failures. During Decius' brutal attacks on the church, Origen, a great theologian of the Eastern church, was first tortured and then exiled from his home city of Alexandria. So impressive were

The catacombs of Rome

In the first century, Rome's Christians had no cemeteries of their own. If a family owned land, they buried their relatives there, otherwise Christians used the same cemeteries as the pagans. The apostle Peter was probably buried in the great public necropolis on Vatican Hill, and Paul in a necropolis on the Via Ostiense.

During the first half of the second century, Christians in Rome started to bury their dead underground, which is how the catacombs began. The catacombs were by Roman law inviolable, but had to be built outside the city walls. Many catacombs started as family tombs; but their newly converted Christian owners often did not restrict them to family members, but opened them up to brothers and sisters in their faith. Gradually, these burial areas grew larger. For instance, the church of Saint Callixtus administered a large catacomb cemetery complex for its community.

When persecution of Christians ended in the Roman empire at the beginning of the fourth century, Christians became free to build churches and buy plots of land. Nevertheless, the catacombs continued to function as

Christian cemeteries until the beginning of the fifth century.

The barbarian invaders systematically destroyed many monuments, including catacombs. Between the late eighth and early ninth centuries, the popes ordered saints' and martyrs' relics to be removed from the catacombs to city churches, for safety. As a result, the catacombs were no longer visited; and in the course of time, landslides and vegetation hid their entrances, so all trace of them was lost. During the late Middle Ages, most people never knew that they had ever existed.

Re-exploration of the catacombs started with Antonio Bosio (1575–1629), nicknamed the 'Columbus of subterranean Rome'. In the nineteenth century, Giovanni Battista de Rossi (1822–94), sometimes considered the father of Christian archaeology, undertook a systematic exploration of the catacombs, particularly the well-known Catacomb of Callixtus.

The head, hand and other fragments from a colossal statue of Constantine I, 'the Great', Palazzo dei Conservatori, Rome.

many of those who died for their faith that they were more than replaced by new converts. As the Christian thinker Tertullian famously and pithily observed: 'The blood of the martyrs is seed.'

The last sustained persecution of Christian believers came under the emperor Diocletian (reigned AD 284–305). After this, the tide turned. The emperor Galerius announced that Christianity was officially to be tolerated; and, as we shall see, Constantine finally granted Christians religious freedom.

CONSTANTINE I

By the time of the emperor Constantine I (reigned AD 312–37), the Christian church had become firmly established in the Roman empire. Constantine declared himself a convert to Christ, and in AD 313 proclaimed the faith a recognized religion of the empire, on a level with all other state religions. Later, in AD 395, the Christian emperor Theodosius (reigned AD 378–95) recognized the majority position of Christianity in the Roman state by making this faith the only official state religion.

Apostolic Christianity had 'conquered' a mighty empire. In other parts of the world, particularly in Africa and western Asia, the church had also made significant progress. However, time would show that, in its rapid sweep across the Greco-Roman world, Christianity had lost something of its original zeal and much of its early simplicity.

CHAPTER 2

People of the Book

Most Christians' beliefs are based, to a greater or lesser extent, on the Bible. But what exactly is the Bible? How did it come into being? And what happened when its authenticity or authority was challenged?

As Christian communities and churches formed, believers began to ask questions concerning their faith. What precisely did Jesus do and say? Who was to lead the church? What should they do if church members erred or changed their ideas? How should they celebrate the Eucharist? How should they relate to the civil authorities?

As long as the apostles were alive, such questions could be referred to them; those who had lived alongside Jesus were happy to retell his teachings and acts and try to apply his sayings to life issues. But as that first generation died, it became increasingly vital to preserve a more permanent record of these teachings.

The Jewish Scriptures

Of course, the Jews already had their holy books – they are often known as 'people of the book'. All Jews acknowledged the five 'Books of Moses' – also known to them as 'the Pentateuch' (five scrolls) and the *Torah* (Hebrew for 'the Law'): the books of Genesis, Exodus, Leviticus, Numbers and Deuteronomy (the first five books of what Christians now call the 'Old Testament').

The *Torah* is displayed for a Jewish boy's *barmitzvah* at Jerusalem's Western Wall.

The Pentateuch told the story of creation and the beginnings of humanity, and then narrated the genesis of the Jews, the epic journey of the patriarch Abraham from Ur of the Chaldees to Canaan – 'the Promised Land' – the liberation of the Hebrews from Egyptian slavery and forced labour at the Exodus, and their receiving the Ten Commandments on Mount Sinai as the basis for their religion and ethics. The Pentateuch was complete and recognized by all Jews by the fifth century BC.

Probably by around 165 BC two other sets of Hebrew sacred texts, known by the Jews as the 'Prophets' (*Nebhiim*) and the 'Writings' (*Kethubim*), had also been recognized and organized into discrete collections. The 'Writings' included books narrating the history of the Jews in Canaan, the rise and fall of Israelite kings and foreign empires, the ebb and flow of the Jews' faithful worship of Yahweh, the Jewish deity (see, for example, the books of 1 and 2 Samuel, 1 and 2 Kings, 1 and 2 Chronicles), as well as Hebrew poetry, wisdom and hymns (see, for instance, the books of Psalms, Proverbs and the Song of Songs). The 'Prophets' consisted of the messages of Jewish

Christian music

Spiritual songs
Jesus and his disciples would probably have sung the psalms from memory. Early Christians probably continued to sing the psalms as they were sung in the synagogues. The apostle Paul encouraged the church at Ephesus to speak to each other 'in psalms and hymns and spiritual songs, singing and making melody in your heart to the Lord'. He also encouraged the church at Colosse to teach each other with 'psalms and hymns and spiritual songs'.

Plainsong
Following the fall of the Roman empire, monks seem to have regarded musical instruments as fit only for secular music – for minstrels and troubadours. They opted for the human voice alone. Several traditions of plainchant – a form of monophonic, unaccompanied singing – developed in the Christian West: Celtic chant in Ireland, Mozarabic chant in Spain, Gallican chant in France, Ambrosian chant in Milan, Beneventan chant in Benevento and Old Roman chant in Rome.

Gregorian chant
In time, Gregorian chant became the musical basis for most of the Western church. Named after Pope Gregory, who in around AD 600 is supposed to have collected and codified the tunes used in worship, it included music for every service and every festival of the church. Many of the tunes are much older; some come from classical Greece and Rome, others from Jewish synagogue worship.

During the Carolingian Renaissance there appeared the first manuscripts of Gregorian chant with musical notation, paving the way for the development of medieval church music. By the twelfth century, Gregorian chant had effectively supplanted all other traditions of Western plainchant, except for the Ambrosian chant of Milan and Mozarabic chant in a handful of Spanish chapels.

The texts chanted were mostly from the Bible, and mostly in Latin (although there are some Greek texts such as *Kyrie eleison* and *Hagios Theos*). Plainsong has no harmony and its tunes cover only a narrow span of notes; its rhythm is the rhythm of the words chanted. Yet heard in a vast cathedral it resonates magnificently. Plainsong is still widely used in the Eastern churches – in the chants of the Byzantine, Syrian and Armenian churches, for example. Gregorian chant has been sung unchanged for more than a thousand years.

Some chants are simple enough to be sung by regular congregations; others are more complex and best left to the choir. Historically, every cathedral in the West had its own specially trained choir, led by a choirmaster and organist who was normally a composer too. Performing standards gradually improved and the music became increasingly elaborate. In the great churches, performances at the major festivals became more like concerts than services – so much so that one pope tried to ban performances by exhibitionist musicians.

prophets – denouncing godlessness and sometimes looking forward to a golden age and the coming of the Messiah (see, for example, the books of Isaiah, Jeremiah and Ezekiel). Some were lengthy, others very short.

So, by the beginning of the Christian period, the collected books of the Jewish Hebrew Bible as we know them today existed. They were not bound up into a single volume, but written out painstakingly on bulky and much-valued sets of scrolls. (Even today Jewish synagogues keep scrolls of their Scriptures in a special cupboard known as 'the ark'.)

At a Jewish council at Jamnia in AD 85, it is possible that the twenty-seven books of the Hebrew Bible, which Christians now know as the Old Testament, were authoritatively recognized. However, this council was not making novel decisions about Jewish holy books so much as confirming general Jewish opinion. A few 'apocryphal' books such as Ecclesiasticus, Tobit, Judith, Susanna and 1 and 2 Maccabees were rejected; sometimes known as the Deutero-canonical books, these are today accepted, but accorded less authority, by some Christian churches.

The mass

Elaborate church music continued to be written, particularly settings of parts of the mass. These were played in the great churches and cathedrals for special church festivals. But inevitably they had the feel of 'performances', calling for large choirs and orchestras. Today they are often performed in concert halls by professional musicians.

Among the greatest settings of the mass are those by J. S. Bach (*Mass in B Minor*), Haydn, Mozart, Beethoven (*Missa Solemnis*), Schubert and Bruckner. Some of the profoundest settings have been of the Mass for the Dead, or Requiem Mass; for instance, Verdi's operatic *Requiem*, Berlioz's *Grande Messe des Morts* and Benjamin Britten's *War Requiem*. Johannes Brahms also wrote a moving Protestant *German Requiem* based on passages from the Bible.

Christian music has not been confined to the church and concert hall. Noisy, colourful processions feature in Christian festivals throughout the world, especially in Spain and Latin America. Similar events attracted the people of medieval Europe. In addition to music from choirboys, religious plays were performed – at first inside church buildings, later outside in the market-place. Craftsmen's guilds would mount their own plays, and music was provided at appropriate points: for the angel choirs, the trumpet on Judgment Day, and so on.

Oratorios

Not all sacred music was composed for performance in church. The oratorio, invented in the mid-seventeenth century, was a close relative of opera. Like opera, it has a dramatic form, and uses arias, recitatives, choruses, ensembles and orchestral music; but it is not staged. The earliest oratorios were by the Italian composer Carissimi, and the first significant German examples were by Schütz. J. S. Bach's passions, *St John* and *St Matthew*, are similar in form, and retell the events of Holy Week – but were always intended for church performance.

The best-known English oratorios are by Handel: *Saul*, *Theodora*, *Samson* and above all *Messiah*. During the writing of the celebrated 'Hallelujah Chorus' for *Messiah*, the overwhelmed composer declared: 'I did think I did see Heaven opened and the Great God himself.'

Almost equally famous are Joseph Haydn's *Creation*, an oratorio in the classical style, and Mendelssohn's more romantic *Elijah*. Twentieth-century English composers contributed such works as *The Dream of Gerontius* (Edward Elgar), a setting of a long poem by Cardinal John Henry Newman, and *Belshazzar's Feast*, (William Walton).

THE MAKING OF THE NEW TESTAMENT

At first Christians passed on their faith by word of mouth ('oral transmission') – the apostles recounting what they had seen and heard of Jesus' ministry, believers listening carefully and remembering word for word. In a largely non-literate culture, memorization was a powerful and ubiquitous tool: such epics as Homer's *Odyssey* and *Iliad* were probably initially passed on using the same processes.

However, as the Christian movement expanded, and as the apostles who had known Jesus began to die, a more permanent record of the beginnings of the faith was required. The earliest Christian writings we possess are probably some of the letters the missionary apostle Paul wrote to various Christian communities during the AD 50s.

Paul's letters

Paul's earliest letter was probably that written to the believers in Galatia – the letter (or Epistle) to the Galatians – around AD 50. This was followed by two letters addressed to Christians in Thessalonica (1 and 2 Thessalonians) and two to Corinth (1 and 2 Corinthians – though there were probably originally at least three letters to Corinth). Paul's closely argued letter to the Romans probably dates from around AD 55/56, while his letters to the churches at Ephesus, Philippi and Colosse were probably written by Paul from jail in Rome between AD 59 and 61.

Paul also wrote to a slave-owning Christian called Philemon, asking him to forgive Onesimus, an escaped slave of his who subsequently converted; and at the end of Paul's life he sent more personal letters to his aides, Titus and Timothy.

From early on, the church seems to have regarded Paul's letters as normative – presumably both because of their important content, setting out and defining Christian beliefs and practices, and from his credentials as an apostle and one who claimed to have encountered the risen Christ.

The Gospel-makers

In addition to Paul's corpus of letters, there are of course the four Gospels – obvious foundation documents for Christianity. These are not biographies of Christ in the modern sense, but a written record of the remembered words and actions of Jesus. Scholars have devoted years of inconclusive debate to identifying the sources, authorship and dates of writing of these vital texts.

Traditionally attributed to the apostles Matthew and John, Luke the physician, and Paul's co-worker, John Mark, the Gospels undoubtedly contain first-hand knowledge and experience of Jesus. Often known as the 'Synoptic Gospels', Matthew, Mark and Luke share considerable amounts of material, making it possible to view them in three parallel columns – 'synoptically' – enabling the reader to note similarities and differences of content and wording. John's distinctive Gospel is at pains to demonstrate the eternal truth of Jesus' mission, while equally maintaining its historical factuality. It is suggested that the writer combined Jewish and Greek terms and ideas in a new way.

Tentative dates of writing could be around AD 64 for Mark's Gospel, AD 65 for Luke and Matthew, and around AD 95 for John's Gospel, though all these dates can be, and often are, challenged.

Other early Christian writings proved more controversial; there were arguments over whether such books as the letters of Jude and

James, the anonymous letter to the Hebrews, and the Revelation of John could and should be included among the set of basic texts for the young church. This was in part because their authors were not necessarily drawn from the original apostles, and in some instances because part of the contents or emphases of these books seemed questionable. Some churches also set value on additional Christian writings – for example, the *Shepherd of Hermas*, the *Letter of Barnabas*, and *1 Clement* – none of which have found a permanent place in the Christian Bible.

Varieties of Christian belief

By the second century AD, with Christian communities spread widely around the Mediterranean, it was becoming clear that Christians were not all speaking with one voice. Various movements, splinter-groups, emphases and viewpoints arose – some of them considerably shocking to their Christian brothers and sisters.

A movement calling itself the 'New Prophecy' ('Montanism' to its opponents) arose in the second half of the second century. Its leader, the eponymous Montanus, claimed to have received a new revelation, which appointed him leader of the church until Christ returned. The movement, which had both ascetic and ecstatic strands, spread rapidly from Phrygia, in modern Turkey, throughout the Roman empire, even developing structures and hierarchies parallel to those of the existing church. Montanism also celebrated secret mystical rites, which made it appear not dissimilar to pagan religions such as Mithraism, with its male initiations and rites of ordeal.

As early as the first century, other believers had claimed it was impossible to accept that the Christ was truly human: they claimed instead that Jesus merely *appeared* to be human, and that his coming was a temporary visitation by God, rather than an incarnation in human form. Those holding this view were labelled 'Docetists', from the Greek verb *dokeo*, meaning 'to seem' or 'to appear'.

In the following century, another group of Christians began to take a directly opposite view, regarding Jesus as *solely* a human being. Known as 'Ebionites' (a transliteration of the Hebrew word *ebyon*, meaning 'poor'), they seem to have been Jewish believers who repudiated Paul and Gentile Christianity.

The largest of these controversial groups within early Christianity was the multi-faceted movement known as 'Gnosticism'. The term 'Gnostic' (from the Greek word *gnosis*, meaning 'knowledge') refers to someone who knows, and the movement centred on acquiring secret, mystical knowledge. There was no single Gnostic sect, but a number of groups and movements holding overlapping ideas. Common to all of them was the dualistic belief that the physical world is totally evil, while the spiritual world is good. Hence they thought that salvation required escape from the evil, physical world into the divine, spiritual world. Since the Gnostics believed all matter to be evil, clearly Jesus could not be both God and human. To resolve this dilemma, some Gnostics claimed Jesus was not material, while others made a distinction between Jesus the man and the spiritual Saviour who spoke through him.

Many Gospels

As anyone following the debate about *The Da Vinci Code* and the *Gospel of Judas* will know, there are reams of Christian or purportedly Christian writings dating from the first centuries AD that are unknown to the modern New Testament. The Gnostics in particular produced a large number of such writings: some of the better-known of these include the Gnostic *Gospel of Thomas* (which collected together various alleged sayings of Jesus to fit the Gnostic worldview), the *Gospel of the Twelve Apostles*, *The Story of Joseph the Carpenter* and the *Gospel of Pseudo-Matthew*. Some of these writings survive in their entirety, others only in fragments. The many 'Gospels' claim to describe aspects of Jesus' ministry and life: but a cursory reading, and comparison with the four New Testament Gospels, quickly shows them to consist largely of pious and often far-fetched tales and to be mainly fictitious.

The early church recognized Matthew, Mark, Luke and John as different in kind from the other alleged 'Gospels'. Nevertheless these documents are useful in illuminating the beliefs of the wide variety of Christian communities in the early years of the faith, and in showing where these beliefs differed from what began to be regarded as correct or 'orthodox' Christian belief.

Marcion

Amid this growth of varying interpretations and practices, some Christians began to see it as essential to define much more clearly the historic, 'true' Christianity. Something of a crisis faced the church when an extremist Gnostic named Marcion, a wealthy ship-owner who came to Rome in AD 140, drew a black-and-white contrast between what he saw

A page from the Gnostic *Gospel of Thomas* discovered at Nag Hammadi, Egypt.

as the morally reprehensible God of the Old Testament and the ethical God of the New Testament. Having summarily dismissed the entire Old Testament, he then proceeded to reject also the Gospels of Matthew, Mark and John, leaving a severely stunted Christian scripture consisting of edited-down versions of Luke's Gospel and Paul's letters. Marcion was attempting to remove all traces of Judaism from his scriptures, and set up a sect of his own that persisted for many years.

With such men as Marcion making their own selection from Christian texts, it was obviously increasingly important to be clear which Christian writings actually were definitive. Just as physical weights and measures are standardized by comparison with a single reference set of measures, Christian writers such as Irenaeus (c. AD 130–200) and Tertullian (c. AD 160–225) held that it was possible to list a set of Christian writings that defined and delimited the faith, and which should act as measuring instruments for discerning the validity of other ostensibly Christian writings and traditions.

Essentially, the books of the New Testament were identified and recognized by their content, and specifically by their witness to the gospel as taught by the apostles. However, they were accepted as part of the 'canon' of Scripture also as the outcome of discussion and a gradual consensus arrived at by believing Christian communities. (The word 'canon' derives from a Hebrew word for a 'reed', which was sometimes used as a measuring rod. It also has the sense of a list or index – probably derived from the series of marks on a measuring rod – hence the 'list' of books reckoned to be Scripture.)

Significantly, Tertullian also wrote of 'two testaments that are divine Scripture', referring to the Old and New Testaments. By this time, Christians had apparently come to regard the apostolic writings as on a par with the Jewish Scriptures.

Bringing it all together

As early as the end of the first century AD, the four Gospels seem to have been brought together into a single collection, known as *The Gospel*. Previously, Mark's Gospel had 'belonged' to the church in Rome, Matthew's to the church in Syria, a Gentile church held Luke's Gospel, and the important church at Ephesus John's Gospel.

Similarly, and around the same time,

Paul's letters were collected under the title *The Apostle*. The second part of Luke's writings, a narrative history of the early years of the church, was omitted from *The Gospel*, as it continued beyond Jesus' death and resurrection. However, since it was by the author of Luke's Gospel, and also presented Paul's credentials as an apostle, it remained part of the core writings of the Christian church. Now known as 'The Acts of the Apostles', its opening verses clearly show it is a continuation of Luke's Gospel; it contains detailed descriptions of Paul's missionary activities as well as reports of early Christian preaching and other practices.

However, it is not true to say that the grounds for inclusion of a book in the canon were simply that it should be written by an apostle (the apostles were the twelve whom Jesus chose to help in his mission; later, Paul was added to their number). Mark and Luke were not strictly speaking apostles (though Mark is often regarded as having been close to the apostle Peter), yet there seems to have been little doubt that their Gospels should be accepted as canonical. Rather, the early Christians seem to have been able to distinguish clearly between books that they regarded as possessing divine authority and those they did not.

What's in, what's out?

In AD 180, Irenaeus (who had been taught by the martyr Polycarp, himself a disciple of John, and who could trace a direct line from there back to apostolic times) recognized a Christian Scripture canon consisting of the four Gospels, Acts, Romans, 1 and 2 Corinthians, Galatians, Ephesians, Philippians, Colossians, 1 and 2 Thessalonians, 1 and 2 Timothy, Titus, 1 Peter, 1 John and Revelation.

An early list of New Testament books, called 'the Muratorian fragment' after its eighteenth-century Italian discoverer, Cardinal L. A. Muratori, includes the four Gospels and Acts, Paul's nine letters to churches and four personal letters, the letters of Jude, 1 and 2 John and 1 Peter, and the book of Revelation. It adds that the *Shepherd of Hermas* is fit to be read in church, but not to be included among the apostolic writings. Other lists, which agreed on almost all the New Testament books, but disputed such writings as 2 Peter, 2 and 3 John, James, Jude and a few other books, were made by Origen (c. AD 185–254) around AD 230 and the pioneer church historian Eusebius of Caesarea (c. AD 265–340) in the early fourth century.

By AD 367 the first known list of the twenty-seven New Testament books as Christians recognize them today was recorded by Athanasius, Bishop of Alexandria (c. AD 296–373). He made a point of adding that the *Shepherd of Hermas* and *1 Clement* were also useful, but not part of the recognized canon of the New Testament. Shortly afterwards, both Jerome and Augustine, leading figures in the church, listed the same twenty-seven books.

The canon approved

With the state recognition of the church, its organization could be publicly developed and councils of bishops openly called. Accordingly, Athanasius' list was formally approved at the Synod (a gathering of bishops) of Hippo in AD 393 and the Synod of Carthage in AD 397, making the New Testament as we know it 'official'.

However, these councils were simply recording the previously established canonicity of the books – not conferring some new or arbitrary authority upon them. The scholar F. J. Foakes-

Jackson has succinctly summed up the origin of the Christian canon: 'The Church... did not make the New Testament; the two grew up together.' And another biblical scholar, F. F. Bruce, wrote:

Inclusion in a canon conferred on no book an authority which it did not already possess; the books were included in the canon because of the authority accorded to them individually throughout the Christian world from the end of the first century onwards.

Early manuscripts

It is from this period, too, that the oldest known complete copy of the New Testament dates. Known as the *Codex Sinaiticus*, and rediscovered by a nineteenth-century German scholar named Konstantin Tischendorf at St Catherine's Monastery, near the foot of Mount Sinai, Egypt, it consists of almost the entire Bible – Old and New Testaments (as well as the books of Barnabas and Hermas). Today the *Codex Sinaiticus* may be viewed in the British Library, London, as can the slightly later *Codex Alexandrinus*, while another important very early manuscript, the *Codex Vaticanus*, is now preserved in the Vatican, Rome. Such early manuscripts are vital for scholars checking that the text used to translate modern Bibles is identical to that used by the early Christians – and that copyists' errors or well-meaning 'corrections' have not mutilated the original words.

But these important manuscripts are far from being the only or even the oldest early texts of the New Testament. The oldest fragment yet found is a scrap of papyrus codex dating from the first half of the second century, containing some verses from chapter 18 of John's Gospel. It is now housed in the John Rylands Library, Manchester.

Professor F. F. Bruce, who was also based at

A page from the fourth-century Greek Bible known as the *Codex Sinaiticus*, now in the British Museum, London.

Manchester University, compared the manuscript witness for some major classical authors with the early texts of the New Testament. He noted that, for instance, we have only nine or ten good manuscripts of Caesar's *Gallic War* – well known to generations of Latin students – of which the oldest dates from 900 years after the author's time. The Greek writer Thucydides' *History*, written in the fifth century BC, is known to us only via eight texts, the earliest of which dates from around AD 900, some fourteen centuries after the writer's day. By contrast, we have some 5,000 surviving early manuscripts of all or part of the Greek New Testament.

UNDERSTANDING THE BIBLE

Even in the early years, literate Christians encountered many problems in reading, understanding and interpreting Scripture. (Even the apostle Peter, at the end of his second letter, said that some of Paul's letters were 'hard to understand'!) The third-century theologian Origen discovered what he considered to be internal inconsistencies and contradictions in the text, and felt that the endless battles, genealogical lists and legal codes of the Old Testament were difficult to regard as aids to a spiritual pilgrimage through life. Origen's own response was to evolve a two-pronged principle for the interpretation of Scripture. When the biblical passage has an obvious meaning, truth lies in that plain sense of the text. However, when the plain sense seems flawed or even wrong, then the text needs to be interpreted allegorically, finding a spiritual meaning that the reader can apply to his or her life.

The Old Testament in Greek

With the adoption of the Jewish Scriptures by the Christian church, it became important for believers who could not read Hebrew – the original language of the Old Testament – to be able to access the text.

In the third century BC a translation usually known as that of 'The Seventy' (the Septuagint) was begun by Jewish scholars in Alexandria. A popular legend arose that seventy individual translators working in separate cells produced in seventy-two days seventy identical Greek versions of the original Hebrew text! Even at the time, this 'miracle' was widely ridiculed. Nevertheless, the translators produced the desired result in the form of a serviceable Greek version of the Old Testament. It was this translation that, from the first century AD onwards, Christians adopted as their version of the Old Testament.

The Bible in Latin

In the fourth century, Pope Damasus commissioned the learned but incorrigibly quarrelsome and cantankerous monk Jerome (c. AD 345–420) to create an accurate Latin translation of the entire Bible, to supplant various inaccurate versions currently available. After wandering through Antioch, Egypt and the Holy Land, Jerome finally settled for monastic seclusion in Bethlehem in AD 386, and devoted the remainder of his life to the pope's commission, meanwhile also writing commentaries on Scripture at break-neck speed.

Jerome initially used the Greek Septuagint as the basis for his Latin translation of the Old Testament. However, he later decided that greater fidelity to the meaning would be

The Scriptures... have both a meaning which is obvious and another which is hidden from most readers... The inspired meaning is not recognized by all – only by those who are gifted with the grace of the Holy Spirit in the word of wisdom and knowledge.

ORIGEN (C. 185–C. 254)

Mosaic from the interior of the Mausoleum of Galla Placidia, Ravenna, dating from the fifth century, depicting the martyrdom on a red-hot grid of St Lawrence. To the left is a cupboard containing the Gospels of Matthew, Mark, Luke and John.

assured by going back to the original Hebrew text and reworking his initial translation from the Greek. (For this, he was roundly condemned by some who regarded the Septuagint as itself inspired.) Jerome explained that he wanted to 'give my Latin readers the hidden treasures of Hebrew erudition'.

Jerome's Latin version of the New Testament was derived from the current Greek texts. Finally, in AD 405, after twenty-three years' work, Jerome's revised Latin Bible was finished. It became popularly known as the 'Vulgate', and was eventually accepted in the Christian West as the authorized Latin version.

During the Middle Ages, as a result of copyists' errors, various attempts at correction and editors' interventions, Jerome's text became badly corrupted. Around AD 800, Alcuin of York (c. AD 735–804) attempted to create a more dependable version of the text, as instructed by the emperor Charlemagne, as did Theodulf of Orleans (c. AD 750–821). A Paris version made in the thirteenth century was used in the earliest printed editions of the Vulgate. After the Reformation, the epochal Council of Trent (1545) confirmed the Vulgate as the authoritative Latin version of the Bible for the Roman Catholic Church, and an authorized revised text, known as the 'Clementine Vulgate', was printed between 1592 and 1598.

The unread Bible

With the fall of the Roman empire, literacy fell, and the general lack of public education meant that in practice the reading, study and interpretation of Scripture was increasingly restricted to the monasteries. Rather than returning to Scripture to re-assess their understanding of the faith, medieval theologians were often content instead to refer back to the teachings and interpretations of earlier Christian writers.

If they did actually study Scripture, medieval scholars tended to follow and elaborate on the allegorical process proposed by such earlier writers as Origen. They developed a four-fold analysis for biblical interpretation: The literal teaches the events, allegory what you are to believe, the moral sense what you are to do, the spiritual where you are to aim.

Ironically, it was Jewish scholars such as Rabbi Solomon ben Isaac (Rashi) of Troyes (1040–1105) who in the eleventh and twelfth centuries began to revive the search for 'the simple sense of the Bible'. Their path was then followed by Christian academics such as Nicholas of Lyra (1265–1349), whose insistence 'upon the literal sense' is believed in turn to have moulded the reformer Martin Luther's approach to biblical interpretation.

The print revolution

In 1452 an event occurred that was radically to affect the story of the

Bible: the invention of printing (or rather the re-invention – the Chinese had been printing books since AD 868). In Mainz, Germany, Johann Gutenberg (or Gensfleisch, 1398–1468) first experimented at printing on parchment with wooden letters dipped in dye. From this, he moved to using metal type and could soon print many pages from a single block.

Almost inevitably, the first book printed by Gutenberg was the Vulgate Bible. It was published in two large volumes, with headings and chapter openings printed in red. Gutenberg produced two editions – one printed on parchment, the other on paper. Although he printed only 150 copies of this first Bible, it took him two years to complete, since typesetting just a single page took a whole day and printing ten copies of that page at least one hour.

Nevertheless, book production had suddenly leapt from being a solitary craft pursued by monastic copyists to an industry with a potentially huge output. Other editions rapidly followed the 'Gutenberg Bible', including 'poor Bibles' which were available at more affordable prices, the first German language Bible in 1466 – a literal translation of the Latin Vulgate called the 'Mentel Bible', and an illustrated Bible produced by Joducus Pflanzman. Soon print works were springing up throughout western Europe. The age of the affordable book had commenced.

THE BIBLE AND THE REFORMATION

The iconoclasts of the Protestant Reformation rejected religious imagery such as statues, stained-glass windows and wall paintings. Instead, the Protestant Reformers looked to the printed word of the Bible and the spoken word of the sermon for instruction and encouragement in their faith.

If the Bible was to be the source of such spiritual nourishment, it needed to be accessible to the ordinary Christian in his or her own language, without the mediation of a Latin-speaking priest. Hence the work of such Bible translators as Martin Luther (German, 1534), William Tyndale and Miles Coverdale (English, 1526 onwards), Lefèvre d'Étaples (French, 1523), Jaacob van Liesveldt (Dutch, 1526), Giovanni Diodati (Italian, 1607) and Laurentius Petri (Swedish, 1541).

The Authorized (King James) Version of the English Bible, commissioned by James I and first published in 1611, became a seminal work not only for the church but also for English literature and the English language. Although translated by a committee – famously a recipe for a hybrid satisfying no one – in this case, by a happy mix of circumstances, the result was a text that remains memorably resonant and that has influenced generations of both believers and non-believers, as well as most subsequent English translators and translations.

Luther's German translation performed a similar role for the German church and German language. He completed his translation with a version of the Old Testament in 1534; and by 1584 100,000 copies had been printed in Wittenberg alone. Most Germans continued to use the Luther Bible in some form for the four succeeding centuries.

Catholic vernacular Bibles

But Protestants were not alone in translating the Bible into the vernacular. Encouraged by the introduction of printing and equipped with the new learning of the humanist renaissance, many Catholic scholars also laboured to produce versions of the Bible in their own language. A French translation known as the Louvain Bible – after the university where it was produced –

I wish that the Scriptures might be translated into all languages… that the farm-labourer might sing them as he follows the plough.

ERASMUS OF ROTTERDAM

A page from the Gutenberg Bible, the first printed Bible (1454/5). The red ink and illumination was added by hand.

appeared in 1550; an Italian version, translated by Antonio Brucioli, was published in the 1530s; and a Dutch translation, by Nicolaas van Winghe, was published by the Catholic Church in the Low Countries in 1548. Even in Orthodox Russia, a Slavonic Bible, based on the ninth-century version by the missionary brothers Cyril and Methodius, originally from Thessalonica, was published in 1581. (The Russians had to wait until 1821 for a New Testament in Russian.)

The authority of the Bible

Through the centuries, Christians assumed generally that the Bible was historically – and even scientifically – accurate throughout. Then in the early seventeenth century, Galileo Galilei (1564–1642) took up the banned ideas of Copernicus: 'I hold that the… Earth rotates itself and moves around the sun.' This was in clear opposition to the Catholic Church's teaching that the earth was at the centre of the universe.

But it was not only the results of his researches that threatened the church's authority: it was Galileo's very methodology: 'In disputes about natural phenomena one must not begin with the authority of Scriptural passages, but with sensory experience and necessary demonstration,' he declared. Here was the dynamite ready to ignite beneath the church's dogmatism. Aged sixty-nine, suffering from chronic arthritis and threatened with torture by the Inquisition, Galileo recanted his Copernican views: I 'abjure, curse and detest my errors' he said. Then he is alleged to have added *sotto voce*, *'eppur, si muove'* – yet it does move!

But during the nineteenth century, and in part as a result of Enlightenment critical thinking, it became increasingly respectable to throw doubt on the historicity of such stories as Noah's ark and Jonah and the whale: far fewer people took these stories as fact in 1914 than in 1800. Yet though such doubts might have seemed shocking, they were probably

A contemporary painting of the trial of Galileo before the Inquisition in Rome (1633).

in the event much less momentous in changing people's religious beliefs than current social changes such as population movement and industrialization.

The nineteenth century also saw a fearsome battle between those Christians who believed that they had to defend the literal truth of every verse of Scripture and scientists and their defenders who were making discoveries and proposing theories that seemed incompatible with such a stance. Foremost among the latter was, of course, Charles Darwin (1809–82), whose *Origin of Species* (1859) propounded the theory of evolution, which seemingly completely contradicted a literal understanding of the Genesis account of a seven-day creation. However, this

might well be regarded as a confusion of categories. Most informed scientists did not claim to be proving that the universe had a purely mechanical purpose, making it incompatible with religion in general or Christianity in particular.

CRITICAL THINKING

Emanating from the European Enlightenment, theological liberalism first appeared in Germany in the early nineteenth century, anticipated in the work of the German Pietist scholar Friedrich Schleiermacher (1768–1834). This movement commenced as an attempt by theologians to come to terms with modern knowledge and thought, especially the new historical study of the Scriptures. Its effect was to strip

The Bible and the Bible only is the religion of Protestants.

WILLIAM CHILLINGWORTH

Christianity of its supernatural elements – in particular the miracles and the doctrine of the deity of Christ – as in David Friedrich Strauss' book, *The Life of Jesus* (1835–36), translated into English by the novelist George Eliot. The Bible was no longer considered trustworthy, but was seen as containing errors and contradictions. Critical studies seemed to have undermined its authority.

Conservative reaction

Such liberal thinking was deeply worrying to many Christians. The Roman Catholic Church, which in this period appeared to lack the great scholars it boasted in earlier centuries, was troubled by this apparent conflict between the truth of the Bible and the consequences of the discoveries of scientists and historians.

Pope Pius X (reigned 1903–14), who had little claim to being an intellectual, cut through the knot drastically by lumping together any supposed threats to orthodoxy as 'modernism', and then rejecting and condemning all those who allegedly held such beliefs. This crude catch-all approach, reminiscent of political McCarthyism in 1950s America, unfortunately blackened not only those who espoused agnosticism, but also Christian scholars who were genuinely battling to interpret their faith for the modern world. Even the saintly English Cardinal John Henry Newman came under dark suspicion of such 'modernism' not long after his death in 1890.

Fundamentalism and the word of God

Some Protestants met the perceived intellectual challenge with not dissimilar strategies. Liberal theologians were teaching a 'new theology', in which the essential Christian virtues were seen to consist of the fatherhood of God, the brotherhood of man [sic] and the necessity for humanity to live in love. The world was basically on an ever-upward course of progress, leading eventually to the establishment of the kingdom of God on earth. (Such views received an irrecoverable shock with the outbreak of the catastrophic 'war to end all wars' in 1914.)

Looking to the book of Revelation for their answers, conservative Protestants countered that life on earth was deteriorating, and would continue to do so until Christ returned for a thousand-year rule here on earth. The main – even sole – purpose of the Christian 'remnant' was to evangelize and convert the rest of humankind before it was too late.

Conservatives also reacted to biblical criticism, with a kind of chop-logic. They argued firstly that the Bible is God's word, and secondly that God is perfect and cannot err. Therefore the Bible cannot err. And not only can it not err on matters of theology, but it cannot err geographically, historically or even scientifically – and the original manuscript of the Bible is also inerrant.

This reactionary movement was strongest in the USA, where in the 1910s a series of booklets called *The Fundamentals* (hence 'Fundamentalism') appeared to argue its case. Following the First World War, a bruising confrontation took place in the so-called Fundamentalist-Modernist controversy. For almost a generation Christians fought an exhausting battle for the minds and souls of American churches, seminaries and their members. Every major denomination was affected and a number were split by the quarrel.

During this period, the debate between theological conservatives and liberals often centred on evolution. Fundamentalism suffered a major set-back in the notorious Scopes monkey trial held in Dayton, Tennessee, in July 1925, when a young Tennessee high school teacher,

John T. Scopes, was charged with teaching evolution illegally. Progressive politician and three-times Democratic Party presidential candidate William Jennings Bryan, who championed American Fundamentalism, although technically winning the case, used ill-founded arguments that allowed the press mercilessly to ridicule him and his cause as obscurantist. As a result, many people henceforward tended to equate Fundamentalism with bigotry.

The text of the Bible

The revolution in ideas that had begun before the First World War spread through the West in the 1920s. Numerous thinkers rejected faith in progress and human rationality, and prophets of doom spoke of the decline of Western civilization. Doubt, uncertainty, alienation and pessimism marked this intellectual crisis. The new physics depicted a universe with no absolute, objective reality. Everything was relative. Freudian psychology explained human behaviour in terms of the irrational unconscious, driven by desires in conflict with the rational and moral parts of the mind.

Logical positivism held that the only valid concepts were those that could be tested by scientific experiments or by mathematical logic. Therefore, concepts such as God, freedom and morality were meaningless.

The Swiss theologian Karl Barth (1886–1968) published a commentary on Romans (1919) that argued the inadequacy of liberalism and the need for faith in God. The only hope lay in the 'crisis of faith', when one repents before God. Barth did much to re-establish the message of the Bible, the mission of the church, the importance of theology and the relevance of the Christian gospel to life.

The nineteenth century also saw a greater critical study of the actual text of the Bible, which affected both learning and belief. As we saw earlier, at the turn of the nineteenth century Catholics were still using Jerome's Vulgate, translated in the late fourth century, as the authoritative basis of faith. Similarly English-speaking Protestants depended on the 1611 King James Version, and Germans on the Luther Bible. While these literary masterpieces contributed richly to their respective cultures,

Karl Barth

Born in Basel, Switzerland, Barth was trained in Protestant Liberalism, against which he reacted in the First World War, believing his teachers had been misled in claiming divine support for a war they said was in support of German culture. In his commentary on Romans Barth argued that God as revealed in the cross of Jesus challenges any attempt to ally God with human cultures, achievements or possessions.

In 1934, as the German Protestant Church tried to come to terms with Hitler's Third Reich, Barth was largely responsible for the Barmen Declaration, which argued that the church's allegiance was to the God of Jesus Christ and should resist other 'lords', such as the *Führer*, Adolf Hitler. Barth was forced to resign from the University of Bonn for refusing to swear an oath to

Hitler and returned to his native Switzerland. In 1938 he wrote to a Czech colleague, saying that soldiers who fought against the Third Reich were serving a Christian cause.

Barth's theology is summed up in his *Church Dogmatics*, regarded by some as one of the most important works of theology. When a reporter once asked Barth to summarize his theology, he replied: 'Jesus loves me, this I know, for the Bible tells me so.'

After the Second World War, Barth co-authored the Darmstadt Statement (1947), a statement of German guilt and responsibility for the Third Reich and for the Second World War.

the scholarship they represented clearly no longer reflected modern findings.

Scholars had been busy unravelling the history of the text of the Bible, which meant that well-loved translations such as the King James Version badly needed revising and correcting. These studies were greatly helped by the discovery in 1844, by the German Lutheran Konstantin Tischendorf, of the *Codex Sinaiticus* at the monastery of St Catherine at Mount Sinai, and by the release by the pope of the *Codex Vaticanus* in 1859. These two manuscripts, dating from the fourth century, together with the *Codex Alexandrinus*, a slightly later manuscript, allowed scholars to settle upon an agreed, sound original text which then formed the basis for a much more accurate translation of the Bible.

These nineteenth-century discoveries were greatly enhanced in the twentieth century by archaeologists' discoveries of numerous papyri fragments of the Scriptures, mostly dating from the third and fourth centuries AD – particularly those found by the English scholar Chester Beatty and hence named after him. Beatty's finds included large fragments of the Gospels, Acts, Paul's letters and Revelation, all between 100 and 150 years older than any previously known text for the New Testament. These, together with evidence provided by the Dead Sea Scrolls, first discovered at Qumran in the Dead Sea Valley in 1947, made yet further revisions of the biblical text necessary.

New translations

The creation of a more reliable and authentic Greek and Hebrew text made possible and indeed imperative new and more accurate translations of the Bible. The nineteenth and particularly the twentieth century saw, too, growing demands for translations in

contemporary language – rather than in the language of William Shakespeare and Martin Luther. In English, the Revised Version appeared in 1881–85, the Revised Standard Version in 1962 and the New English Bible in 1970. The German Herder Bible (1965), which evolved into the Jerusalem Bible (1966), was the first Catholic Bible not based on the Vulgate text to enter widespread use.

From the mid-twentieth century onwards, the Evangelical movement in the USA was responsible for a number of popular translations, including the Living Bible, translated by Dr Kenneth Taylor, the New International Version, the Good News Bible (made by the American Bible Society), and the New Living Translation.

CHAPTER 3

Defining Belief

Clearly, despite some twenty-first-century Christians' appeal to the Bible or to primitive Christianity for justification of the minutiae of their beliefs and practices, the church did not emerge fully formed by some heavenly fiat, with precise specifications for the architecture of ecclesiastical buildings, the nature of priests' robing and the wording of hymnbooks.

Gradually, over the early centuries, believers in Christ's resurrection, 'followers of the Way', defined their faith, developed their spiritual practices, discovered a unique morality and recognized a definitive literature. However, because they were from the outset despised, uneducated, persecuted and remote, we have pitifully few early external records about them to help chart this process.

Lifestyle differences

Since their lifestyle was radically different, Christians excluded themselves from many aspects of pagan society. When they refused to take part in the ceremonies of Roman religious life, declined to engage in violence and rejected luxury and personal adornment, they were suspected of being anti-social fanatics.

Because they were so obviously different from non-Christians in the Roman world, the early believers were sometimes dubbed 'the third race' – neither pagan nor Jewish, but a race apart. And many early Christians did consider earthly citizenship unimportant, because they believed themselves to be citizens of heaven. Indeed, some were expecting Christ's imminent return. On the other hand, Christians were also concerned to give proper respect to duly constituted government.

The hallmarks of apostolic Christianity might be summarized as simplicity, community, evangelism and love. It was simple because it had little or no formal organization, no church buildings, relatively easy-to-comprehend teachings, and it encouraged alms-giving. This simplicity appealed especially to the poor and oppressed, who could both understand and take part in the new faith. The sense of community was fostered by frequent meetings for worship, sharing and the celebration of a love feast – a communal religious meal called the *agape*, closely linked with the Eucharist, where rich and poor met together. The early Christians were also often aggressively evangelistic, as they wanted to spread their good news,

This catacomb wall-painting depicts early Christians sharing a Eucharistic meal.

convinced that they had discovered truth in the resurrected Jesus and his teachings.

The Eucharist

The first Christians faced misunderstanding and malicious opposition. Enemies claimed they were composed of the dregs of society, and were ignorant people who attended nocturnal gatherings, solemn feasts and barbarous meals. They were even accused of cannibalism. Such accusations were based on a total misunderstanding – deliberate or otherwise – of the central focus of early Christian meetings: when bread and wine were shared as Christ's 'flesh' and 'blood'.

At first the Eucharist was a common meal, during which bread and wine were shared as a reminder of the death and resurrection of Jesus and of the believers' sharing in it: they believed that through Jesus' death they too had 'died' to, or left behind, their old way of life, and that through Jesus' resurrection they had been given a new life.

RIGHT TEACHING

After the first century, the growth of Christianity was greatly aided by the fact that it began to attract increasing numbers of able converts who gave the young faith the leadership necessary to stabilize it as it spread. Some Romans realized that the growth of the church posed a threat to traditional Roman values. Yet educated Christians hoped that the church and the empire could co-exist, and several Christian writers during this period used classical philosophy to explain aspects of Christian teaching.

Over the years statements summing up basic Christianity began to emerge. They probably evolved as part of baptismal, or other, services in which the beliefs of new converts were normally summarized.

Gnostics

In the second century, establishing how Christians could know what was right teaching and practice was a major problem for the church. One way of doing this was by deciding which early writings were to be regarded as standard – as discussed in chapter 2. Another was by trying to trace a direct line back to the apostles, through subsequent pastors, bishops, elders and teachers. This uninterrupted 'apostolic succession' was seen by some as a guarantee that what was being handed on was the genuine apostolic teaching.

But as Christianity expanded so did the potential for deviating from the faith. To refute the claims of movements such as Gnosticism, Marcionism and Montanism, Christian leaders of the second and third centuries attempted to set down systematically exactly what it was that Jesus and the apostles taught.

Some educated Greek converts believed that any deity would be contaminated by contact with flesh, and while they accepted that Jesus had a body, they thought this unimportant, since they held that he saved the world not by his suffering and death but by bringing it knowledge – *gnosis* in Greek, hence their name, 'Gnostics'. This group claimed that their teachings had been passed along in secret Gnostic groups since the days of the apostles.

Ignatius of Antioch
Some Christian writers attempted to justify their faith by writing arguments for what they believed. Others tried to explain the faith on the basis of the remembered teachings of Jesus as set out in early Bible texts. Among these was Ignatius of Antioch (d. c. AD 117), who in the early second century strongly defended the church against the misleading teachings of the Gnostics and Docetists, both of whom taught that Jesus was something other than God in human form.

Irenaeus
In the middle of the first century, a conservative

reaction broke out when Montanus claimed the Holy Spirit was speaking through him, and that his prophecies did away with the need for sacred books or church organization (see p. 23). He and his followers regarded themselves as a spiritual 'elite'.

So where was truth to be found – in Gnostic secret traditions, in Montanist prophecies or in the mainstream Christian communities? A Gallic theologian named Irenaeus of Lyons – who as a boy had heard the venerable martyr Polycarp speak – suggested answers, carefully basing his arguments on biblical teaching. He wrote five tomes opposing Gnostic views as well as a book called *Proof of the Apostolic Preaching*. Irenaeus re-emphasized the basic Christian beliefs that seemed challenged by Gnosticism: that the world was created by one God, that Jesus, son of the Creator, died to save humans, and that there will be a resurrection of the body. He also developed further the idea that Jesus was fully man and fully God.

Justin Martyr
In the mid-second century, Justin Martyr (c. AD 100–65), who came to Christianity as a pagan philosopher, skilfully exposed Marcion's heresy (discussed on p. 24), which was similar to Gnosticism, and other aberrations of the Christian faith. He tried to show that Christianity could debate on equal terms with other beliefs and schools of thought. Justin addressed his *First Apology* directly to the Roman emperor Antoninus Pius (reigned AD 138–61), pointing out that the popular prejudice that Christians were immoral and atheistic was baseless, and that Christian belief and practice demonstrated an elevated reason and morality. As his name implies, Justin himself died for his faith in Rome.

Tertullian

New Christian thinking was also beginning to emerge from North Africa, where the theologians Tertullian (c. AD 160–c. AD 220) and Cyprian (d. AD 258) composed the first important theological works in Latin, using for the first time an important technical vocabulary such as *sacramentum* (sacrament) and *Trinitas* (Trinity). The North African Christians had a narrower view of the church, seeing it as a community of the elect few; and unlike thinkers elsewhere, they feared and rejected pagan culture.

From Carthage, Tertullian was trained as a lawyer and could defend his beliefs keenly. More forthright than Justin Martyr, Tertullian had no patience with earlier attempts to make Christianity fit in with Greek philosophy: 'What is there in common between Athens and Jerusalem?' he demanded rhetorically. For him one of the glories of the Christian faith was its very uniqueness. Tertullian's masterpiece was his *Apology* (c. AD 200) in which he argued effectively for the toleration of Christianity. Tertullian also coined the unforgettable phrase, 'the blood of the martyrs is seed [of the church]'.

Origen

From the Christian centre of Alexandria, Egypt, where Greek philosophy rivalled Christianity, the intellectual Origen (AD 185–254) was largely responsible for introducing new thought-forms to express Christian

All judges, city-people and craftsmen shall rest on the venerable day of the Sun.

CONSTANTINE'S EDICT

beliefs. Together with Clement (d. c. AD 215), Origen pioneered systematic theology, attempting to harmonize Christians' understanding of God, Christ and the church. He also founded the discipline of biblical study and interpretation, or 'exegesis'.

These Alexandrian leaders took what they felt was good from pagan culture, and incorporated Greek philosophical elements into their Christian theology. This was to become a standard theological method, especially among the theologians of the later Middle Ages known as the Scholastics.

A STATE RELIGION

The fourth century saw the Roman emperor, Constantine I (reigned AD 306–337), converted to some form of Christianity, ending the persecutions and allowing the Christians finally to evangelize freely. They succeeded, and by the end of the century the Roman empire had become officially a Christian state. But the emperors still considered themselves to be sacred – chosen by God to rule – and tensions rose whenever church and state mixed, tensions that were to grow in the Middle Ages.

Some believe that the recognition of Christianity as the official state religion during the fourth century seriously damaged the church, as Christian leaders became confidants of emperors and Christianity became popular with the masses. Others even see this period as the 'fall' of the

39

church from pristine purity – the beginning of a new era, in which the right relationship between church and state needed resolution.

Whatever the case, the fourth century marked a major turning-point in the history of Christianity which deeply affected how Christians would live in the world. It also saw the beginning of a new theological sophistication and of the rapid growth of the institutional church.

Church councils

The church now set about defining orthodoxy in carefully argued and worded statements. A series of church councils met in this and succeeding centuries with the difficult task of expressing clearly two particular paradoxes of the Christian faith:

➤ There is one God – yet God has revealed himself as Father, Son and Holy Spirit.

➤ Christ has both a divine and a human nature; he is both God and man.

Theologians had great difficulty with the concept of the Trinity – not a term found in the Bible – afraid that if they said that the Father and the Son were both divine, this would compromise the essential monotheism of the faith. The belief that the Son was divine but inferior to the Father (called 'Subordinationism') became common, though theologians recognized it was inadequate.

If you ask anyone in Constantinople for change, he will start discussing with you whether the Son is begotten or unbegotten.

GREGORY OF NYSSA

A fourteenth-century depiction of the three persons of the Trinity by Nardo di Cione (d. 1365).

The whole world groaned in astonishment at finding itself Arian.

JEROME

It took many meetings and much debate to come to anywhere near satisfactory conclusions, with councils meeting at Nicea, Constantinople, Ephesus and Chalcedon between AD 325 and AD 451 to grapple with these complex questions.

Arius

An Alexandrian presbyter named Arius (d. AD 336) denied the divinity of the Son, teaching that the Son was subordinate to the Father. At the emperor's urging, the bishops of the inhabited world (*oikumene* in Greek) assembled at Nicea, Asia Minor, in AD 325 for the first ecumenical council, to debate the question. The council concluded by affirming both the equality and divinity of the Father and Son, using Greco-Roman philosophical terminology – stating, for example, that the persons of the Trinity 'share in the one divine substance'. Their statement was later expanded into the Nicene Creed, which continues to be used in many churches across the world today. Christians had thus decided it was acceptable to use elements of Greco-Roman culture.

Arius himself was excommunicated. But the questions raised by him did not die out, and in AD 381 a second ecumenical council, Constantinople I, re-affirmed the conclusions of the Council of Nicea, and affirmed, additionally, the equality and divinity of the Spirit.

Athanasius (c. AD 296–373), a tenacious opponent of Arius, later came up with what has become the orthodox statement on the question:

We believe in one Lord Jesus Christ, the Son of God, begotten of the Father, only-begotten, that is, of the substance of the Father, God of God, Light of Light, true God of true God, begotten not made, of one substance with the Father, through whom all things were made...

Fifth-century debates

While the fourth century dealt with questions about the Trinity, the fifth faced up to equally difficult questions about the nature of Christ. How could Christ be both human and divine, without the divine swallowing up the human? A theologian named Nestorius (d. c. AD 451) separated out the human and divine persons in Christ, but the third ecumenical council of Ephesus (AD 431) insisted on their unity.

In AD 449 a theologian named Eutyches was teaching that Christ had two natures before the incarnation; after the incarnation, the divine swallowed up the human, so that there was only one nature. Such a view gained support at another church council at Ephesus in the same year. But Pope Leo of Rome proceeded to denounce this council in undiplomatic language as a 'synod of robbers' (*latrocinium*). When a fourth ecumenical council met at Chalcedon in AD 451, the bishops – mostly Greeks – endorsed Leo's position: that Christ is one person with two natures, one human, one divine, each distinct but both united in the one person. (The crucial words are translated: 'one and the same... Son, Lord, Only-begotten, to be acknowledged in two natures without confusion, without change, without division, or without separation'.) This has been the Western church's understanding of the person of Christ (Christology) ever since. But in Egypt and other parts of the Near East 'one-nature' (Monophysite) Christians, who rejected the consensus of Chalcedon, became a powerful force – the ancestors of today's Coptic Christians.

With such carefully defined statements of belief, the church now felt it could resist opponents who ridiculed such apparent complexities as the Trinity.

Augustine of Hippo (AD 354–430)

Like Janus, the Roman god of the New Year, whose characteristic was to look both ways, Augustine of Hippo (not to be confused with Augustine of Canterbury, the first Archbishop of Canterbury) stands at a turning-point. He lived at the end of the period of the church's initial growth, when the Roman empire was crumbling into decay. But he also looked forward to the church of the Middle Ages, which he strongly influenced.

Brought up in Roman North Africa, by his pious mother Monnica, the worst childhood sin Augustine could remember was stealing pears! As an adult he taught in Carthage, Rome and Milan, and espoused a series of philosophical systems, while leading a dissolute personal life. Then one afternoon in AD 386 he heard a child's voice chanting, 'Pick it up, read it; pick it up, read it' ('*tolle lege, tolle lege*'). Because the words were unusual he took them as God's instruction to read the Bible. Augustine accordingly read at random Romans 13:13: 'Let us behave decently… not in sexual immorality.' 'It was as though the light of faith flooded into my heart and all the darkness of doubt was dispelled,' he wrote later.

Augustine now turned to a life of preaching, teaching and celibacy, becoming a redoubtable defender of what he regarded as orthodox Christianity. He returned to North Africa, where in AD 391 he was ordained a priest in Hippo Regius, and set up a monastic foundation at Thagaste. He soon became celebrated as a preacher, noted for combating the Manichaean heresy, to which he had formerly adhered. In AD 396 he was made Bishop of Hippo, but continued to lead a monastic existence. Augustine died in AD 430, during the siege of Hippo by Vandal invaders.

Augustine left his mark in a tightly argued theological system based on the writings of the apostle Paul. He developed a doctrine of predestination: No reason can be given why some are saved and the rest damned – it is due solely to God's inscrutable choice. Similar ideas were taken up later by Bernard of Clairvaux, Martin Luther and especially John Calvin.

No less significantly for coming centuries, Augustine redefined the early Christian adherence to non-violence to allow participation in what he termed a 'just war'. He also advocated the use of force against the heretical Donatists.

Augustine's classic books, the autobiographical and possibly exaggerated *Confessions* – often called the first Western autobiography – and the *City of God*, have affected generations of Christians. Some contemporaries claimed Christianity had caused the Roman empire's downfall by turning people away from Roman gods. In the *City of God* Augustine argued that Rome was being punished for its past sins, not its new faith. Living through the turmoil of a collapsing empire, he encouraged believers to seek the peace of the kingdom of heaven.

Augustine of Hippo, portrayed by Konrad Witz (c. 1400–c 1445).

The Church of North Africa

As we have noticed, by the end of the second century the African Church had become a significant theological force. Tertullian and Cyprian of Carthage laid the foundations for major Christian doctrines, including the Trinity and original sin. Augustine of Hippo (AD 354–430) developed these and other doctrines when he laid out his own teachings on the church and sacraments, predestination and grace during his controversies with both the Donatists and the Pelagians.

Donatism

A bitter controversy in the early church was known as the Donatist schism. Many bishops from Numidia, North Africa, refused to accept as Bishop of Carthage a man called Caecilian, because he had been consecrated by someone who had 'lapsed' during the harsh persecution under Emperor Diocletian (reigned AD 303–313). Named after their first leader, Donatus, the Donatists formed what they regarded as the 'true' or pure church. Donatism remained the more powerful church in North Africa until Augustine argued a strong case for Catholicism.

Augustine was also obsessed with original sin, and his work formed the basis of much medieval thinking on the subject. Pelagius, a British monk, rejected the idea, insisting that the tendency to sin is humanity's own free choice – hence there is no need for divine grace; individuals simply need to decide to do the will of God. Countering this, Augustine elaborated his ideas on the fall and original sin, asserting that God's grace was necessary to free a person's will to turn to God; and that a fixed number of the 'chosen' were predestined by God for salvation.

Give me chastity and celibacy – but not yet.

AUGUSTINE OF HIPPO

There is no salvation outside the church.

AUGUSTINE OF HIPPO

CHAPTER 4

Rome and the Papacy

The first Christian community we know of in Rome was that to which Paul addressed his letter to the Romans, written around AD 58. (As we have seen, Paul almost certainly did not found the church there; the apostle Peter has long been attributed with that role.) According to a strong tradition, both Paul and Peter were martyred in Rome, following the fire of Rome during Nero's reign. During a later persecution under the emperor Decius (AD 249–51), Fabian, an early Bishop of Rome, was also martyred in the imperial capital.

THE BISHOP OF ROME

As the church became a more organized institution, the bishop emerged as a leading figure, with responsibility for an area rather than merely for a single church. The Bishops of Rome increased in authority disproportionately, in time coming to be regarded as 'first among equals'. An early document attempted to demonstrate that the Bishop of Rome stood in a direct line from the apostle Peter, who was claimed as the city's first bishop. In addition, the Bishops of Rome started to assume the right to intervene in local disputes in other dioceses, which inevitably led to an increasingly centralized church.

In the second century AD, the Christian writer Irenaeus stated that all Christian teaching derived from the apostles, and that their teaching was to be found in both the Bible and tradition. He located tradition in the public teachings of bishops of 'sees' founded by the apostles, with Rome the chief among these.

After Constantine

By the third century AD, the church in Rome had steadily increased in influence, and was beginning to dominate Mediterranean Christianity. In AD 256 the Roman Church had a disagreement with African believers over whether Christian heretics and backsliders needed to be baptized when received back into the church, as Africa claimed (Rome said the laying on of hands was sufficient). In this debate, Pope Stephen I became the first pope to claim to speak with the authority of Peter.

Rome rose in importance particularly following Emperor Constantine's declaration of tolerance for Christians, the Edict of Milan (AD 313). With Constantine's conversion, the Bishop of Rome received new honours, and the emperor commenced the construction of an ambitious basilica to stand over the shrine of St Peter, on the Vatican Hill –

You are Peter, and upon this rock I will build my church.

MATTHEW 16:18

replaced in the sixteenth century by the St Peter's that still stands today. It was only during Constantine's reign that the churches were permitted to own property without restriction.

In AD 330, Constantine moved the political capital of the Roman empire to Constantinople; in the resulting power vacuum, Rome and the rest of Italy came increasingly under the authority and influence of the Bishop of Rome.

As the authority of the papacy grew, so did its estates, known later as the 'Patrimony of St Peter'. With a new liberty for Christians, and relaxed property restrictions, Pope Sylvester I (AD 314–35) and his successors built many new churches – sometimes over pagan temples – in the ancient city.

Frescoes of the passion of Christ in the twelfth-century crypt of Aquileia Cathedral, Italy. Rebuilt over a very early church, remains of a fourth-century pavement and fifth-century baptistery are still visible.

Barbarians at the gates

At the end of the fourth century AD an ominous warning sounded when the Germanic barbarians, kept at bay for so long, finally began to enter the Roman empire. In the following century the dam burst: barbarian tribes crossed the River Rhine into France, moved into Spain and crossed the seas into Britain and North Africa. In AD 410, Germanic Visigoths under Alaric sacked Rome itself – a terrible shock for a city that had stood inviolable for some eight hundred years.

The Roman empire was now in its death-throes. As the barbarian invaders from the north and east – Ostrogoths, Visigoths, Vandals, Angles, Saxons, Jutes and Franks – swarmed across the once proud empire in the West, the church eventually was left as the main institutional link with the imperial past. The last emperor in the West, Romulus Augustulus, was deposed in AD 476 and with him went the Roman empire in western Europe.

Attila the Hun

Christian Europe now found itself increasingly under siege. While the Germans were taking over western parts of the empire, the Asiatic Huns, under the leadership of Attila, 'the scourge of God', crossed the Rhine in AD 451, only to be defeated by Roman forces near Verdun. Attila then turned south to northern Italy with plans to attack Rome, but in AD 452 disease, lack of supplies and the determined resistance of Leo I ('Leo the Great' – AD 440–61), Bishop of Rome, forced him to retreat to the plains of eastern Europe.

The Bishops of Rome continued to claim supreme power, sometimes backed by emperors desperate for support. Leo himself claimed that, as Peter's successor, the pope possessed the apostle's authority. However, by the end of the fifth century the popes found themselves bishops of a decaying city ruled by barbarian Goths.

Justinian

Although for many years the emperor in the East continued to claim jurisdiction over the West, the last emperor to retain any semblance of authority outside the Byzantine East was Justinian I (reigned AD 527–65). Justinian, who temporarily re-conquered Italy and regarded himself as a second Constantine, took a lively interest in both the church and theology, but allowed little deviation by anyone – including the pope – from what he himself considered to be orthodoxy. When he took it upon himself to call the Council of Constantinople II in AD 553, he actually kidnapped Pope Vigilius (reigned AD 537–55) to make him attend.

Then in AD 568 Lombard barbarians invaded Italy and pushed Byzantine rule back to small pockets around seaports, such as Ravenna. The West was to be barbarian, not Byzantine.

An imposing mosaic image of Justinian I ('the Great') from the cathedral of St Vitale, Ravenna, Italy, underlining the emperor's domination of church and state.

Rome, which captivated the whole world, has herself been taken captive.

JEROME

RIGHT: A ninth-century ivory relief of Gregory the Great at his writing desk.

GREGORY THE GREAT

After Justinian, the empire in the West was mostly a fiction, and by the time of Pope Gregory I (AD 590–604) only a memory. Under Gregory, the papal office was fully established, papal leadership became decisive in the creation of a unified church in western Europe, and the pope was widely recognized as the single most important public figure in the West. When Rome itself was threatened by the Lombard invaders at the end of the sixth century AD, it was Gregory who took over civil and military control of the city.

The most influential figure in the sixth-century Western church, Gregory 'the Great' realized that the barbarians were there to stay. So he made it his aim, with the help of his bishops, to evangelize the rest of Europe. He devoted considerable time and resources to this task, attempting to Christianize the Visigoths in

A Year in the Life: The Church's Calendar

There is a natural cycle for all living things: day follows night; summer follows spring. Similar patterns are reflected in many religious rituals and traditions. Christians accepted this, and often adapted pagan festivals for themselves.

Events in the life of Christ and anniversaries in the church's life are celebrated at set times in the year. As varied traditions grew up in different parts of the church, different dates and contrasting celebrations evolved.

The liturgical – or Christian – year, is the cycle of liturgical seasons, each with its own mood, theological emphasis and prayers. These seasonal changes are reflected in some churches by different ways of decorating the building, different clerical vestments, different Bible readings and sermon topics. Distinct liturgical colours may also be displayed at different seasons of the liturgical year.

The dates of the festivals vary between the Western – Roman Catholic, Anglican and other Protestant – churches and the Eastern Orthodox churches, though the actual sequence is the same.

Easter – a moveable feast

In both East and West, the dates of many feasts vary from year to year; this is mainly because the date of Easter varies, and all other dates follow from this. From the outset, Easter has been regarded as the most important annual Christian festival. At first, it was often called the Christian Passover, and coincided with the Jewish Passover. It was the time to remember particularly Christ's death and to celebrate his resurrection.

As early as the second century AD, animated debates focussed on the appropriate date to celebrate Easter. Some churches preferred to stick to the Jewish calendar, while others used a different dating system. At Nicea in AD 325 it was decided that Easter should be celebrated on the first Sunday after the vernal full moon. All the Western churches agreed on this date at the Synod of Whitby, north-east England, in AD 664.

At first, Easter was only a one-day festival, marking both Jesus' death and resurrection. But as pilgrims began the custom of spending the festival in the Holy Land, retracing Jesus' steps during his final week in Jerusalem, a series of Easter services was introduced to mark the various events. So, by the fourth century AD, Palm Sunday, Maundy Thursday, Good Friday and Easter Sunday were all celebrated in their own special ways.

At the same time, it became customary for those wanting to be baptized to be prepared during the forty days of 'Lent' (marking Jesus' own period of preparation in the wilderness), leading up to Easter.

Lent and Passiontide

Lent begins on Ash Wednesday (which follows Shrove Tuesday, the traditional day of confession before the fast) and ends on Easter Day. There are forty days of Lent, not including Sundays. The final week of Lent is known as 'Holy Week', and starts on Palm Sunday. The last three days of Lent are sometimes known as the Easter *Triduum* (to denote the 'three days' from dusk on Holy Thursday to dusk on Easter Sunday):

❧ Holy Thursday, or Maundy Thursday, when some churches engage in ceremonial foot-washing, to re-enact Jesus' washing of his disciples' feet at the Last Supper.

❧ Good Friday – the commemoration of Jesus' death on the cross.

❧ Holy Saturday – remembering the day Christ lay in the tomb.

❧ Easter Vigil – held after sunset on Holy Saturday, or before dawn on Easter Day, anticipating the celebration of Jesus' resurrection.

Then comes Easter Day itself, which celebrates Jesus' resurrection.

But the celebrations do not end on Easter Day. The next seven weeks culminate in the celebration of the coming of the Holy Spirit on the Day of Pentecost – the fiftieth day. The celebration of Jesus' ascension, Ascension Day, on the fortieth day of Easter, is always a Thursday. The first Sunday after Pentecost is celebrated as Trinity Sunday.

Christmas

The major fixed point in the Christian year is Christmas, celebrating Jesus' birth in Bethlehem. Christians observed Christmas on various dates from at least as early as the fourth century AD. In the West, most churches fixed Christmas as 25 December; in the East, 6 January was the chosen date. Probably both dates were previously pagan holidays. In the fifth century AD, the churches of East and West agreed that 25 December should mark Jesus' birthday, and 6 January (known as Epiphany) the coming of the wise men to worship the baby Jesus.

Advent

Just as Easter has its preparatory period (Lent), Christmas is prepared for by the season of Advent, when Christians also look forward to Jesus' second coming. In the West this is in fact the first season of the liturgical year, beginning four Sundays before Christmas and ending on Christmas Eve.

High days and holidays

By AD 600, many other minor festivals had appeared in the Christian calendar – for example, saints' days, remembering such figures as the first martyr, Stephen, and the apostles James and John; and Holy Innocents' day, marking King Herod's massacre of the baby boys in Judea after the birth of Jesus. The Virgin Mary and local saints and martyrs were also allocated their own days. The Celtic church even added 'All Saints' Day'.

Many of these festivals are still celebrated:

➧ The Assumption of Mary (15 August) – a Roman Catholic festival celebrating the bodily entry of Mary into heaven.

➧ Corpus Christi – eleven days after Pentecost in the Catholic and some Anglican traditions.

➧ All Saints' Day – celebrated in most Western traditions on 1 November.

➧ St Michael's Day ('Michaelmas') – celebrated in some traditions on 29 September.

➧ St Martin's Day ('Martinmas') – celebrated in some traditions on 11 November.

➧ Reformation Sunday – celebrated on the Sunday preceding 31 October, especially by Lutherans, to commemorate Martin Luther nailing up his 95 Theses.

The extent to which these fasts and festivals are celebrated varies between churches; Protestants generally observe far fewer than Catholics and the Orthodox, and are much less likely to celebrate feasts of the Virgin Mary and the saints. Some sections of the Anglican/Episcopal church have retained minor festivals and commemorations, as have Lutheran churches. Most other Protestant churches – including Anglicans/Episcopalians, Lutherans, Methodists, Presbyterians, the Reformed churches and the United Churches of Christ, USA, the United Church of Canada and the Uniting Church in Australia – recognize the liturgical year, but only observe the main seasons.

The liturgical calendar

The church calendar has a practical purpose, too. The high days and holidays were times of great celebration. But in between, the calendar provided a framework for the church's teaching. A scheme of Bible readings called the 'lectionary' was designed to take people through the core of the Bible's teaching over the course of the year.

Spain, the Franks in France, and the pagan tribes of England, Germany and the Balkans, and parts of Italy. The success of his campaign signalled the gradual evolution of Christianity from a Mediterranean to a European religion.

In AD 596, Gregory sent the Roman monk Augustine to convert the Anglo-Saxons of Britain. Augustine completed this task by AD 600 and was duly appointed the first Archbishop of Canterbury. Yet he was not entering a completely non-Christian land; Celtic monks had already established the faith strongly in parts of the north. The differing traditions of Celtic and Roman Christianity finally came to terms at the Synod of Whitby (north-eastern England) in AD 664, when representatives of both expressions of the faith argued their case before King Oswy of Northumbria, who decided in favour of the Roman party – mainly persuaded by the claim that the pope was Christ's vicar on earth and 'the keeper of heaven's gate'.

Byzantine influence

In the face of the Muslim threat to Constantinople (Islamic armies besieged the city three times between AD 670 and AD 718), many fugitive Eastern scholars came to Rome, where their knowledge of Greek theology proved invaluable. Pope John IV (reigned AD 640–42) became the first of eleven Greek-speaking popes between AD 640 and AD 752. Yet he firmly supported Roman traditions against the Byzantines, insisting upon the papacy's primacy and independence from the emperor. His successors followed the same policy. But Greek influence became paramount; an English bishop visiting Rome wrote home that the entire papal court spoke Greek.

These Greek-speaking popes introduced some Greek customs; for example, portraits of saints in Roman churches now took on Byzantine characteristics. They also increased the veneration of the Virgin Mary, made the liturgy more formal and introduced Byzantine procedures to the papal court, emphasizing that the pope was successor to the apostle Peter.

Charlemagne

Time and again in the ensuing centuries the pope and the Western emperor were to struggle for power. When the leaders of the Christian community in the West were not attempting to stem the Muslim tide or absorb the invaders from the East, they were battling with great temporal leaders such as Charlemagne ('Charles the Great', reigned AD 800–814) for control of the institutional church.

A pious man, Charles attempted to reform the church by encouraging Benedictine monasticism, appointing effective bishops, abolishing paganism, spreading the Roman liturgy and sponsoring an intellectual revival known as the 'Carolingian Renaissance', largely guided by Alcuin, and which included the first serious Latin (in other words, Western) theology in three centuries.

But Charles made it clear that he – and not the pope – was to govern the church in his expanding Frankish kingdom. The popes tried to restrain his ambitions, but when some Roman aristocrats accused Pope Leo III (reigned AD 795–816) of misconduct, drove him out of office and tried to murder him, Charles rescued the beleaguered pope. Leo was restored to his office – but at the cost of dependence upon the emperor.

On Christmas Day, AD 800, Leo, in an attempt to establish his independence from the Eastern church, revived the empire in the West by crowning Charlemagne emperor. However, Charlemagne for his part did not warm to the idea of owing his crown to the pope, and for the next fourteen years strove to dominate the papacy.

Charlemagne was king of the Franks, but the pope had made him emperor. Did this mean only the pope could create an emperor? The popes thought so, but Charlemagne's descendants disputed it. As the century wore on, the imperial title went to the strongest, and the popes found themselves constantly embroiled in politics.

POPE VERSUS EMPEROR

For the next two centuries, emperors routinely interfered in church affairs, and popes and emperors competed for the loyalty of the church. This continual intervention in church matters by rulers such as Charlemagne led to further attempts by the papacy to strengthen itself to

prevent such intrusions. This consumed the energy of successive popes, sometimes diverting them from spiritual issues.

The noble families of Rome regarded the papacy as a means by which they could rule the city, and did not shrink from using violence. Leo V (reigned AD 903–904), John X (reigned AD 914–29) and Stephen VIII (reigned AD 939–42) were all murdered. Nor did these Roman aristocrats worry about the dignity of the papal office; John XII (reigned c. AD 955–64) was only eighteen when his family procured the papacy for him. The tenth century saw the papacy at a low ebb.

The German king Otto I (reigned AD 936–73), having beaten the Magyars, wanted an imperial title, which was duly offered him by Pope John XII in AD 962 – in order that Otto would save the pope from

Pope Leo III crowns Charlemagne in St Peter's Rome, Christmas Day, AD 800. The dispute between emperor and pope over superiority rumbled on for the next two centuries.

his Italian enemies. Otto marched on Rome in AD 962, and John accordingly crowned him emperor – thus setting up the Holy Roman empire, which was to survive until the nineteenth century.

Restoring papal power

The Holy Roman emperors now dominated the papacy, personally appointing and deposing popes. So a group of reforming popes tried to break this stranglehold, and put the papacy to the fore of the reform movement.

Pope Gregory VII (reigned c. 1023–85) and, above all, Innocent III (reigned 1198–1216) were militantly jealous of the church's rights. As Archdeacon Hildebrand, Gregory had already demonstrated his zeal for a Cluniac-style reform of the papacy. Intellectually brilliant, spiritually gifted, strongwilled and arrogant, he set out his claims for the papal office in his *Dictatus Papae* of 1075: 'The Roman Church has never erred and never will err till the end of time… The Pope can be judged by no one.' He was claiming not just supreme spiritual authority, but also superior temporal power, including that of deposing the emperor! All this stemmed from the belief that the pope derived his authority from the apostle Peter, whom Jesus had given authority over the church.

Gregory now set the papacy on a collision course with the secular princes. He chose to fight on the question of 'lay investiture' – a

The magnificent crown created for Otto I in an attempt to reinforce his imperial claims.

For no power on earth may judge the Apostolic See.

SYNOD OF ROME, AD 800

ceremony in which a lay noble gave the bishop his tokens of office (including vestments, hence 'investiture'). Gregory claimed, on the contrary, that only the pope could do this.

When the German emperor opposed him, Gregory excommunicated him, which so weakened the emperor politically that he begged (and received) the pope's forgiveness. But the emperor soon reasserted his control over the German church, ignored a second excommunication and drove Gregory from Rome. In 1085 the pope died in exile in southern Italy.

Yet, from Gregory's reign onwards, the papacy was to play the dominant hierarchical role in Roman Catholicism. The claims for papal supremacy and for church reform were now backed by a papal court that became increasingly sophisticated in its bureaucracy and communications,

See where all this damnable business is leading you! … Why [do] you sit from morning to evening listening to litigants? What fruit is there in these things? They can only create cobwebs.

BERNARD OF CLAIRVAUX, IN A LETTER TO THE POPE IN 1150 COMPLAINING ABOUT THE CHURCH'S BUREAUCRACY

overseeing a network of agents and advisers throughout the Christian West.

The early Norman kings of England, from William the Conqueror onwards, successfully remained under the control of the church. When Henry II attempted to wrest back control that had weakened during the chaotic reign of Stephen, he was defied by his erstwhile faithful servant, Archbishop Thomas Becket. Although Henry professed penitence following the murder of Becket – supposedly on the king's wishes – the English church remained *de facto* under the control of the English crown. Becket's rapid canonization did however give England a new saint and a new pilgrimage centre – Canterbury.

Innocent III

Innocent III (reigned 1198–1216), building on foundations laid by Gregory VII a century earlier, reached the zenith of papal power in the thirteenth century, establishing a virtual 'papal monarchy' in western Europe. Using a variety of means, during his papal reign Innocent brought the major rulers of Europe to heal, to the extent of subduing King John of England by excommunication.

Another indication of new vitality, as well as the increased power of the papacy, was the ability of the church to mount a series of crusades to recover the Holy Land from the Muslims. Innocent also called, and presided over, the Fourth Lateran Council in

The Angelic Doctor

Thomas Aquinas (c. 1225–74), a giant in body and mind, gained the nickname 'dumb-ox', as he was fat, slow and rather serious. Yet these characteristics masked a brilliant mind and a prolific pen. Among a shelf-full of works, Aquinas wrote the hugely influential *Summa Theologiae*, a kind of encyclopedia of Christian thought.

Aquinas ranked supreme in the medieval Christian thinkers' self-imposed task of synthesizing reason with revealed truth. But when the two appeared to clash, Aquinas opted for revealed truth. Known as 'the Angelic Doctor', he is considered by many Catholics to be the church's greatest theologian – only Augustine has exerted a similarly profound influence on the theology of the Western church.

Born in Naples, Italy, Thomas Aquinas became a Dominican friar at seventeen and followed the great philosopher–theologian Albertus Magnus (1193–1280) – the most important influence on his own thought – from Cologne to Paris.

After 1256, when he was made Doctor of Theology, Aquinas' life was one of unceasing work. He served his order, made frequent long journeys and constantly advised the pope on matters of state. He preached daily, while also assembling his greatest work, the *Summa Theologiae*, in which he sets out his systematic theology.

On 6 December 1273, Aquinas had a mystical experience, after which he set aside his *Summa* with the words, 'I cannot go on... All I have written seems like so much straw compared with... what has been revealed to me.'

Aquinas believed 'that for the knowledge of any truth humanity needs divine help, in order that the intellect may be moved by God'. He is well known for his five rational proofs for the existence of God. In Aquinas' thought, the goal of human existence is union and eternal fellowship with God, achieved through the 'beatific vision', in which a person experiences perfect, unending happiness by comprehending the essence of God. This vision, which occurs after death, comes as a gift of God to those who have experienced salvation through Christ on earth.

1215 – the most important ecumenical gathering of the Middle Ages – which dealt with problems of renewal and reform, and also authorized crusades against Christian 'heretics' such as the Albigensians in southern France.

The Lateran Council

Named after its meeting place, the Church of St John Lateran in Rome, the Lateran council embodied the revival in the power of the papacy and the church that had been taking place over the previous two hundred years.

All of this added to papal prestige. Never before or since has the papacy wielded so much power.

The Lateran Council pronounced as official the doctrine of transubstantiation – that the blood and wine were miraculously transformed into Christ's body and blood during the Mass: 'The Body and Blood are truly contained in the Sacrament... under the appearance of bread and wine, after the bread has been changed into the Body, and the wine into the Blood, through the power of God.'

The council not only backed the

This fresco by Andrea da Firenze (c. 1343–77) depicting 'The Triumph of Catholic Doctrine' graphically symbolizes the zenith of papal power.

Crusades against the Muslims of Palestine, but also decided to try to control Jews living in the West. The Jews, like all Christians, were now required to pay tithes to the clergy and, ominously, to wear a distinctive piece of clothing – yellow or red – or, in Italy, a hat of a particular colour.

Boniface VIII

A growing number of disputes between the popes and secular rulers as to their respective authority proved seriously damaging to the church, and with Pope Boniface VIII (reigned 1294–1303) papal claims outran actual power. The duel came to a head in 1303 when Boniface confronted King Philip IV of France (reigned 1285–1314) over who had ultimate jurisdiction over the Gallican (French) Church – the pope or the king. With a boldness not seen since the days of the twelfth-century

German emperors, and using military force, the king challenged, imprisoned and humiliated the pope.

Philip added insult to injury by securing the election as new pope of the Frenchman Clement V (reigned 1305–14), and moving the College of Cardinals to Avignon – a new papal state, surrounded by the kingdom of France. From 1309 to 1377, the seat of the papacy remained at Avignon, a period the Italian writer Petrarch called 'the Babylonian Captivity'.

THE GREAT PAPAL SCHISM

During this Avignonese period, the fortunes of the papacy declined as it became obvious it had fallen under French control. Because France was the dominant power of the period, this raised problems for Christians elsewhere in Europe. Eventually, under increasing pressure to return to

The Palace of the Popes, Avignon, France, where the papacy was located for much of the fourteenth century.

Rome, the College of Cardinals elected an Italian pope, Urban VI (reigned 1378–89), who returned to the Eternal City. This, however, only precipitated a split among the cardinals, with a majority voting to depose Urban, elect a new French pope and return once more to Avignon. This, in turn, led to 'the Great Papal Schism' (1378–1417) when first two, then three, popes all claimed to be the true successor of the apostle Peter.

This scandalous schism was inevitably a major cause of a decline in papal prestige and authority. The rulers and people of Europe divided according to their loyalties to the competing popes in Rome and Avignon, and to the third 'pope-at-large'. Finally, in an effort to end the chaos, the roving pope John XXIII (now declared an 'anti-pope'), with the aid of the Holy Roman emperor Sigismund (reigned 1410–37), convened the Council of Constance (1414–18). With the election of Martin V (reigned 1417–31) to replace all three papal claimants, the papacy was restored to Rome and the schism at last came to an end.

The success of Constance led to the summoning of a further council at Basel (1431–49), to try to solve the most pressing problems of the church. Some historians have dubbed this 'the Conciliar Age'.

Reform

The popes continued to claim supreme authority, while still weakening their claims to holiness by meddling in power politics. The papacy was coming under increasing criticism and the appetite of the popes for taxes, tithes and tolls scandalized many across Europe. There were, of course, attempts at reform. During the fifteenth century, much hope was vainly invested in the series of church councils mentioned above.

RENAISSANCE POPES

By the mid-fifteenth century, the papacy had begun to recoup its fortunes with the election of Nicholas V (reigned 1447–55). Nicholas was the first of a long line of 'Renaissance popes', in tune with the new culture. However, the holiness and humanist

Pope Alexander VI, born Roderigo de Borgia, generally reckoned to have been one of the worst popes.

learning of a pope such as Nicholas was soon nullified by his successors. Pius II (reigned 1458–64), Innocent VIII (reigned 1484–92), Alexander VI (reigned 1492–1503), Julius II (reigned 1503–13) and Leo X (reigned 1513–21) were worldly, urbane, sophisticated, talented – but seldom religious. They were noted more for their paganism, nepotism, immorality and Machiavellian politics than any saintliness or wise statesmanship.

Probably the greatest damage to the church was inflicted by Rodrigo Borgia (reigned 1431–1503), Pope Alexander VI, who was uniquely unfitted for this supreme position. He fathered – and acknowledged – numerous children, including Lucretia and Cesare Borgia, the latter the model for Niccolo Machiavelli's pragmatic handbook for politicians, *The Prince* (1513).

Renaissance popes continued to dominate Rome. Leo X dismissed the uproar of the Reformation in the north as 'a monk's quarrel' and spoke with disdain of 'drunken Germans'. In the end, as we shall see in the next chapter, the church was too late in taking the issues seriously, and the Lutheran dispute soon evolved into the Protestant Reformation.

CHAPTER 5

Monks and Monasteries

In the search for God, most religions include practitioners who take their beliefs more literally, more seriously or more exactingly than the rest. Sometimes this entails rejecting what others consider normal and good – for example, marriage and sex. Sometimes it's a matter of increased piety – more praying, at more inconvenient times. And sometimes it involves withdrawing from society either to a solitary life, devoted to cultivating the soul, or to a community life, apart from the world but with others of similar persuasion.

Jewish ascetics

There had always been such a strand of asceticism within Judaism. 'Nazirites' made vows of abstinence from wine. Old Testament prophets such as Elisha gathered groups of male followers for special teaching and prayer.

In the time of Jesus, John the Baptist was such a solitary ascetic, living on a restricted diet in the Judean wilderness and preaching a stern message of repentance. Probably the best-known religious community of this same period is that which settled at Qumran, on the north-west shore of the Dead Sea, well below sea-level: as barren a spot as you could wish for. Even today, the exact beliefs of this group are fiercely debated; but it is probable that they were a splinter-group from the Jewish sect known as the 'Essenes' – an extremist offshoot of an ascetic minority – cultivating a particularly austere and exclusively male way of life. (Another recent theory is that it wasn't a religious colony at all, but an isolated pottery!)

A thread of asceticism can also be traced through some early Christian groups in the centuries immediately following. James, the first leader of the Jerusalem church, was held up as an exemplar for his frequent fasting and prayer. Some early Syriac-speaking churches seem to have restricted baptism to those who were celibate rather than extending it to all believers. (Syriac was a Semitic language, originally a dialect used in Edessa, northern Mesopotamia.) Martyrdom too was viewed as a pinnacle of devotion by many believers within the early church. And asceticism was common among some of the fringe Christian movements, such as the Montanists and the followers of Marcion, whom we encountered in chapter 3.

The call to asceticism

With the beginnings of official toleration and recognition of

Christianity, from shortly before the time of the emperor Constantine, the church started to attract many new members. However, more meant less: that is, standards of ethical and spiritual practice within churches apparently fell noticeably as membership grew and less seemed demanded of their adherents. In reaction, believers desiring a purer form of Christianity began to withdraw both from the existing churches and from society itself. Martyrdom was no longer an attainable goal for most, as the faith was now licit. So, as bishops wrestled with emperors for control of the church, and nominal, formal Christianity became increasingly common, the monastic life came to replace the martyr's crown as the ultimate form of sacrifice for many of the most devout.

A later writer, John Cassian (c. AD 360–435), described this process. As Christian fervour and devotion cooled in the churches, he wrote:

…many combined their belief in Christ with wealthy living; but those who retained the ardour of the apostles… withdrew from their cities and the society of those who thought this lax living was acceptable for themselves and the church as a whole, and there practised alone or in groups what they recalled the apostles had instituted for the whole church.

ANTONY IN THE DESERT

Developing from this practice of private asceticism among the first Christians, some of the faithful began to pursue the life of the hermit, dedicated to God. Antony (c. AD 256–356), a young Egyptian, is the earliest celebrated Christian hermit (though, confusingly, there is some doubt as to his

Hieronymous Bosch (c. 1450–1503) depicts the temptations Antony confronted in the desert.

historicity: possibly he is a fictitious figure, employed to inform readers about monasticism – and temptation). There is doubt, too, as to whether Antony (if historical!) was indeed the innovator and pioneer he is claimed to be, as at the time he himself decided on an ascetic life, he is said also to have entrusted his sister to a convent of previously existing nuns. (There were certainly a number of women's monastic communities in Egypt before Antony's time.)

Antony's life was evidently turned around by hearing a preacher expound Jesus' words: 'If you want to be perfect, go, sell your possessions and give to the poor, and you will have treasure in heaven. Then come, follow me' (Matthew 19:21). Antony did exactly and literally as the Bible verse required. (Centuries later, Francis of Assisi experienced a similar 'conversion'.)

Antony spent his first fifteen years as a hermit living among tombs in the desert, but even this existence, he decided, was insufficiently austere – so he then moved to an old fort deep in the middle of the desert. All this in an effort to get away from the busyness of human society and to cultivate a closer relationship with God.

The flaw in Antony's plan was that he soon became well known for his reclusive life, and increasing numbers of the curious and dissatisfied began to visit him in the desert. Consequently, Antony believed he had no alternative but to provide Christian instruction for those who arrived to gawp at him in his desert hide-out. However, eventually he decided enough was enough, and left his fort to set up a community of monks near the Red Sea, at Mount Colzim.

Antony was far from being the sole monastic – and as we have seen, may not even have been the first. Many similar hermits withdrew to the deserts of Syria and Egypt in temporary or permanent retreat from society and in search of a more spiritual form of life. Living alone or in small groups, they devoted their time to prayer and meditation, and often attempted unusual feats of spiritual and physical endurance, such as fasting while standing for long, sleepless hours in prayer.

Such deprivation sometimes precipitated hallucinations and nightmare visions, often with a strong sexual content – Antony's biography includes lurid accounts of such

Simeon Stylites (c. AD 390–459)

Some of the earliest monks and hermits took asceticism to extraordinary extremes. Simeon, who lived near Antioch in Syria, started his career as a monk by living for forty days in a cave, with his right leg fastened to an iron chain. Deciding this was insufficiently rigorous, he later built and took up permanent residence on top of a pillar that eventually reached 60 feet (18 m) in height. He passed messages to others, and received what he needed to survive, by means of a bucket winched up and down from his perch atop the column.

Ironically, though presumably he had retired to the desert to seek seclusion as well as bodily discipline, his exploits attracted vast numbers of spectators, many of whom were apparently convinced and converted by his

devotion. In time, a church was constructed around his pillar, and he became known as 'Simeon (or Simon) Stylites' (*style* being the Greek word for column or pillar).

Although he may appear to modern eyes as an outlandish eccentric, clearly to contemporary men and women – both Christian and non-Christian – he provided not just a tourist attraction, but an outstanding example of devotion to God.

'temptations', with the devil appearing to him as a 'little black boy… with flashing eyes and fiery breath, and horns on his head, half man, half ass'. The great Christian leader and writer Athanasius (c. AD 296–373), who was for a time in exile, hiding among the hermits in Egypt, wrote the important *Life of Antony*, which in turn helped stimulate many others to follow his example in fleeing to the desert to lead an ascetic and solitary existence.

Pachomius and communal monasticism

The first communal Christian monastery we know of was set up around AD 320 by Pachomius (c. AD 287–346), formerly a soldier serving in Constantine's army. After converting to Christianity as a result of encountering hermits in Egypt, he spent some time as a solitary hermit himself. Pachomius then proceeded to found an ascetic community at Tabennisi, by the River Nile. He renounced the rigorous extremes of asceticism of the likes of Simeon Stylites, laying down regular routines for meals and worship, and trying to ensure that his community was self-supporting – for instance by growing and selling its own fruit and vegetables. The monks even owned some Nile fishing-boats.

Candidates for admission to the order set up by Pachomius were, if necessary, taught to read and write, and as part of their qualifications to join the community they had to recite from memory entire sections of the Bible. Further communities followed and, although the first were for men only, Pachomius later also superintended early communities for women.

Pachomius had set an important pattern for monasticism for the future: that of a community of monks, sometimes even living in a single building, who followed a set rule. For the present, however, a looser arrangement tended to prevail, in which the group of monks spent most of their time alone in their individual huts, but joined together for communal meals and prayer.

The monastic movement spreads

A fourth-century historian of Egyptian monasteries believed that they provided a kind of defensive wall, protecting the entire Christian community by their prayer and spiritual power:

There is no town or village in Egypt… that is not surrounded by hermitages as if by walls, and the people depend on their prayers as if on God himself… Through them the world is kept in being.

By the end of the fourth century AD, monastic life had spread from Egypt throughout the Christian world, both town and country. There were now at least 300 monastic houses in Constantinople, and others in spectacularly remote spots such as St Catherine's Monastery, Mount Sinai, the unique rock-cut monasteries of the lunar-like landscape of

Cappadocia, and the Holy Mountain of Athos, Greece.

Church and monastery
Basil the Great (AD 330–79) who became Bishop of Caesarea in Cappadocia in AD 364, founded a community of his own which introduced further important new trends. He was concerned that monks and hermits should be more closely integrated with the local church, that the local bishop should have overall authority over a monastery, and that community rather than solitary prayer should be paramount within the monastery. Basil also wanted to ensure that monasteries served society; his own community offered medical help, poor relief and education to those living nearby. His model for monastic life was summed up in two 'rules', which Eastern Orthodox monks still observe today.

WESTERN MONKS
Martin of Tours (d. AD 397) pioneered monasticism in western Europe. Much like Pachomius, Martin founded his first community after initially serving as a soldier, and subsequently living as a solitary hermit. The monastery he set up at Marmoutier in France became noted for its austerity and holiness, and provided a catalyst for the spread of Christianity into France.

Further monasteries were founded on the island of Lérins, near Cannes, by a monk named Honoratus, and in AD 415 at Marseilles by John Cassian (d. c. AD 433). Cassian wrote widely on monasticism, discussing such varied topics as monks' clothing, monastery services and monks' spiritual warfare. Another innovator, a Roman senator named Cassiodorus (AD 490–583), founded a monastery at Vivarium, in Calabria, southern Italy, which introduced to monasticism a new emphasis on the study and copying of ancient manuscripts – an activity that in due course became particularly closely associated with Christian monasteries and literally saved much of ancient civilization.

St Benedict
It was Benedict of Nursia (c. AD 480–c. 547), the so-called 'Father of Western Monasticism', who provided what was to become the definitive 'rule' for monasteries in western Europe. Little is known about Benedict, outside a hagiography ostensibly written by Pope Gregory the Great, and there is considerable doubt whether (like Antony) he actually existed.

Benedict is supposed to have been born in Nursia, Umbria, to have studied in Rome and, after living for a time as a hermit in Subiaco, southern Italy, is said to have set up in AD 528 what became an influential monastery at Monte Cassino (perhaps better remembered today for a particularly savage battle during the Second World War). Benedict's 'Rule' was written at Monte Cassino, but only after his death, when a copy reached Pope Gregory in Rome, did it become more widely known.

Benedict of Nursia preaches to his monastic followers near Monte Cassino, from a fifteenth-century Flemish illumination by Jean de Stavelot (1388–1449).

Are you hurrying towards your heavenly home? Then with Christ's help, keep this little rule that we have written for beginners. After that, you can set out for loftier summits of the teaching and virtues… and under God's protection you will reach them.

THE CONCLUDING WORDS OF THE RULE OF BENEDICT

The Rule

Regardless of Benedict's personal historicity, his Rule is of huge historical significance. Benedict's Rule, based in part on an earlier document known as the 'Rule of the Master', and drawing on the ideas of both Basil of Caesarea and John Cassian, divides a monk's life into two essential activities: prayer and work (in Latin, *orare et laborare*). The work usually consisted of hard manual labour in the monastery's fields, orchards or workshop, though Benedict's Rule was less concerned to encourage a life of extreme austerity and penance than to achieve a harmonious community life. The Rule required vows of obedience, stability and 'continual conversion', which were later succinctly summarized as poverty, chastity and obedience.

Benedict was also concerned that the monastery should provide care for the weak and the sick, as well as offering hospitality to strangers. He insisted that a monk should stay at the monastic house where he had originally taken his vows; that the abbot should be the spiritual head of the monastery, and be responsible for its discipline; and that monasteries should be well organized and centred on worship. Daily life in a Benedictine monastery was constructed around a set liturgical pattern of seven lengthy prayer services: Matins (or Lauds), Prime, Terce, Sect, Nones, Vespers and Compline.

Gradually the Rule of Benedict supplanted all other Rules for monasteries in western Europe. Benedictines established monasteries throughout western Europe, supported education and promoted culture in the early Middle Ages and beyond. Even today, most monasteries observe the Rule of Benedict largely as it was originally set out.

IRELAND

Meanwhile, in north-west Europe, and outside the orbit of Rome, a rather different expression of Christianity had sprung up among the Irish. Building upon earlier vestiges of Christianity, Patrick spearheaded from Britain the conversion of the Irish people in the fifth century AD (though there is no definitive evidence that he was himself a monk or founded monasteries – or even, some scholars claim again, that he actually existed!)

Irish monasticism seems to have taken on something similar to the pattern of the Egyptian monastic communities. The Irish monks became renowned for their devotion to Christ, mystical spirituality, thirst for scholarship, ascetic rigour, restlessness and evangelistic zeal. Today, some New Age devotees have laid claim to Celtic Christianity; they would probably be shocked if they bothered to investigate the rigorous but distinctly orthodox tenets of the original Celtic Christians' faith.

The Irish monasteries also became renowned for their libraries and richly illuminated (illustrated) manuscripts, with their distinctive and intricate Celtic designs. A prime example is the famous *Book of Kells*, conserved today at Trinity College, Dublin. But while monks elsewhere were required by the Rule of Benedict to stay put in one geographical location, the Irish monks had a strong wanderlust – a tendency to adopt a travelling style of life.

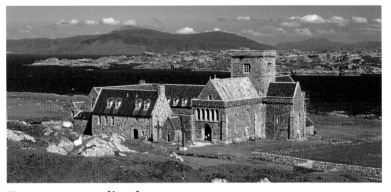

Iona Abbey, Iona, Scotland, centre of Columba's mission.

Europe evangelized

Much of the British Isles and many regions of central and western Europe were evangelized in the sixth century AD by Irish missionary-monks, such as Columba and Columbanus. Columba (AD 521–97) sailed from Ireland to the island of Iona, off the west coast of Scotland, where he soon established what became a particularly influential monastery. (A modern Church of Scotland community on the island has attempted to take up the baton.)

In turn, a monk from Iona, Aidan (d. AD 651), was sent to help King Oswald of Northumbria (c. AD 605–42) convert his people to Christianity, setting up headquarters on Lindisfarne (Holy Island) – a name that has become synonymous with a consummately illuminated manuscript of the Gospels, now preserved at the British Museum, London. Further Celtic monks proceeded to Christianize the East Saxons, Mercians and East Anglians of England.

However, this dynamic Christian growth was not contained by the English Channel. The Irish monk Columbanus (c. AD 543–615), an aristocrat by birth, travelled to Gaul, founding monasteries at Anneguy and Luxeuil, and later at Bobbio, in Burgundy. Bobbio, like the Irish-founded abbey of St Gall, in due course earned a high reputation for its scholarship. Columbanus also preached to the Alemanni, launching the spread of Christianity into southern Germany. And yet another monk, Amandus (c. AD 584–679), took the Christian message to the Basques, Slavs, northern Franks and Netherlanders.

Anglo-Saxon monk-missionaries

In time, this Irish evangelistic impulse was disrupted by Viking invasions and internal wars. But the newly confident Anglo-Saxon church was now ready and prepared to take up the challenge. The Venerable Bede (c. AD 673–735), regarded as the foremost scholar of his age, spent almost his entire life as a monk at the monastery of Jarrow in Northumbria. Learned in Latin, Hebrew and Greek, he numbered a Bible translation and the great *Church History of the English People* – the first history of the English – among his impressive achievements.

Another Anglo-Saxon, Wilfrid of York (AD 634–709), was the first to take Christianity to the Frisians, and was followed by his own pupil, Willibrord (d. AD 739), who set up a pivotal monastery at Echternach, Germany. Winfrith of Crediton, Devon, better known as Boniface (AD 680–754) – 'the apostle to the Germans' – carried the faith from the Low Countries into Germany, evangelizing the regions of Bavaria,

Boniface, 'the apostle to the Germans', confronts pagan priests in a dramatic early-twentieth-century depiction by Johannes Gehrts.

Thuringia and Hesse. Boniface had set out with a commission from the pope to convert anybody, anywhere. He carried this open brief through with a firm will and dramatic flair: he is remembered for boldly chopping down an oak tree sacred to the northern god Woden at Geismar; from its wood he is said to have constructed a new Christian chapel. Boniface also founded the leading Benedictine monastery of St Fulda, near Frankfurt on Main, Germany.

Anglo-Saxon missionaries worked with unparalleled vigour in these years: one historian even claimed Boniface 'had a deeper influence on the history of Europe than any Englishman who has ever lived'.

To the north

Further north, the Frankish monk Anskar (AD 801–865), the 'apostle of the north', who came originally from the Benedictine monastery of Corbie, France, brought Christianity to Denmark, setting up a little wooden church at Hedeby. However, it took the 'official' conversion of Denmark by King Cnut to make a lasting impact. Subsequently invited to help by King Björn, Anskar went on to build the first Christian church in Sweden.

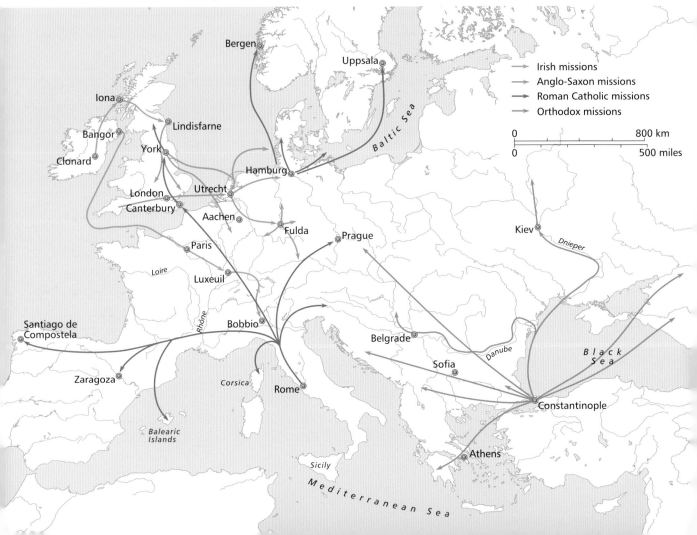

Medieval monastic missions.

Irish missions
Anglo-Saxon missions
Roman Catholic missions
Orthodox missions

0   800 km
0   500 miles

Eastern monastic missions

But it was not just Celtic and Anglo-Saxon monks who were at work. In the ninth century Eastern monks, the intrepid brothers Cyril (AD 826–69) and Methodius (c. AD 815–85), travelled from Thessalonica to central Europe, translating the Bible and liturgical texts into Slavonic, and establishing the Orthodox Church in parts of Moravia and Bohemia. Known as the 'apostles of the southern Slavs', they were sent to Moravia by the emperor Michael III. They are still revered by Bulgars, Serbs, Croats and Czechs.

Noble monks

As we have seen, from the sixth century AD there was a tendency for almost all monasteries in the West to follow the Benedictine Rule. Other changes also occurred. For example, instead of monks largely consisting of individuals following up a personal call to the monastic life, increasingly the nobility offered their sons or daughters to monastic houses, to devote their lives to God. This influx of more literate and educated candidates to monasteries gradually led to less emphasis being placed on manual labour and more on the liturgical practice of the monastery, as well as on such cultural activities as copying ancient literature and sometimes brilliantly illuminating the texts. Much of the secular Latin poetry and prose we know today has been passed down to us via manuscripts copied in medieval monastic houses.

The 'devoting' of nobles' children to monasteries is one way in which during this period monastic houses evolved from being retreats from civil society, where a life of perfection could be cultivated, to being regarded as religious bodies that served the wider society by praying for, and on behalf of, the rest of humanity.

MONASTIC REFORM

However, these changes did not go unchallenged. A second Benedict, Benedict of Aniane (c. AD 750–821), in AD 817 called upon monks to observe greater discipline and asceticism, to undertake more manual work, to study less and to be less closely involved with the outside world. But this had little immediate effect; the Christian West was at the same time being battered by external assaults from the Magyars, the Muslim Saracens and the much-feared Vikings, as a result of which many monasteries were destroyed or fell into serious decay.

However, from the tenth century, spiritual renewal began to sweep across the Western world, starting with the foundation of the monastery of Cluny in Burgundy, central France, by William the Pious around AD 910. A succession of diligent abbots made Cluny a model of monastic reform, and many daughter houses followed, eventually numbering more than a thousand.

Cluny was founded mainly to rejuvenate Christian monasticism by the stricter observance of the Benedictine Rule. It attempted to revert to the purity of the original monasteries started in the West by Benedict of Nursia, and to the early emphasis on the daily cycle of worship as the core activity of the monks. But whereas Benedict had sought to segregate his monks from society, Cluny tried to integrate monasticism with society. The reforming monks wished to present to ordinary, lay people a radically alternative way of life from that of the ordinary clergy – some of whom, in the opinion of many, had become both dissolute and excessively affluent. Cluniac monks usually joined as young boys and received all their necessary training within the cloister.

By contrast with most earlier monasteries, which had essentially been independent – linked only by shared practices and beliefs, and sometimes shared founders – the powerful and long-ruling abbots of Cluny insisted that in the many daughter houses that they spawned, every monk owed ultimate obedience to them rather than to the prior of his respective monastery. These reforms were mirrored in reforms to monasteries in the Low Countries, Lorraine and Anglo-Saxon England.

Cluny became the catalyst of a wider reform movement in the church at large in the West. Among other things, the Cluniac leaders wanted to stamp out the practice of buying and selling church offices and positions (simony), to recall the clergy to celibacy, to eliminate corruption from the church and to encourage greater piety among ordinary Christians. Their aim was to achieve these reforms from the top downwards, through a spiritually revitalized pope who shared their reforming goals. This they finally accomplished with the election of Hildebrand as Pope Gregory VII (AD 1073–85) in the following century.

Meanwhile in England, Dunstan (AD 909–88), Archbishop of Canterbury, worked to reform the English church and promote Benedictine monasticism, while his contemporary the Bishop of York, Oswald (d. AD 992), eliminated abuses in the church and established monasteries.

Charterhouse

The Cluniacs were not the only reforming movement within medieval monasticism. Indeed, they began to attract some criticism from others for their excessive attention to ceremony and splendour. In 1084 Bruno of Cologne, former master of a cathedral school in Rheims, founded a monastery named La Grande Chartreuse in southern France, 'on a high and dreadful cliff under which there is a deep gorge in a precipitous valley'. Against the general pattern, this house reverted to a hermit-type organization, with the monks essentially living solitary lives in a cluster of individual cells. The Carthusian order (English, Charterhouse), which started here, remained the most austere form of monasticism throughout the Middle Ages. Its leaders claimed it was never reformed because it was never corrupted.

Cistercians

Others too believed that Cluniac reform did not go far enough. A much more austere model of monastery was founded at Cîteaux, near Dijon, Burgundy, in 1098, and rapidly gave rise to the new order of Cistercian monks. This order reverted to a particularly strict observance of the Benedictine Rule.

Cistercian monasteries were deliberately built in utterly remote spots in order to avoid contact with town-dwellers. Their sites were chosen for their inaccessibility 'by

[The monks] all have their own separate cells round the cloister in which they work, sleep and eat. On Sunday they get their food from the cellarer, that is, bread and beans, the latter, their only kind of relish, being cooked by each in his own cell... They have fish and cheese on Sundays and the major festivals... Gold, silver, ornaments for the church they get from no one, having none in the place but a silver cup... They hardly ever speak anywhere, for when it is necessary to ask for anything, they do so by signs. Their dress is a hair shirt and few other clothes... Although they submit to every kind of privation, they build up a very rich library. The less their store of worldly goods, the more do they toil laboriously for that meat which does not perish, but endures for ever.

GUIBERT DE NOGENT ON THE MONASTIC LIFE AT LA GRANDE CHARTREUSE

reason of thickets and thorns and inhabited only by wild beasts'. The Cistercians (often known as the 'White Monks' from the colour of their habits) stressed silence and rigour, and renewed the emphasis on hard manual work. They rejected 'the use of coats, capes, worsted cloth, hoods, pants, combs, counterpanes and bed-clothes, together with a variety of dishes in the refectory'.

Like the Cluniacs, the network of Cistercian monasteries had a centralized form of organization, headed by the Abbot of Cîteaux, with an annual assembly of all abbots held at the mother house. Leading Cistercians included Bernard of Clairvaux (1090–1153), celebrated for his spirituality and his impact on both church and state and on the first Crusade.

By the year of Bernard's death in 1153, there were already some 360 Cistercian monasteries in Europe, with 122 in Britain, 88 in Italy, 56 in Spain and 100 in German-speaking countries; by the end of the thirteenth century, there were in total 694 Cistercian monasteries in western Europe.

In order to survive, the Cistercian monks cultivated the wasteland around their monasteries, soon becoming expert at sheep farming. Ironically, this proved to be the seed of their downfall. To help clear the land, and to meet the growing demand for wool, the monasteries employed illiterate 'lay brothers', who were only part-members of the order, thus diluting the purity of the monastic ideal. The Cistercians' financial success resulting from the sale of wool soon made the order extremely rich. So the order that set out in search of extreme austerity ended by being fiercely criticized for its greed and avarice.

Other new medieval orders included the less austere Augustinians (known in England as

The abbey of La Grande Chartreuse depicted in a panel painting that also shows the resurrection of the dead.

'Austin Canons'), founded in the mid-eleventh century, who claimed that their rule of life was based on principles first set out by Augustine of Hippo. Among other activities, they helped set up schools and hospitals for the care of the sick, hospices for those suffering from leprosy and hospitals for pregnant women.

Like all human institutions, the monasteries were not slow in succumbing to worldly temptations. Wealthy benefactors made lavish donations to monastic houses in an attempt to buy prayers for their success in this world and the next; this led to successful monasteries acquiring vast estates, and developing the administrative and financial expertise that their upkeep entailed. The monastic life started as a calling, but all too often was corrupted into a profession. Similarly monastic scholarship frequently stultified into dry traditionalism.

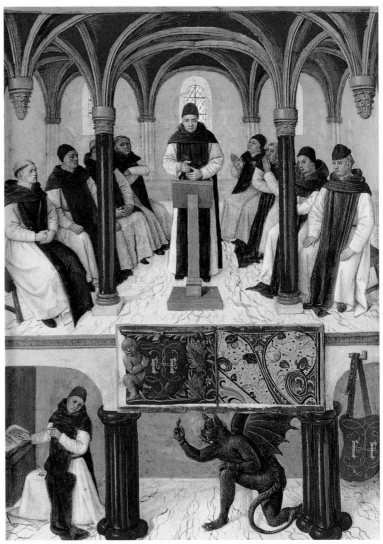

NEW ORDERS
Francis of Assisi
The saintly Francis of Assisi (1182–1226) was motivated not so much by a reaction to monastic decline as by a direct response to the Scriptures. Born into the family of an Assisi cloth-merchant in 1112, Francis enjoyed all the luxuries his father could afford. But suddenly, in his twenties, he rejected all this, in literal obedience to Christ's command in Matthew chapter 4 to reject the devil's offer of worldly power and glory and serve only God. He left home, clad in rough clothes, to take up a wandering life, followed by a few like-minded friends. They begged from the rich, gave to the poor, tended the sick and preached to anyone they met.

Francis instructed his early followers to preach: 'The kingdom of Heaven is at hand. Heal the sick, cleanse the lepers, raise the dead, cast

These illustrations by Jean Fouquet (c. 1415–c. 1477) from a Book of Hours show Bernard of Clairvaux teaching monks and wrestling with temptation.

out devils. Freely you have received, freely give.'

In time Francis' followers became recognized as a new order: the Franciscans. Though they took similar vows to other monks, the Franciscans were known as 'friars' and were 'mendicants' – constantly on the road, not based in a single location or building. The friars broke away from the accepted monastic ideal of living apart from the sinful world, but they were still concerned to exhibit the excellence of the Christian way of life. They wanted to bring the faith to ordinary people, not simply by cloistered prayer, but by living among them.

Francis is often linked with the birds and wild creatures that, legend claims, listened spellbound to his sermons. In fact, most of his efforts were devoted to the expanding cities of medieval Italy, where he preached and cared practically for the poor.

Francis' friend, Clare (c. 1193–1253), established an order for women similar to the Franciscans, called the Poor Clares.

Francis warned all his followers that they would be tempted with riches and power following his death. Despite this perceptive warning, soon after his death in 1226 a massive basilica to Francis' memory was erected in the town of Assisi itself.

Missionaries

Missions were a key concern of the Franciscans. Francis himself managed to travel to Egypt in 1219 where, dirty and penniless, he surrendered to Muslim guards, demanding an audience with the Sultan. The Muslim leader heard him preach but dismissed Francis' offer to firewalk to demonstrate to them the strength of his faith.

The Franciscans went on to send brothers to Hungary, Spain and the East, and in the thirteenth century established houses in eastern Europe, North Africa and the Middle East. Later, Franciscan missionaries travelled as far as Central Asia and India, and in the fourteenth century an Archbishop of the East was appointed near Peking.

The Franciscans continued to lead the way as missionaries. The Spanish and Portuguese conquest of the New World was rapidly followed up by the friars – with Franciscans to the fore. They immediately set about converting the population, and often attempted to adapt and accommodate Christianity to the culture of the new adherents.

As we will see in chapter 9, Catholic orders played a huge part in evangelizing the world, from the time of Francis onwards. Orders such as the Jesuits saw a major part of their task as evangelizing non-Christian parts of the world. From the Catholic Reformation onwards, and peaking in the nineteenth century, many new orders were formed specifically to take the faith to all parts of the globe.

Lord, make me an instrument of thy peace...

FRANCIS OF ASSISI

Francis of Assisi, detail from *Saint Francis Preaches to the Birds* by Giotto (1267–1337).

Dominic (1170–1221)

Francis' followers, the Franciscans, were often nicknamed 'Grey Friars' from their grey habits which distinguished them from the 'Black Friars', the Dominicans – or more properly the Order of Friars Preacher, founded by Dominic de Guzman (1170–1221) in 1214. The Dominican friars were a new force in the church: preaching monks, who spent much of their time in the towns and cities, gaining popular respect by their simple living and their caring attitudes. Their churches were plain and undecorated, designed for effective preaching as much as for celebrating the Mass.

Education

Education was at this time still almost entirely in the hands of the church. Until around the tenth century, the exposition of doctrine was the responsibility of bishops or monks in monasteries. Over the next four centuries, however, they were gradually superseded by masters teaching in the new cathedral schools and universities. The Dominicans keenly pursued learning and were closely involved in the rise of these new universities – Paris, Bologna, and later Oxford and Cambridge. But the Franciscans had their intellectuals too, such as Bonaventura (1221–74), Duns Scotus (1266–1308), William of Ockham (c. 1280–c. 1349) and Roger Bacon (c. 1214–92).

Paris was the main centre of learning, and was adopted by both the Franciscans and the Dominicans as their main training centre. Major scholars such as Anselm of Bec, Peter Abelard, Peter Lombard, Albert the Great, Duns Scotus and Thomas Aquinas studied and taught at Paris during this period. They were striving to harmonize the theology of Augustine with the philosophy of classical Greek thinkers – especially Aristotle – in an intellectual system known as scholasticism.

Anselm (c. 1033–1109), Archbishop of Canterbury in the late eleventh century, is remembered for his logical ('ontological') argument for the existence of God. He wrote of his method: 'I do not seek to understand that I may believe, but I believe that I may understand: for this I also believe, that unless I believe I will not understand.' He also wrote importantly on Christ's death on the cross – *Cur Deus Homo* (Why did God become man?). His answer: Only God-Man (Christ) could make a satisfactory compensation for human sin.

Peter Abelard (1079–1142) attacked some of Anselm's ideas, but is better remembered for his illicit love affair with his pupil Héloïse. He was daring too in his thinking, and attracted the suspicions of other scholars for his radical views of the Trinity and of Christ's death on the cross.

Bringing together the Catholic articles of faith and the method of reasoning by logic was the crowning achievement of Thomas Aquinas in his *Summa Theologiae*, which was to form the chief basis of much future Catholic theology.

Crusading orders

Fervently supported by monastic leaders such as Bernard of Clairvaux, the Crusades led to the founding of further new monastic orders. The Knights Hospitaller were set up (as their name implies) to provide care for sick pilgrims and wounded crusading knights; however, it was not long before they also actively took up arms.

Similarly, the Knights Templar were founded with the purpose of defending the Holy City of Jerusalem and the rest of the Holy Land. To this end, they constructed elaborate castles across Palestine. They soon became exceedingly wealthy, and were suppressed by Philip IV of France in 1312, after being accused on apparently flimsy grounds of homosexuality and necromancy. (More recently they have been accused, on equally flimsy grounds, of being responsible for sustaining the essential ingredients of *The Da Vinci Code* myth.)

A third crusading order, the Teutonic Knights, originally set up in 1189 as a tent hospital for German pilgrims at the port of Acre, on the Mediterranean coast of Palestine, soon took an actively militant role in conquering and forcibly Christianizing regions of the Baltic and Russia.

The monks' contribution

Both monks and friars contributed hugely to medieval life in western Europe. Their churches were seen as praying power-houses for society. Many monasteries became vital centres of scholarship and learning. Some monks devoted years to copying and illuminating Christian and classical manuscripts, thereby ensuring their transmission to modern times. Monastic orders founded and ran schools, hospitals, hospices and shelters for the poor and destitute. They were also known widely for their hospitality both to religious pilgrims and to ordinary travellers.

NEW HOLINESS

In the Low Countries, a new form of Christian semi-monastic community was introduced in the fourteenth century. Named the Brotherhood of the Common Life, it was less tightly disciplined than earlier monastic orders, and encouraged both devotion

and learning. This group called for a return to the clear preaching of the Bible and to holy living.

The author of the famous *The Imitation of Christ*, Thomas à Kempis (c. 1380–1471), was probably attracted to join one such community at Windesheim. The emotional and spiritual depth of his book is typical of the Christ-centred devotional nature of the Brotherhood, which also set up schools. The leading humanist scholar Desidirius Erasmus became a pupil at one of these schools in Deventer.

But by late medieval times, many in western Europe had become critical of monastic wealth, suspicious of monastic morality and jealous of monastic power.

Dissolution

In England, the English Reformation had been set in motion by King Henry VIII, who was angered by the pope's refusal to annul his marriage to Catherine of Aragon, to free him to marry the younger Anne Boleyn. The king proceeded to make a frontal assault on the monasteries, encouraged by his reforming chancellor, Thomas Cromwell. The monasteries were regarded as the bastion of the Roman Catholic tradition, and held the added attraction for their greedy enemies of being the richest landowners in the country. The king, at one stroke, filled his coffers and removed a main buttress of Roman Catholicism.

A soul cannot live without loving...

CATHERINE OF SIENA, A DOMINICAN TERTIARY

Christian mystics

Throughout Christian history (as in Judaism and Islam) there have been those who sought a more immediate and heightened experience, or vision, of God – usually by means of meditation, prayer and ascetic discipline. Often misunderstood and suspected by fellow believers, these seekers after higher spiritual experience are often known as mystics. The search for such mystical experiences has usually been more common among monastics and hermits, who have already decided to devote their lives completely to God.

Early Christian theologians taught that the mystics' desired vision of God is attained hereafter; in the present life few can reach it, and then only by special grace. Many mystics have written of their experiences in poetic language: fire, an interior journey, the dark night of the soul, a knowing that is an un-knowing are some of the images and descriptions used to express their mystical experiences.

Origins

Much Christian mysticism derives from the third-century thinker Plotinus, whose beliefs became known as 'Neo-Platonism'. These stated that an ultimate One lies behind all experience. This One is known by a method of negation: that is, by saying what it is not like.

A distinct mystical Christian theology emerged in Alexandria, Egypt. Origen (c. 185–254), drawing on Neo-Platonism, taught that each soul has individually fallen and must find its way back to God with the help of the *Logos*, Christ.

The medieval monk Bernard of Clairvaux (1091–1153) promoted an anti-intellectual mystical vision of overwhelming love, in which the church is described in erotic terms as the bride of Christ.

Mysticism was also found in the Eastern church. Gregory Palamas (1296–1359), a prominent Eastern Orthodox mystic, was a monk at Mount Athos in Greece, and later Archbishop of Thessalonica. Fellow monks were accused of wasting time in contemplative prayer when they should have been studying, but Gregory claimed that prophets had greater knowledge of God than the learned, because they had actually seen or heard God. He upheld the orthodox doctrine that although it is impossible to know who God *is* in and of himself, it's possible to know what God does, and who he is in relation to creation and to humanity, as he reveals himself to us.

The Imitation of Christ

In the fourteenth and fifteenth centuries, there was a revival of mysticism, represented by such men as Jan Van Ruysbroek (1293–1381) and Jean Gerson (1363–1429). A leading Rhineland mystic, Johannes Tauler (1300–61), stressed the importance of the inner person rather than outer deeds, and later became popular among Protestants and Pietists.

One of the best-known late medieval mystics is Thomas à Kempis (c. 1380–1471), writer of *The Imitation of Christ*. An Augustinian monk, his writings are the finest expression of the *devotio moderna*, a spiritual movement developed in the Low Countries, which stressed the practice of simple piety and asceticism.

A concern with practical and methodical prayer motivated the sixteenth-century mystics Ignatius Loyola and Teresa of Avila (1515–82), a Spanish Carmelite nun who formed the Discalced (Barefoot) Carmelites with John of the Cross. Her writings describe the stages of the mystical journey, while John of the Cross (1542–91), in his book *Dark Night of the Soul*, emphasizes mysticism as union with God, attainable only through the denial of self. Another classic of Roman Catholic spirituality is François de Sales' *The Introduction to the Devout Life*.

Mainstream Protestantism has generally mistrusted a mystical dimension to the spiritual life. Exceptions include the Lutheran mystic Jakob Böhme (1575–1624), who influenced George Fox, the founder of the Quakers in seventeenth-century England, and the English writer William Law (1686–1761), most famous for his devotional work *A Serious Call to a Devout and Holy Life*.

As mentioned, mysticism has always been closely tied to monasticism, where the disciplines associated with it have their most rigorous application. The monastic orders continue to encourage mysticism and contemplation – the mystic writer Thomas Merton (1915–68), a Trappist monk, is a case in point.

A powerful portrayal of Henry VIII of England (1491–1547), instigator of the English Reformation, by Holbein.

Following a commission organized by Thomas Cromwell to investigate the state of the monasteries, the resulting reports met the requirements of the king and his adviser. Furnished with written reports of financial, spiritual and sexual corruption, in 1536 Cromwell was able to force the smaller monasteries to yield their estates. The great monastic houses followed in 1539.

The impact of the dissolution of the English monasteries was enormous. Henry used much of the revenue gained to sweeten the aristocracy and strengthen their adherence to the new Protestant religion. However, by no means all the monasteries were corrupt: many fine and worthy institutions were irretrievably wrecked, their properties razed and their communities expelled and scattered. England lost a rich and extensive architectural, cultural and spiritual heritage, today represented by numerous ruins and gothic fragments scattered across the countryside.

Catholic Reform

When the Roman Catholic Church began to reform itself in the sixteenth century, as ever the papacy looked to the monasteries to set the pace. Pope Pius V encouraged reform in the Franciscan and Cistercian orders. The Spanish visionary and mystic Teresa of Avila (1515–82) – who herself came under scrutiny at one point by the Spanish Inquisition – set up the order known as the Discalced (Barefoot) Carmelites, which was patronized by King Philip II of Spain. A strict order of Observant Franciscans was also established by John of God, as well as the Brothers of Mercy, which was dedicated to caring for the sick.

In 1624 the French monk Vincent de Paul (1581–1660) set up the Congregation of the Mission, devoted to taking the Catholic faith into the country from its Paris base at the priory of St Lazare. As a young man, Vincent had been captured by Barbary pirates and forced to work as a slave in Tunis. He organized his order not only with the purpose of evangelizing rural areas and setting up retreats to improve the quality of priests, but also of trying to help galley-slaves in circumstances like those he had earlier suffered.

Unlike the older monastic orders, which had largely confined their work behind monastery walls, these new orders were visible and active in the community, teaching, visiting the sick and prisoners, and evangelizing in towns and villages.

Enlightenment thinking
The eighteenth century brought new pressures on monasticism. Although a fervent Catholic herself, Archduchess Maria Theresa of Austria had no compunction in exercising her power to limit clerical privileges – such as the clergy's right to sanctuary and to freedom from taxation – and in initiating monastic reform. Not to be outdone, her son, Emperor Joseph II, took this Enlightenment policy a stage further, confiscating monastic property without notifying the pope, and abolishing monastic houses that had no 'useful' function apart from spiritual contemplation. Joseph's actions resulted in the closure of about 400 monasteries within his realm and the reduction in the number of monks and nuns from 67,000 to 27,000.

REVOLUTION
The experience of religious orders in Austria was mild in comparison with that of monastics in revolutionary France. Before the Revolution, the eighteenth-century French church did not appear to be markedly corrupt or in decline, though church attendance in Paris seems to have been falling. However, free-thinking intellectuals had encouraged much sceptical thinking in preceding years, and a dormant anti-clericalism was soon aroused when the Revolution actually broke out in 1789.

After first confiscating and selling off church lands, in February 1790 the French National Assembly suppressed all mendicant and contemplative religious orders. As in Austria, orders that had educational and charitable objectives, and which were thereby

regarded as having some social purpose, were allowed to continue for the time being; but no one was allowed to take new monastic vows. Anti-Catholic opinion and activities increased as the Revolution became increasingly extreme and brutal. In total, between thirty and forty thousand French priests fled the country, and thousands of those who stayed were murdered.

Gradually the storm passed. By February 1795, free exercise of religion was again guaranteed. Though lacking in leadership as a result of the persecution of the clergy, French Catholics began to hold Mass again, at first in private houses and with priests dressed in lay clothing.

But the French government known as the Directory then proceeded to revive the anti-religious policy, which was also imposed in countries conquered by France: Italy, Switzerland, the Rhineland and Belgium. The Cisalpine Republic in northern Italy dissolved its monasteries, while the Roman Republic banned monasteries. However, Catholicism was far from spent, and popular uprisings in Belgium, Switzerland and Rome called for its return.

Similarly, anti-clericalism in Spain in 1820 resulted in the closure of Spanish monasteries and the expulsion of religious orders; but the defeat of the political liberals just three years later soon restored the old order of the church. Meanwhile Tsar Nicholas I ordered the dissolution of some 500 Catholic monasteries and nunneries in Russia in the same period.

MONASTICISM TODAY
During the twentieth century, religious orders continued to spearhead missionary work. However, by the second half of that century, the older orders were shrinking visibly in numbers and in influence. The Capuchin order numbered

15,710 in 1965, but by 1984 was down to 11,497; the Jesuits dwindled from 36,038 in 1965 to 29,426 in 1974. Fighting the trend more successfully, women's orders declined much less rapidly, possibly because as part of their calling they cared for the sick and disabled. Meanwhile, nuns' habits were modified to make them less distinctive – and less uncomfortable.

Bucking the trend, new Catholic orders were founded in the twentieth century, but these were often rather unorthodox in form compared with traditional monasticism. A French army officer named Charles de Foucauld (1858–1916) first joined an ascetic Trappist order, then the Poor Clares in Nazareth, before his murder in obscure circumstances in Algeria. However, posthumous publication of his writings led to the setting up of the Little Brothers of Jesus in 1927, on the edge of the Sahara Desert, and subsequently to the establishment of the Little Sisters of Jesus in 1936 (see p. 160).

The Swiss Protestant Roger Schütz set up a community in Taizé (not far from Cluny, Burgundy) in 1940, but returned to his homeland after the German military occupation of France. When France was liberated, at the end of the Second World War, Schütz came back accompanied by seven other men, all of whom took monastic vows. Brother Roger was stabbed to death during an evening service in Taizé in August 2005.

Taizé gradually built a worldwide reputation for its programme of Christian unity and prayer, particularly attracting young people, who were encouraged to carry their mission to the urban poor and oppressed. Other experiments in community living included the Protestant Iona Community, on the Scottish island of Iona, which had been hugely significant for the early Celtic church. The new community prepared its members to go back into Scottish cities or overseas as Christian workers.

Extremely well known – even perhaps over-publicized – was the work of the Albanian nun, Mother Teresa, for the sick, destitute and dying in the slums of Calcutta. In 1950 her community received official recognition as the Missioners of Charity, with about 2,000 members.

It seems doubtful whether monasticism will ever recover the strength and importance it attained at the height of the Middle Ages. Celibacy is today regarded as an oddity if not an affliction; poverty as a weakness; obedience as an infirmity. Scandalous stories of sexual abuse in some monastic houses have probably also turned many against taking vows. In an increasingly driven and busy world, fewer and fewer seem to feel the call of the monastery cloister and cell.

CHAPTER 6

The Eastern Church

From the time of the ecumenical Council of Chalcedon (AD 451) two increasingly different Christian traditions were developing, one focussed on Rome, the other on Constantinople. The tradition now known as Orthodox Christianity, Eastern Orthodoxy and the Orthodox Church began as the Eastern half of early Christendom.

With their differing emphases, these Western and Eastern traditions of the church gradually grew apart. The Eastern church developed its own traditions of spirituality, worship and church life, and Western Christians increasingly lost regular contact and communication with believers in the East.

The state's spiritual arm

Unlike the Western church, the Eastern church never attempted to claim independence of the state; rather, it formed a kind of spiritual arm of the state. The pattern was set by the emperor Constantine, who chaired the Council of Nicea (AD 325), and guaranteed the church unity at the cost of its independence. Ensuing emperors continued to work for Christian peace and unity by browbeating and overawing the church. The Bishop of Constantinople was in a way the emperor's court-preacher, and was well advised to curry the emperor's favour if he was to succeed. Those who, like John Chrysostom (c. AD 344–407), criticized the emperor were liable to be punished.

JUSTINIAN I

After Constantine I moved the capital of the empire to Constantinople (formerly Byzantium) in AD 330, Rome and the rest of Italy came increasingly under the influence and control of the Bishop of Rome. Although for many years the emperor in the East continued to claim authority over the West, the last emperor to maintain any real control beyond the Byzantine East was Justinian I (reigned AD 527–65). As the political division of the Roman empire into East and West became permanent, the Latin Catholic Church of the Roman West and the Eastern Orthodox Church of the East similarly took on separate identities.

Justinian, who took a lively interest in the church and its theology, allowed little deviation from what he considered to be orthodox belief and practice. He was intolerant of other Christian traditions and beliefs, which led to divisions within the Eastern empire, a debilitating effect that helped bring about the

One empire, one law, one church.

JUSTINIAN

relative lack of resistance by many Christians to the arrival of Islam in the following century.

The rise of Islam
After the return of Muhammad to Mecca in AD 622, Islam exploded into a holy war. Led by Abu Bakr, Islamic forces swept across the East. Egypt, Syria, Palestine and many of the Mediterranean islands were quickly overrun by Muslim forces. The Eastern church was cut back drastically, whereas the West felt the impact only later. (This is described in more detail in chapter 7.)

Rome and Constantinople
With the capture of Jerusalem, Antioch and Alexandria by the Muslims, the two surviving major centres of Christianity emerged as rivals, following the collapse of the Western empire: Rome under the guidance of the pope, and Constantinople under the leadership of the patriarch. At first the Orthodox patriarch appeared to be the more powerful, since he presided over the wealthier – and still viable – Eastern Roman empire (Byzantium). However, as time passed it became increasingly clear that the patriarch would continue to be subservient to the Eastern emperors who, in effect, ran both church and state.

The nature of Christ
In the East, Islam kept up the pressure on the increasingly besieged Byzantine empire. Meanwhile, complex theological controversies raged within the Eastern empire, especially concerning the nature and person of Jesus Christ; and these failed to be resolved at the Third and Fourth church Councils of Constantinople in AD 680 and AD 879.

There was a tendency in the East to emphasize the divine nature of Christ at the expense of his humanity. Some Eastern Christians, known as 'Monophysites', rejected the Nicene Creed of AD 325, with its statement that Jesus is 'truly God and truly man', and emphasized solely Jesus' divine nature. The Fourth Council of Constantinople, summoned by the learned patriarch Photius (c. 820–95), specifically condemned both the Monophysites and the 'Iconoclasts'. Since large numbers of Eastern believers were both Monophysites and Iconoclasts, this only created further dangerous divisions within the empire.

ICONOCLASM
The East contrasted visually with Rome in its veneration of images and representations of God. Such images were disapproved of in the West; but the Eastern churches luxuriated in icons, decorated with gold and extravagant colours, symbolically representing Christ, Mary (the '*Theotokos*', Greek for 'God-bearer') and the saints. These images were used both to help people in worship, and to illustrate the mystery of holiness.

But even within the Eastern church, icons provoked controversy. The Second Council of Nicea in AD 787 approved the making and veneration, but not worship, of religious images against the attacks of the iconoclasts. Rome also accepted this decree.

Iconoclasts still fought to rid their church of icons, but were successfully resisted by the emperor Leo III (c. 680–741). Eventually he and the icons triumphed, and the latter have continued as an essential feature of Eastern Christianity.

Differences in theology
During these years, the Western and Eastern churches made several efforts to find common ground and reunify. As we have seen, the two

wings of the church had been drifting apart since the Council of Nicea in AD 325, for many reasons of theology, church government and liturgy.

For example, the Eastern church never accepted the so-called *filioque* clause added to the Nicene Creed in the sixth century, which stated that the Holy Spirit proceeded from both the Father 'and the son' (*filioque*). This addition was intended to reaffirm the divinity of the Son, but Eastern theologians objected both to the unilateral editing of a creed produced by an ecumenical council and to the actual editing itself. For Eastern Christians, both the Spirit and the Son have their origin in the Father.

Other differences between the two churches included the question of whether the clergy could be married (East) or must remain celibate (West). The two churches also differed over the Christian calendar and over the date on which Easter should be celebrated.

THE GREAT SCHISM

In 1054, a serious dispute over authority finally brought matters to a head. The papacy claimed

Orthodox icons

Icons are of major significance to Orthodox Christians. These beautiful and elaborate paintings, sometimes described as 'windows into the kingdom of God', are used in worship and to decorate the church and family homes. Icons are regarded both as a form of prayer and as a means *to* prayer.

An icon is usually an elaborate, non-perspectival painting, often with a gold-leaf background, and usually made on wood. It depicts such subjects as Christ, Mary, the saints, Bible scenes and stories about the saints.

Before painting an icon, the iconographer prepares carefully by praying and fasting. When finished, the icon is venerated and candles and oil lamps are often burnt before it. The worshipper kisses the icon, makes the sign of the cross and may often kneel before it.

In most Orthodox church buildings, the sanctuary is separated from the main body of the church by a solid screen (known as the 'iconostasis') pierced by doors. This screen is decorated with icons, the main ones portraying Christ and Mary, normally flanked by icons of John the Baptist and of the saint, or feast, to which the church is dedicated.

Icon of 'The Holy Trinity' the best-known work of Andrei Rublev (c. 1360/70–1427/30), the most celebrated Russian iconographer.

direct succession from the apostle Peter, and thus supreme church authority, supported by a document known as the 'Donation of Constantine' (later discovered to be a fake). Ultimately an immovable pope, Leo IX, excommunicated an equally uncompromising patriarch, Michael Cerularius (reigned 1043–59), the intransigent leader of the Eastern church. In response, the patriarch excommunicated the legates of Pope Leo IX (reigned 1049–54), who delivered the actual sentence of excommunication, and also anathematized the pope.

Following this apparently irrevocable so-called 'Great Schism', a faint glimmer of hope for reconciliation appeared later the same century, at the beginning of the Crusades, when the West came to the aid of the East against the Turks. But especially after the Fourth Crusade (1200–1204), when Western crusaders brutally sacked and occupied Constantinople, the ultimate result was in fact increased hostility between the two churches. The sacking of Constantinople eventually led to the complete loss of the Byzantine capital to the Muslim Ottomans in 1453, and has never been

The Eastern Orthodox year

In the Eastern Orthodox Church, the liturgical year is characterized by alternating fasts and feasts, and is not dissimilar to the Roman Catholic year. However, it begins on 1 September, not the first Sunday of Advent, and includes twelve 'Great Feasts', in addition to Pascha (Easter) itself, the 'Feast of Feasts'. These festivals generally mark significant events in the lives of Jesus Christ and of the Virgin Mary (*Theotokos*).

'Winter Lent' is a name for the extended fast leading up to the Feast of the Nativity of Jesus Christ (Christmas). 'Great Lent' is the extended fast leading up to Holy Week and Pascha. Two other extended fasts are the 'Apostles' Fast', usually one to two weeks leading up to the Feast of Saints Peter and Paul, and the fast leading up to the Dormition of the *Theotokos*, in the two weeks before that feast, 1–14 August.

The twelve Great Feasts

- Nativity of the *Theotokos* (8 September): The birth of Mary to Joachim and Anne

- Elevation of the Cross (14 September): The re-discovery of the original cross

- Entrance of the *Theotokos* into the Temple (21 November): Entry of Mary to the Temple, aged about three

- Nativity of Our Lord and Saviour Jesus Christ (25 December): Birth of Jesus (Christmas)

- Theophany (6 January): The baptism of Jesus, Christ's blessing of the water, and the revelation of Christ as God

- Presentation of Jesus in the Temple (2 February): Christ's presentation as an infant in the Temple by Mary and Joseph.

- Annunciation of the *Theotokos* (25 March): Gabriel's announcement to Mary that she will bear the Christ-child

- Entry into Jerusalem (Sunday before Pascha): Palm Sunday

- Ascension (Forty days after Pascha): Christ's ascension into heaven

- Pentecost (Fifty days after Pascha): The Holy Spirit comes to live in the apostles and other believers

- Transfiguration of Our Lord (6 August): Christ is transfigured before Peter, James and John.

- Dormition of the *Theotokos* (15 August): The falling asleep of Mary (known as the Assumption of Mary in Western Christianity)

forgotten by the Eastern Orthodox Church.

It was by now clear that the East/West break was final: the unity of the church was truly severed. Although the Schism was the last straw, the separation was in fact neither sudden nor unexpected. For centuries there had been a number of significant religious, cultural and political differences between the Eastern and Western churches.

Organization and authority

The Orthodox Church is organized into a number of regional churches, each governed by its own head bishop (technically known as autocephalous, or self-governing, churches). The Patriarch of Constantinople has theoretical primacy, but this does not carry the same weight as the Roman Catholic pope's primacy within his church.

Bishops in the Orthodox Church are considered direct successors of the original apostles. Although priests in the Orthodox Church are allowed to be married, bishops must be celibate.

For Orthodox Christians, religious authority is not in the pope – as in Catholicism – nor with the individual Christian and his or her Bible – as in Protestantism – but is vested in the Bible as interpreted by the seven ecumenical councils of the church: Nicea AD 325, Constantinople 1 (AD 381), Ephesus (AD 431), Chalcedon (AD 451), Constantinople 2 (AD 553), Constantinople 3 (AD 680) and Nicea 2 (AD 787). The Orthodox

also set great store by the writings of early Greek theologians and writers, such as Gregory of Nyssa (AD 330– c. 395), John Chrysostom and Basil the Great (c. AD 329–79).

WHAT IS TRUTH?

However, the Eastern churches approach the question of religious

The Muslim Ottomans besiege Constantinople in 1453, by Bertrandon de la Broquiere.

truth differently from the Western church. The word Orthodox itself derives from the Greek *orthos* ('right') and the word *doxa* ('belief'): hence 'Orthodox' means correct belief, or right thinking. For Orthodox Christians, truth must be experienced personally. Within Eastern Christianity there is less focus on defining religious truth, and more on the practical and personal experience of truth in an individual believer's life and in the church. Precise theological definitions are intended primarily for the negative purpose of excluding error.

Orthodoxy

Eastern Christianity stresses a way of life and belief that is expressed particularly through worship. By maintaining the correct ('orthodox') way of worshipping God, passed on from the very earliest Christians, Eastern believers hold that they confess the true doctrine of God in the right forms.

Culturally, the Greek East has tended to be more philosophical, abstract and mystical in its thinking; whereas the Latin West tends toward a more pragmatic and legal-minded approach to Christianity. While the Eastern churches believed that the church should express itself through the language of the local community, in the West Latin became the accepted language of the church.

Salvation

Orthodox theology holds that humans were created in the image of God. The full communion with God that Adam and Eve enjoyed meant complete freedom and true humanity; thus humans are most human when they are completely united with God. However, sin led to the blurring of the image of God and a barrier being set up between God and humanity. Salvation is the process of re-establishing humanity's lost communion with God. This process – repairing the unity of human and divine (sometimes known as 'deification') – doesn't mean humans *become* gods, but that humans join fully with God's divine life.

Worship

The theological richness, spiritual significance and variety of worship in the Orthodox Church are major factors in its continuity and identity, and help to explain the survival of Christianity during the many centuries of Muslim rule in the Middle East and Balkans, when liturgy was almost the sole remaining source of religious knowledge and experience.

Fasting and prayer

Fasting and prayer play an important part in the Orthodox Church: Orthodox Christians believe discipline of the body can help the mind prepare for prayer.

There are four main periods of fasting in the Orthodox Church:

- The Great Fast (Lent)

- The Fast of the Apostles: Eight days after Pentecost until 28 June, ending with the Feast of Saints Peter and Paul

- The Dormition Fast, from 1 to 14 August

- The Christmas Fast, from 15 November to 24 December

In addition, all Wednesdays and Fridays are supposed to be days of fasting.

Reunion?

During the twentieth century, re-opened contacts led to a renewing of friendship between the Orthodox and Roman Catholic churches, with some Western churches studying and learning from the spirituality and devotion of Eastern traditions. Attempts at actual reconciliation between East and West were renewed in the second half of the twentieth century. In 1964, the Second Vatican Council praised the Eastern churches:

The Catholic Church values highly the institutions of the Eastern Churches, their liturgical rites, ecclesiastical traditions and their ordering of Christian life. For in those churches... is clearly evident the tradition which has come from the Apostles through the Fathers and which is part of the divinely revealed, undivided heritage of the universal church.

On 7 December 1965, the mutual excommunication of 1054 was officially lifted by Pope Paul VI and Patriarch Athenagoras.

ORTHODOXY TODAY

The two most widely known Orthodox traditions are the Greek and Russian Orthodox, and Orthodoxy is found today in numerous countries throughout the world. Membership of the Russian Orthodox Church – the largest of the Orthodox churches – is claimed at between 40 and 80 million. Orthodox churches also thrive in Bulgaria, Serbia, Australia, Romania, Albania, Cyprus and the United Kingdom, and there are strong Orthodox communities in Japan and Korea. In Finland the Orthodox Church is a state church, in parallel with the Lutheran Church. There is also an Orthodox Church of Alexandria, Egypt, and an Orthodox Church of Jerusalem.

The Orthodox faith was originally taken to North America by Russian missionaries, via Alaska, where an Inuit Orthodox Church still flourishes. The Russian Orthodox Church in the USA was eventually granted independence by Moscow and is now largely American. There are also thriving Orthodox mission churches in East Africa. It is reckoned that today some 225 million people worldwide are Orthodox Christians.

RUSSIAN ORTHODOXY

Some claim the Russian church was founded by the apostle Andrew, who is said to have visited Scythia and Greek colonies on the Black Sea during the first century AD. We do know that between AD 863 and 869, Eastern Orthodox missionaries, the brothers Cyril and Methodius, with the blessing of the pope, travelled to eastern Europe and translated parts of the Bible into the Old Slavonic language for the first time – having first, by some accounts, invented the Glagolitic alphabet. They paved the way for the Christianization of the Slavs.

Foundations

The first Christian bishop to travel to Kiev seems to have been sent from Constantinople by Patriarch Photius or Ignatios (c. 797–877) around AD 866. Princess Olga of Kiev was the first ruler to convert to Christianity, in AD 955 or 957, and there was soon a Christian community among the Kievan nobility led by Greek and Byzantine priests, although paganism remained predominant in the region. Then in AD 988, Olga's grandson, the regent Prince Vladimir I of Kiev, accepted Byzantine Christianity and was baptized in Constantinople. This marks the official founding of the Russian Orthodox Church.

Initially the Russian Church was part of

Бислышавъ володимиръ рё. ацщенна пна боудеть
отопойстисъ велик къ христаненск . аповельстре
стити . еппъ же корсоуньскый . спопы цэчны ё
гласнъ крти володимира . иıаковъ злож роукоу
чань . набне прозре . видеж же володимеръ . на
прасное исцеленне и прослав бга рёте первоъ ведеъ бäı

Fifteenth-century Russian illuminated manuscript depicting the baptism of Prince Vladimir I in 988, and the acceptance of Christianity as the state religion.

Неже вид евши дроумае . мнози кртиша . крти же са в црки
стоебуй . не црки истойци . в корехни грамам есте по
сретал . идете торгъе . пола та володимиравъ кра црки
стоить . и оседмиацрчнаполата за олтаре . покре
щенни же при ве црцю наш богу чапне :·

the Patriarchate of Constantinople, but in 1051 a Russian primate was established and a separate and distinctive Russian Orthodox Church began to grow, which was eventually to claim to be the true successor of Rome and Constantinople. By the twelfth century, the Russian Church had become an important force unifying the Russian people at a time of serious division.

The Russian Metropolitan's residence was originally in Kiev. However, since Kiev was losing political importance as a result of the Mongol invasions, which started in 1237, Metropolitan Maximus moved to Vladimir in 1299. Maximus' successors, Metropolitans Peter and Theognostus, in turn moved to Moscow by 1326.

THE THIRD ROME

By 1448, the Russian Church was independent of Constantinople. Metropolitan Jonas, installed by the Council of Russian bishops in 1448, was given the title of Metropolitan of Moscow and All Rus'. The fifteenth- and sixteenth-century Russian tsars claimed they were heirs of the Caesars, Moscow was 'the Third Rome', and the Patriarch of Moscow was head of the Orthodox Church.

[The Russian rural churches] trip up the slopes, ascend the high hills, come down to the broad rivers, like princesses in white and red, they nod to each other from afar, from villages that are cut off and invisible to each other they soar to the same heaven.

ALEXANDER SOLZHENITSYN

St Basil's Cathedral, Moscow, Russia.

During the fifteenth century the Russian church was pivotal in the survival and life of the Russian state. Such holy figures as Sergius of Radonezh (c. 1314–92) and Metropolitan Alexis helped the country to withstand years of Tatar oppression, and to expand both economically and spiritually. Sergius encouraged resistance to the Mongols and also set up the Monastery of the Holy Trinity, which became the greatest in the land. The Cathedral of St Basil in Moscow, built between 1555 and 1560, is perhaps the best known in the Russian Orthodox Church.

The Mongols were finally defeated in 1480, after which Ivan IV began to develop a powerful Russian state.

Change and reform

Monastic life flourished in Russia, focussing on prayer and spiritual growth. Disciples of Sergius founded hundreds of monasteries across Russia, some of the most famous located in the Russian north to show that the faith could flourish in inhospitable lands.

At a church council of 1503, Nilus of Sora clashed with Joseph, Abbot of Volokolamsk, over the role and duty of monastics. Joseph stressed the social obligations of monks, while Nilus insisted that a monk's primary purpose is prayer and separation from the world. A split now occurred: Joseph's 'Possessors' believed church and state should be closely allied, and that monks should care for the sick and the poor; Nilus' 'Non-Possessors' opted for the life of holy detachment.

In the 1540s, Metropolitan Macarius convened a number of church synods, which culminated in the Hundred Chapter Synod of 1551, which unified church ceremonies and duties in Russia.

Autocephaly and reorganization

In 1589, the Metropolitan of Moscow was elevated to the title of Patriarch of Moscow. During the next half-century, when the tsars were weak, the patriarchs Germogen and Philaret became influential. In 1652, Patriarch Nikon resolved to centralize power, while conforming Russian Orthodox rituals to those of the Greek Orthodox Church. He insisted, for instance, that Russian Christians cross themselves with three fingers, rather than the traditional two.

Nikon aroused great antipathy among a section of believers – especially those who followed Joseph – who saw the changed rites as heretical. This group separated off from the church to become a sect known as the 'Old Ritual Believers' or 'Old Believers', who rejected the reformist teachings of the patriarch. A number of dissidents were burnt at the stake.

Expansion and the Holy Synod

In the late seventeenth and early eighteenth centuries, the Russian church experienced huge geographical expansion. In 1686, the Metropolitanate of Kiev passed from Constantinople's control to that of Moscow, bringing millions more members and several more dioceses under the care of the Russian patriarch.

Missionary efforts reached out across Siberia into Alaska, then on into California, USA. Prominent Russian Orthodox missionaries included Innocent of Irkutsk, Herman of Alaska and Innocent of Siberia and Alaska. They learned local languages and translated the Gospels and hymns, some of the translations requiring the creation of new alphabets.

In 1700, following Patriarch Adrian's death, Peter the Great prevented a successor being named. He abolished the patriarchate and, in

1721, following the advice of Feofan Prokopovich – Archbishop of Novgorod and a tireless innovator – established instead a Holy Synod to govern the church. This remained the situation until shortly after the Russian Revolution of 1917.

THE OCTOBER REVOLUTION

By 1914 there were some 55,000 Russian Orthodox churches, 29,500 chapels, 112,600 priests and deacons, 550 monasteries and 475 convents with a total of around 95,000 monks and nuns.

The year 1917 was a turning point in the history of both Russia and the Russian Orthodox Church. Under the tsars, the church had become closely linked with the ruling regime. When the Russian empire was dissolved, the tsarist government – which had granted the church numerous privileges – was overthrown. After a few months of turmoil, the Bolsheviks seized power in October 1917, and soon declared the separation of church and state. Having defended the old regime both before and after the Revolution, the church was – not surprisingly – regarded as the enemy of the Bolsheviks.

The Russian Orthodox Church found itself for the first time without state backing, which led to a marked decline in its power and influence. The new Communist government declared freedom of 'religious and anti-religious propaganda', giving the church's enemies free rein. The church was also caught in the crossfire of the Russian Civil War, which began later in 1917, with many leaders of the church supporting the losing 'White' movement.

Even before the end of the civil war and the establishment of the Soviet Union, the Russian Orthodox Church was being persecuted by the secular Communist government,

A Russian Communist propaganda poster depicting religion as the enemy of industrialization.

Russian Communists plant an anti-religious banner over a Christian mural in the ruins of a blown-up church building.

Does an honest man go to a theological seminary in our century of science and technology?

SOVIET CRITIC OF THE CHURCH

which stood for militant atheism, viewing the church as 'counter-revolutionary'. When set up, the Soviet Union officially claimed religious toleration, but in practice the government discouraged organized religion and did everything possible to remove religious influence from Soviet society.

Thousands of churches and monasteries were taken over by the government and destroyed or used as warehouses, recreational centres or 'museums of atheism'. It was impossible to build new churches. Bishops – such as Metropolitan Veniamin in Petrograd in 1922 – priests and worshippers were arrested and executed for refusing to hand in church treasures, including sacred relics.

The Orthodox Church was not the sole victim of persecution. Stalin almost wiped out the Lutheran Church and laid waste to the Evangelical Christian-Baptist denominations. In the 1920s many Mennonites emigrated to North America, and those who remained were persecuted, as were all other religious groups – Roman Catholics, Uniate Catholics, Old Believers and even Jews and Muslims.

Practising Orthodox Christians were barred from prominent careers and from Communist party membership. Anti-religious propaganda was encouraged by the government, and the church was given no opportunity to respond. The government youth organization, the *Komsomol*, encouraged members to vandalize Orthodox church buildings and harass worshippers. Seminaries were closed down and the church restricted in its use of the press.

Patriarch Tikhon anathematized the Communist government, which further antagonized relations. In 1927 Metropolitan Sergius, who took over the leadership of the Russian Orthodox Church after Tikhon's death, decided to accept the new government as legitimate, leading to schism with the Russian Orthodox Church outside of Russia.

Life under the Soviets
Relations between the Soviet government and the church improved considerably during World War II, in an effort by the state to buy church support for the war. The Moscow Theological Academy and Seminary, which had been closed since 1918, was re-opened.

A second round of repression, harassment and church closure took place between 1959 and 1964 during the hardline rule of Nikita Khrushchev, and by 1987 the number of open churches in the Soviet Union had fallen to 6,893, the number of monasteries to just 18.

Church and government remained on unfriendly terms until the coming of *glasnost* in 1988. Practising Christians could not join the Communist Party, which meant that they could not hold political office. However, large numbers remained religious: in 1987 it is estimated that between 40 and 50 per cent of babies were baptized and more than 60 per cent of the dead received a Christian funeral.

The year 1988 marked the thousandth anniversary of the founding of the Russian church. Government-supported celebrations took place all summer in Moscow and other cities, and many older churches and some monasteries were now re-opened. An implicit ban on religious propaganda on television was finally lifted and for the first time church services were seen live.

Post-Soviet recovery

The Russian Orthodox Church is the largest of the Eastern Orthodox churches and has seen a resurgence in activity since the end of Soviet rule. Like other Orthodox churches, regular church attendance is not regarded as particularly important, so numbers attending services are quite low – though significantly higher since the collapse of the USSR.

In 2005, the Russian Orthodox Church had more than 26,600 parishes, 164 bishops, 688 monasteries and 102 seminaries in the territory formerly occupied by the Soviet Union, and a well-established presence in other countries. Many buildings were returned to the church, most of them in a dilapidated condition.

In 2002, Pope John Paul II created a Catholic diocesan structure for Russia, which the leaders of the Russian Church saw as a throwback to earlier attempts by the Vatican to proselytize Russian Orthodox Christians. The encroachment of other Christian denominations into Russia is a sensitive issue as the Orthodox Church argues that it is weak after decades of Communist rule, and unable to compete on equal terms with Western churches.

At the same time, smaller religious groups, particularly Baptists and other Protestant denominations, have become active in Russia in the past decade, and claim the Russian state gives unfair support to the Orthodox Church while suppressing other Christians.

CHAPTER 7

Jihads and Crusades

When some of the nomadic peoples of the Arabian Peninsula began to settle permanently in around the fifth century BC, a number of them made their home in Mecca, near the west coast of Saudi Arabia. This city boasted a unique and massive cube-shaped shrine, known as the *Ka'ba*, dedicated to various deities. Mecca soon became a significant religious centre, with merchants relying on pilgrims to the city's 360 shrines for their livelihood. Among the multitude of Arab deities was Allah: creator, provider and determiner of human destiny.

THE PROPHET

In AD 570 Muhammad was born in Mecca. As a young man he worked as a camel-driver, and met people of many nations and faiths, including Jews, Christians and pagans. In AD 610, after meditating in a cave on the outskirts of Mecca, Muhammad told his wife Khadija that the angel Gabriel had appeared to him, and announced that he had been chosen to become God's messenger.

Muhammad's message was that people should turn away from paganism, polytheism, immorality and materialism to the worship of the one

Muslim pilgrims walk around the *Ka'ba*, Mecca, which is covered with a black cloth embroidered with verses from the Qur'an.

91

true God, Allah, whose prophet he was. However, Muhammad gained only forty followers in Mecca in the next three years, and with his disciples he was stoned, beaten, thrown into prison and boycotted by local merchants.

Hijira

When Muhammad heard he had some followers in Yathrib, 280 miles north of Mecca, he and his friend Abu Bakr fled the persecution and escaped to Yathrib – an event celebrated by Muslims as the *Hijira*. The year of the *Hijira*, AD 622, became year one in the Muslim calendar.

The people of Medina were indeed open to Muhammad's teachings and, as an outsider, he found he was able to arbitrate objectively in their tribal disputes. Muhammad was soon regarded as the town's leader, as reflected in the renaming of Yathrib as Medinat al-Nabi, 'the City of the Prophet' – later simply Medina, 'the City'.

In AD 630, Muhammad led an armed force from Medina to assault and defeat Mecca. Having captured his birthplace, Muhammad now re-dedicated the *Ka'ba* to Allah and converted most of the people of Mecca to the new faith, Islam.

By AD 632, the year of his death, Muhammad had conquered most of western Arabia for Islam. And within a hundred years of his death, Islam had reached the Atlantic Ocean in the West and the borders of China in the East.

Muhammad regarded Judaism and Christianity as precursors of Islam, and himself as the 'seal' of a line of prophets, beginning with Abraham and including Jesus. For this reason, he was friendly to the Jewish and Christian populations of towns converted to Islam.

THE CALIPHS (AD 632–61)

A succession crisis followed the Prophet's death. One group of followers claimed

Muhammad had chosen Ali, his cousin and son-in-law, to succeed him; others that Abu Bakr, his friend and father-in-law, should become the new leader, or caliph.

In the event, Abu Bakr (reigned AD 632–34) became first caliph. He soon suppressed a Bedouin uprising, and in so doing secured the entire Arabian Peninsula for Islam. With his army, he next took the new faith to the very frontiers of the Eastern Christian empire in Syria, and declared *jihad* (holy war) against the Byzantine state – but died before he could act on this.

The second caliph, Umar (reigned AD 634–44), won the strategic battle of Yarmuk (c. AD 636) and took Christian Damascus (AD 635) and the Christian holy city of Jerusalem (AD 637) from Byzantium. Umar also moved against the Sassanid empire in the east, conquering its fabled capital, Ctesiphon, in AD 637. Babylon (AD 641) was next to fall to Muslim forces, followed by the major Christian centre of Alexandria (Egypt) in AD 642. By the time of Umar's death, the Muslim empire was second in size only to the Chinese empire.

Uthman (reigned AD 644–56), a member of the influential Umayyad family, succeeded Umar, leaving Ali's supporters frustrated once again. Uthman continued the expansion of Islam, capturing the island of Cyprus in AD 649, and arriving at the eastern borders of Persia in AD 653.

After Uthman's assassination in AD 656, internecine war over the Muslim leadership ensued. Ali declared himself the fourth caliph, but was challenged by Mu'awiya, Uthman's cousin and governor of Syria. Ali was murdered, and the Islamic community now experienced the historic split between the overwhelming majority, the orthodox Sunni, and the Shi'ites, who followed the descendants of Ali.

The Umayyad dynasty

The first Sunni caliphate was the Umayyad dynasty, which ruled from Damascus, and lasted until AD 750, with Mu'awiya as its first caliph. This began a further dynamic period of Islamic military expansion.

By the eighth century, Muslim armies had even crossed the Straits of Gibraltar from North Africa and embarked on the conquest of Christian Spain (AD 711), holding all or part of this region until the last Muslim rulers were expelled from the Iberian Peninsula in 1492. The population remained largely Christian, but Muslims ruled. By AD 732, a Muslim army had crossed the Pyrenees and penetrated as far north as Tours in south-central France, where it was finally checked by the Frankish leader Charles Martel, grandfather of the future emperor Charlemagne. The battle saved Western Christendom.

The spread of Islam

From its original base in central Arabia, the Muslim faith had now spread by force with extraordinary rapidity throughout the Middle East, central Asia and North Africa. One by one, the old Christian centres of Jerusalem, Antioch and Alexandria had succumbed to its military might. Within a century of its foundation

The spread of Islam.

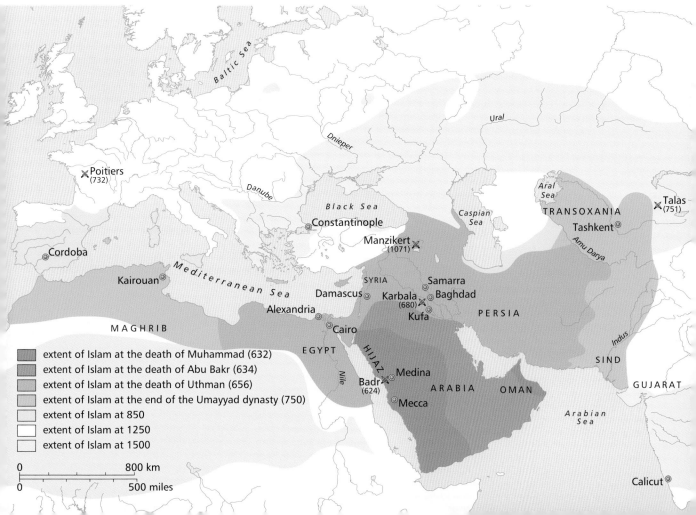

- extent of Islam at the death of Muhammad (632)
- extent of Islam at the death of Abu Bakr (634)
- extent of Islam at the death of Uthman (656)
- extent of Islam at the end of the Umayyad dynasty (750)
- extent of Islam at 850
- extent of Islam at 1250
- extent of Islam at 1500

0   800 km
0   500 miles

Islam had overrun more than half of Christendom. The homes of Jesus and his disciples, of Origen and of Augustine had passed into Muslim hands. The Christians' world became much smaller, and a majority of them now lived in the Latin West as the lost lands had belonged to the Byzantine empire.

The speed with which Islam swept across North Africa and the Middle East is an indicator in part of the tolerance of Islam, allowing the practice of other monotheistic religions, and in part of the receptivity of the conquered peoples to Islam – to them, Islamic supremacy seems to have meant little more than a change of masters.

The majority of the population within the new Islamic empire remained non-Muslim. In these early years, Islam allowed indigenous cultures to continue and there was little attempt at religious conversion. The caliph Umar had introduced a poll tax, the *jizya*, payable by non-Muslims for the privilege of continuing to practise their own religion.

The Monophysite and Nestorian Churches of Egypt, Ethiopia and the Middle East not only survived Islam but had a common enemy with it: Byzantium, the Eastern empire. Nestorian churches flourished in the East, proliferating along the Silk Road into China.

Nonetheless the new religion penetrated deeply. Within just one or two generations most other Christians had converted to Islam, after some six centuries of Roman and Byzantine rule. At times, conversion to Islam was even discouraged by the Muslim victors, since they felt such conversions may have been motivated merely by a desire to avoid the *jizya*, rather than by any genuine faith.

Yet the Umayyads dedicated themselves to conquering the Byzantine empire. Although individual Christians and Jews could be tolerated within the Muslim state, Christian and Jewish states were to be destroyed and their lands conquered. Christianity was the dominant religion; therefore, the Christian world was a prime target for the caliphs – and remained so for Muslim leaders for the next thousand years.

THE CRUSADES BEGIN

In the eleventh century, the Seljuk Turks conquered Asia Minor (modern Turkey), parts of which had been Christian since the missions of the apostle Paul. The Byzantine empire was now reduced to little more than the area of modern Greece. Desperate, in 1095 the Eastern emperor, Alexius I Comnenus (reigned 1081–1118), pleaded for aid from Christian western Europe, as the Seljuk Turks were now threatening Constantinople itself, the very home of Eastern Christianity.

The Crusades were a response to more than four centuries of Islamic conquest, in which Muslims had

Have faith in Allah… and fight for his cause.

QUR'AN

already captured two-thirds of the Christian world. If Christianity did not now defend itself, it felt it would surely be overwhelmed.

The vow of the cross

At the Council of Clermont in 1095, Pope Urban II (reigned 1088–99) called on Christendom to resist and push back Islam. This triggered not just the First Crusade (1095–99) but also the crusading movement that would last for centuries. As a direct result, thousands of knights took a vow of the cross and prepared for war. These crusading knights were often wealthy men, who abandoned all to undertake the crusade in part as an act of penitence.

Urban II presented the Crusaders with several goals: the rescue of the Eastern Christians, the recovery of the Holy Land – particularly the holy city of Jerusalem – from Muslim occupation, and the securing of free access to the Holy Land for pilgrims.

Medieval Crusaders regarded themselves as on a military expedition blessed by the pope, and as pilgrims to the Holy Land, performing righteous acts for which they hoped to receive a special indulgence guaranteeing entrance to heaven. 'God wills it' ('*Deus vult*') was their battle-cry, and their banners proudly displayed the cross. If the Crusaders died on campaign, they believed they would be regarded as martyrs.

It is often assumed that the Crusades aimed at the forcible conversion of the Muslim world. Rather, medieval Christians saw Muslims as predatory enemies, and their task as the defeat and expulsion of Muslim forces from former Christian territories. It was not until the thirteenth century that Francis of Assisi and his followers began to proselytize Muslims – by peaceful persuasion, and not with threats of violence.

The call to Crusade

From the confines of Jerusalem and from the city of Constantinople a horrible tale has gone forth. An accursed race... has invaded the lands of these Christians and depopulated them by the sword, plundering and fire. O most valiant soldiers... start upon the road to the Holy Sepulchre... to tear that land from the wicked race and subject it to yourselves.

POPE URBAN II

Fifteenth-century depiction of Pope Urban II calling for the recovery of the Holy Land.

The First Crusade (1095–99)

The First Crusade seemed always to be on the verge of disaster. It had no leader, no supply lines and no detailed strategy. Many warriors died in battle or through disease and starvation. *En route* a rabble of 50,000 undisciplined soldiers descended on Constantinople.

Yet despite this, by 1098 the Crusaders had restored Nicea and the major centre of Antioch to Christian rule. In July 1099, they went on to capture Jerusalem, and over the next twenty years they managed to set up four Crusader states in the Levant. But the vast majority of the population of the Crusader states were Muslims or Orthodox Christians who loathed the Crusaders.

It seemed for a moment that the tide was finally turning against the Muslims. But the Crusaders

The Crusaders occupy Jerusalem. Illustration from a fourteenth-century edition of William of Tyre's *History of Deeds done Beyond the Sea*.

In the temple... men rode in blood up to their knees... the city was filled with corpses and blood.

THE CAPTURE
OF JERUSALEM

The Temple Mount, Jerusalem: Jewish, Christian, Muslim

Dominating the Old City of Jerusalem is the vast Haram Al Sharif, or Noble Sanctuary, the site today of the Islamic Dome of the Rock and Aqsa Mosque, but in biblical times of the Jewish Temple. Solomon constructed a Temple here whose plan was similar to the portable Tabernacle the Hebrews carried with them during their years of journeying through the wilderness.

Solomon's Temple was destroyed when Nebuchadnezzar captured Jerusalem in 586 BC. After the Babylonian exile, many of the people of Judah returned to the city in 538 BC. They set to work immediately rebuilding the Temple and repairing the city's walls.

During the rule of the Seleucid monarch Antiochus IV Epiphanes, the Temple was profaned in 169 BC – one cause of the successful Maccabean Revolt, which resulted in the Temple being cleansed and rededicated in 165 BC. This event is celebrated by the Jewish festival of Hanukkah.

One of Herod the Great's many ambitious public works was to rebuild the Temple more grandiosely. An Idumean attempting to ingratiate himself with Rome, Herod aimed to make Jerusalem a world-ranking city. Part of the Temple was covered in gold plate, the rest in white marble. In front stood the massive altar of sacrifice, where Herod sacrificed 300 oxen to celebrate the building's completion.

Part of the vast Temple Mount platform, now known as the Western, or Wailing, Wall, is still faced with finely finished stones dating to Herod's time. Just twenty-two years later, in AD 66, the Jews were roused to open uprising against the Romans. After Vespasian had subdued the revolt in Galilee and Judea, he left his son Titus to take Jerusalem. In AD 70 Titus sacked the city and took sacred objects from the Temple for his triumph in the imperial capital, as depicted on Titus' Arch in Rome. The walls of Jerusalem were destroyed and the Temple burned down.

In AD 130, the emperor Hadrian came to Jerusalem with plans to rebuild it as a Roman city. However, when he announced that he intended to place a statue of himself on the Temple Mount, this sparked the Bar Kokhba revolt, which lasted from AD 132 to AD 135.

Following the successful crushing of this Second Jewish Revolt, Hadrian razed Jerusalem to the ground and laid out a completely new city, Aelia Capitolina, from which all Jews were banned.

Only after Constantine declared Christianity a legal religion did Jerusalem start to become the centre of the Christian world. However, in AD 638 Jerusalem was captured by the Muslim Arabs. Although the new ruler, Caliph Umar, did not stop Christians from praying in the Church of the Holy Sepulchre, he cleared the Temple Mount and set up a small mosque on the site of the present Aqsa. Then in AD 691 Caliph Abd al-Malik Marwan completed the amazing Dome of the Rock on the Temple Mount, and it has dominated the Jerusalem skyline ever since.

In 1009 the Crusaders finally captured the city of Jerusalem from the Arabs with great bloodshed. The Crusaders dedicated the Dome of the Rock as a Christian church or prayer hall and made the Aqsa Mosque the headquarters of the Templar Order. But the Crusaders were finally expelled again in 1187, and the city was controlled by the Ayyubids and Mamluks. In 1517 the Ottoman sultan Selim captured the city, and his son, Suleiman the Magnificent, carefully rebuilt the gates and walls, leaving them much as we see them today.

Aerial view of the Temple Mount, Jerusalem, dominated today by the Muslim Dome of the Rock.

had attacked at an opportune moment, when Islam was temporarily split by religious feuds. In the ensuing five centuries of struggle, only the First Crusade significantly pushed back the military progress of Islam.

Anti-Semitism

In 1095, a mob of Crusaders made its way down the River Rhine in Germany, robbing and murdering Jews, heedless of local bishops' attempts to prevent the carnage. These warriors regarded Jews – as well as Muslims – as enemies of Christ, so that plundering and killing them was no crime. Yet the church strongly condemned such anti-Jewish attacks.

Fifty years later, a Cistercian monk, Radulf, again stirred up people against Rhineland Jews. Bernard of Clairvaux himself had to travel to Germany to end the resulting massacres. The purpose of the Crusades was not to kill Jews: popes, bishops and preachers insisted that the Jews of Europe were not to be harmed.

The Second Crusade (1145–49)

When the Crusader state of Edessa fell to the Turks and Kurds in 1144, widespread support was raised in Europe for a second crusade. This time, the crusade was led by two kings, Louis VII of France and Conrad III of Germany, and preached by the spiritual leader Bernard of Clairvaux.

Yet it failed miserably. Most of the soldiers were killed on their way to Palestine. Those who did make it only exacerbated matters by attacking Muslim Damascus, which had until now been a strong ally of the Christians. The continuing growth of Muslim power was unaffected.

By the late twelfth century, crusading had become a society-wide effort. Everyone was

called on to help. Knights were asked to sacrifice wealth and life to defend the Christian East; Christians left at home were rallied to support the Crusaders through prayer, fasting and almsgiving.

Yet still the Muslims grew stronger. The legendary Kurdish Muslim leader Salah al-Din, or Saladin as he is commonly known, made the Muslim Near East into a single entity, while preaching *jihad* against the Christians. At the Battle of Hattin (1187) he wiped out the Christian armies and captured the relic of the True Cross. Christian cities gradually surrendered, culminating with Jerusalem.

The Third Crusade (1189–92)

The Third Crusade, led by Emperor Frederick I Barbarossa of Germany, Philip II Augustus of France and Richard I, 'the Lionheart' of England, was very grandiose. But the aged Frederick drowned crossing a river, so his army returned home without even setting foot in the Holy Land. Philip and Richard's constant arguing only worsened a divisive situation in Palestine.

After recapturing Acre, Philip of France went home. Richard *Coeur de Lion*, a skilled warrior and resourceful leader, took the Christian forces on to victory after victory, eventually reconquering the entire coast of the Levant. But after two abortive attempts, Richard gave up trying to re-take Jerusalem. Promising to return, he agreed terms with Saladin that ensured peace in the region and free access to Jerusalem for unarmed pilgrims.

The Fourth Crusade (1201–1204)

Feuding now broke out between the East and West and led to the diversion to Constantinople of the Fourth Crusade, in 1202, to support an imperial claimant, Alexius IV Angelus, who promised in return generous rewards and

Artist's impression of Saladin's victory at the Battle of Hattin, 1187.

support for the Holy Land. Yet once he was on the throne, Alexius refused to pay up what he had promised. Thus betrayed, in 1204 the Crusaders captured and brutally sacked Constantinople, the greatest Christian city in the world. Their desire for loot supplanted all else, and the campaign became a grotesque perversion of the crusading ideal.

Pope Innocent III (reigned 1198–1216), the same pope who had authorized it, excommunicated this entire crusade and denounced the Crusaders themselves in no uncertain terms. But the tragic events of 1204 succeeded in finally closing the door for centuries between the Roman Catholic and Greek Orthodox churches.

Later Crusades

The rest of the thirteenth-century Crusades were not much better. Numerous squalid military expeditions followed, and a regular traffic of warriors, pilgrims and traders plied between Europe and the Holy Land. A few Crusaders sustained a toe-hold in the Holy Land – but rather than converting local people to Christianity, they often seem to have taken up Eastern customs themselves. The Crusades finally ended in 1270, leaving behind a heritage of vicious ill-feeling between Christians and Muslims which, in a number of places, has lasted down to the present time.

THE TURKISH THREAT

By 1291, Muslim forces had succeeded in ejecting the last Crusaders from Palestine, thus deleting all the Crusader kingdoms from the map. Despite numerous attempts and even more plans, Christian forces never again gained a toehold in the region until the nineteenth century.

The Muslim kingdoms became increasingly powerful during the fourteenth, fifteenth and sixteenth centuries. The Ottoman Turks conquered not only their fellow Muslims, so further unifying Islam, but also continued to press westwards, finally capturing Constantinople and pushing on deep into Europe itself. Europeans now began to fear that Islam would indeed finally achieve its aim of conquering the entire Christian world.

Vienna besieged

In 1480, Sultan Mehmed II captured Otranto as a beachhead for his planned invasion of Italy. Rome was evacuated. But the sultan died shortly afterwards, and his plans with him. In 1529, Suleiman the Magnificent (1494–1566) besieged the city of Vienna. Only a series of unseasonal rainstorms delayed his progress and forced him to abandon much of his artillery, preventing the Turks from taking this city. If they had taken it, Germany would have come under threat.

In 1571, a European Holy League defeated the Ottoman fleet at the battle of Lepanto. Yet in the end, the Muslim threat was neutralized economically. As Europe grew in wealth and power, the once awesome and sophisticated Turks began to seem backward and no longer worth a crusade.

CHAPTER 8

Reformations

A description of the Reformation written by a Protestant fifty years or so ago would probably have opened with a devastating critique of the corruption of the medieval church, the worldliness of the papacy and the indulgence of the priesthood and monks. It would then have retold a heroic story of Martin Luther valiantly hammering his 95 Theses to the Wittenberg church door, single-handedly challenging the mighty pope of Rome to reform the church.

The following is a typical such introduction to the subject:

In 1517, and the years that followed… the power of Rome over the Christian Church was challenged, men broke away from its tyranny, and Christian liberty was at last restored… The people were no less courageous than their leaders. War and persecution did not turn them aside. It was a time of high thinking, and perilous living… The fetters that had bound the people to a religion of superstition and fear had at last been broken, and the Church was once more free to worship God 'in spirit and in truth'.

However, this period and subject matter have been the object of sustained research and lively debate for several decades. Some scholars now talk of 'Reformations' (plural) rather than 'The Reformation'. Some see 'The Reformation' as an essentially medieval theological debate. Other scholars have questioned whether the late medieval church was ever as universally corrupt as had been previously claimed. And yet others have stressed the combination of political opportunities (and opportunism) that allowed the initial protests to build into a major schism within Western Christianity which has continued down to the present, even if today there is much less misunderstanding and hostility on both sides of the divide. Researchers have also re-emphasized the reforming tendencies within the sixteenth-century Roman Catholic Church itself, with its own renewed stress on spirituality and doctrinal orthodoxy.

With the debate still very much in progress, we need to steer a careful path through tricky terrain.

Resentment and resistance

As we have seen, throughout the Middle Ages pope and emperor had been engaged in an ongoing contest for supremacy – a conflict that generally resulted in victory for the papacy, but created bitter antagonisms between Rome and the Holy Roman empire in particular. Such antagonism was exacerbated in the fourteenth and fifteenth centuries by a growth in national feeling, particularly in German-speaking countries. Resentment of papal taxes and against submission to officials of a distant, foreign papacy was also found elsewhere in Europe.

In England the beginnings of a movement favouring independence from papal jurisdiction was marked by political statutes in the thirteenth and fourteenth centuries that considerably reduced the power of the church to withdraw land from the control of the civil government, to make direct appointments to church offices and to exercise judicial authority.

Similarly, Louis XI of France (reigned 1461–83) attempted to remove constitutional restrictions on the exercise of his authority, while in 1516 a concordat between the French king and the pope put the church substantially under royal authority. Papal concordats with other national monarchies had similarly prepared the way for the rise of autonomous national churches elsewhere too.

CORRUPTION AND DECAY

As early as the thirteenth century, there is evidence that the papacy had made itself vulnerable to attack through the greed, immorality and ignorance of many of its officials at all levels. Vast tax-free church possessions – constituting possibly as much as one-third of the territory of Europe – provoked the envy and resentment of land-hungry peasants.

The so-called Babylonian Captivity of the papacy at Avignon (1308–78) and the scandalous Papal Schism

(1378–1416) inevitably weakened the authority of the church (see pp. 55–56); and as it became obvious that the church had come under French political control, Christians elsewhere resented this, too. A new nationalism was beginning to challenge the relatively internationalist world of the Middle Ages. There was also widespread concern over alleged monastic corruption.

Church officials could hardly fail to recognize the calls for reform, and

Louis XI (1423–83) of France.

ambitious programmes to reorganize the entire hierarchy were debated at the Council of Constance (1414–18). However, no proposal managed to gain majority support; the national and theological tensions that had built up over the preceding century were not addressed, and no radical changes were instituted. The failure to reform eventually led to a greater upheaval, since the system needed to be adjusted or it would disintegrate. This failure of what became known as the 'Conciliar Movement' – a movement disliked by some later popes – as represented by the Council of Constance, helped open the way to the Protestant Reformation in the West.

HUMANISM
The revival of classical learning and speculative inquiry – known as

Erasmus of Rotterdam, by Quentin Massys (c. 1466–1530).

Humanism – which started during the fifteenth century in Italy, displaced Scholasticism as the leading philosophy of western Europe. As both a lay and a clerical movement, it deprived church leaders of the monopoly on learning they had held previously. New interest in the learning of the classical world was stimulated in Italy by a steady flow of scholarly refugees from Constantinople in the early fifteenth century, prior to the fall of that city to the Ottoman Turks in 1453. The refugees came carrying both their knowledge of Greek thought and their precious manuscripts.

The Humanists soon began to embrace both the styles and the values of the ancient Greeks and Romans, including their emphasis on 'man the measure of all things', challenging the medieval worldview of a God-centred universe. Debates also occurred concerning the nature of the church, and the source and extent of the authority of the papacy, of councils and of secular princes. This movement was for the time being the domain of an intellectual and artistic elite, and barely affected the masses directly. Educated lay people too began to study ancient literature, and scholars such as the Italian Humanist Lorenzo Valla critically appraised translations of the Bible and other documents which formed the basis for much of church dogma and tradition. However, this elite's activities eventually had a huge impact on the thinking of Christian Europe.

Humanists outside Italy, such as

Desiderius Erasmus (c. 1466–1536) in the Netherlands, John Colet (c. 1466–1519) and Sir Thomas More (1478–1535) in England, Johann Reuchlin (1455–1522) in Germany and Jacques Lefèvre d'Étaples (1455–1536) in France, applied this new learning to the evaluation of church practices – condemning corruption within the church – and to the development of a more accurate knowledge of the Bible.

Erasmus held that true religion was a matter of inward devotion rather than an outward matter of ceremony and ritual – another key emphasis echoed in the coming Reformation. The Humanists' scholarly studies laid the basis on which Martin Luther, the French theologian and religious reformer John Calvin, and other reformers subsequently claimed the Bible rather than the church as the source of all religious authority.

REFORM
John Wycliffe

There were some significant precursors of the Protestant Reformation. The fourteenth-century English reformer John Wycliffe (c. 1329–84), a priest and Oxford don, boldly attacked the papacy, striking at the sale of indulgences, pilgrimages, excessive veneration of the saints and the low moral and intellectual status of ordained priests. To communicate with ordinary people, he translated the Bible into English and delivered sermons in the vernacular

The English reformer John Wycliffe reads from his vernacular translation of the Bible to the influential John of Gaunt, Duke of Lancaster. Painting by Ford Madox Brown (1821–93).

We ask God of his supreme goodness to reform our church...

THE LOLLARD
CONCLUSIONS

instead of in the usual Latin. Wycliffe's work stimulated a movement of lay preachers called the Lollards, who roamed England preaching the Christian faith as they understood it. Wycliffe was burned posthumously as a heretic.

Jan Hus

Wycliffe's teachings also spread to Bohemia, where they found a powerful advocate in the religious reformer Jan Hus, or John Huss (1373–1415), the learned preacher of the Bethlehem Chapel in Prague. After many clashes with the church authorities, Hus – now rector of Charles University, Prague – was summoned by Pope John XXIII to the Council of Constance (1414–18) to defend his views. Although promised safe conduct by the emperor Sigismund, when he arrived at Constance Hus was summarily tried and condemned to be burnt at the stake without any genuine opportunity to defend his beliefs. John XXIII assured Sigismund 'he need not keep his word to heretics'.

The execution of Hus in 1415 led directly to the Hussite Wars, a violent expression of Bohemian nationalism which was suppressed only with difficulty by the combined forces of the Holy Roman emperor and the papacy.

GERMANY AND THE LUTHERAN REFORMATION

The Protestant revolution (sometimes also called the 'Magisterial Reformation' because it was supported by the 'magistrates', the rulers) is seen as having been started by Martin Luther in Germany in 1517, when he published his 95 Theses challenging the theology and practice of indulgences, which allowed people to buy a reduction in the time spent in purgatory, the 'halfway house' to heaven. (A campaign by Pope Leo X to raise major funding to rebuild St Peter's, Rome, prompted the high-pressure selling of indulgences, which served in turn to provoke yet harsher criticism of the church in cities where indulgences were being hawked.)

Papal authorities ordered Luther to retract his theses and submit to church authority; instead he became increasingly intransigent, and now started to appeal for general reform, attacking the church's system of sacraments and insisting that Christianity rested on individual faith based on the truths contained in the Bible. Threatened with excommunication by the pope, Luther publicly burned the papal decree (bull) of excommunication and with it a volume of canon law, by this act of defiance symbolizing his break with the entire system of the Roman Catholic Church.

In an attempt to stem the tide of revolt, Charles V (1500–58), the Holy Roman emperor, assembled the German princes and church leaders at the Diet of Worms in 1521, and ordered Luther to recant. A recalcitrant Luther refused and was now declared an outlaw.

For nearly a year Martin Luther

To go against conscience is neither right nor safe. Here I stand. I cannot do otherwise. God help me. Amen.

MARTIN LUTHER,
18 APRIL 1521

remained in hiding, writing pamphlets expounding his principles and translating the New Testament into German. Although Luther's writings were officially banned, they were openly sold and played a vital role in turning many of the great German cities into hotbeds of Lutheranism.

The reform movement soon made great advances among the people, and Germany now began to divide along religious and economic

Martin Luther

Martin Luther (1483–1546), the German reformer, was born into a miner's family. In 1505, caught in a thunderstorm and almost struck by lightning, he decided to become an Augustinian monk. However, almost paralyzed by guilt, he found that neither confession, penance, nor even a pilgrimage to Rome satisfied his spiritual unease.

Then, while preparing lectures on the book of Romans as a professor at the new University of Wittenberg, Luther grasped at the apostle Paul's words, 'The righteous shall live by faith'. In contrast to most contemporary teaching that salvation was by faith *and* works, Luther now believed from his study of the New Testament that salvation came by 'faith alone'. His discovery of a message of repentance and faith undermined for him the whole complicated confessional system of the medieval church – indulgences, pilgrimages, penances and the rest.

95 Theses
At first, Luther called simply for the reform of the church. But in October 1517 Johannes Tetzel came to Wittenberg, selling indulgences that he promised would reduce the time his customers spent in purgatory. On 31 October 1517 (it is claimed) Luther nailed his 95 Theses attacking the sale of indulgences to the door of the Castle Church in Wittenberg.

Luther's protest was quickly translated into German and, by means of the newly invented printing press, distributed all over Germany. In contrast, the pope's response was slow. Leo X dismissed Luther as 'a drunken German' who, once sober, would 'change his mind'.

Called to defend his views by leaders of the church, Luther found support from other priests, scholars and humanists as well as the German people, but was finally excommunicated by Leo X in 1521. At the Diet of Worms in the same year he declared he would not – could not – recant. He was now outlawed, his books banned and his arrest ordered.

Luther's Bible
In hiding in the Wartburg Castle, under the protection of Frederick the Wise, Luther now set about translating the New Testament from Greek into German to make it more accessible to ordinary people. It was printed in September 1522. Luther then worked with others to translate the rest of the Bible, and the complete 'Luther Bible' was first published in 1534, contributing much to the creation of the modern German language, and becoming a landmark in German literature.

Martin Luther portrayed in a famous painting by Lucas Cranach the Elder (1472–1553).

lines, with those most interested in preserving the traditional order – including the emperor, most of the princes and the higher clergy – supporting the Roman Catholic Church. Luther for his part was supported by the north German princes, the lower clergy, the commercial classes and large sections of the peasantry, who welcomed change as an opportunity for greater religious and economic independence.

A sixteenth-century propagandist depiction of Luther writing on the church door at Wittenberg.

Luther also wrote a number of hymns, including the well-known 'A Mighty Fortress is our God', which contributed to the rise of congregational singing within Protestantism.

Marriage

In 1525, Luther married a former nun, Katharina von Bora, incidentally helping to reintroduce clerical marriage into Western Christianity. 'Katie' moved into Martin's home in Wittenberg, and they started a family. In later life Luther's many illnesses helped make him bad-tempered and harsh. Katie at least once told him, 'Dear husband, you are too rude.'

Anti-Semitism

Luther has also become known for his anti-Semitic writings. In his pamphlet *On the Jews and Their Lies* (1543), he said synagogues should be set alight, Jewish prayer-books destroyed, rabbis forbidden to preach, Jewish houses destroyed and the 'poisonous envenomed worms' be expelled 'for ever'. Luther's violent views fuelled some Christians' suspicion of Judaism, and his coarse language made them dangerously attractive to the Nazis.

The Peasants' War (1524–25)

In 1524, open warfare broke out between the two opposing factions in the principalities of Bavaria, Thuringia and Swabia, with the start of the Peasants' War, which left many Roman Catholics murdered by Protestant bands. The conflict soon gained momentum and a new leader, Thomas Münzer (c. 1489–1525). Many poverty-stricken peasants mistakenly believed that Luther's attack on the church and its hierarchy meant that he would also support an attack on the social hierarchy. Although Luther urged landlords to satisfy any just peasant claims, he soon turned against the peasants and, in a pamphlet luridly entitled *Against the Murdering, Thieving Hordes of Peasants* (1525), utterly condemned their resort to violence, encouraging the nobles to wreak bloody punishment on them.

The peasants were defeated in 1525, but the divide between Roman Catholics and Lutherans continued to widen. Some compromise was reached at the Diet of Speyer (1526), when it was agreed that German princes who wanted to practise Lutheranism should be free to do so; but a second Diet of Speyer three years later abrogated this agreement. The Lutheran minority protesting against this became known as 'Protestants'; thus the first 'Protestants' were Lutherans. The term was later extended to include all Christian groups that developed from this initial break with Rome.

Theologically the divide was wide too. Protestants emphasized salvation by 'faith alone' (not faith and good works); 'Scripture alone' (rather than the Bible plus tradition); and 'the priesthood of all believers' (as opposed to a sacramental priesthood). Because they believed these teachings stemmed from the Bible, they encouraged publication of the Bible in the common language and universal education.

Zwingli

Parallel to events in Germany, a reform movement began in Zurich, Switzerland, led by Huldrych (Ulrich) Zwingli (1484–1531), a milder man yet a more radical reformer than Luther. Born in Wildhaus, Switzerland, Zwingli began to reform when appointed minister of Zurich Minster. He soon became deeply embroiled in politics and died on the battlefield.

This is my body…

Zwingli, like Luther, taught that salvation came solely by God's initiative. Luther and Zwingli also agreed on many other issues, with the recently introduced printing press shuttling ideas rapidly between the two centres of reform. However, the two had a major falling-out over their views of the Eucharist. Martin Luther broke with the Roman church on this as on many other issues, demanding that believers should be offered both bread and wine – not just bread, as in the Catholic Church. Luther likewise rejected the Roman Catholic idea that the bread and wine *became* Christ's body and blood; he believed that these 'elements' benefited those who accepted them in faith, but the act of taking them in itself conveyed no automatic blessing.

But Zwingli went further. For Zwingli, the Lord's Supper was solely a sign or metaphor: 'This is my body' meant 'This stands for my body'. He believed that a vital part of the Eucharistic meal was the bringing together of Christians in communion. This tradition was followed by many later Protestant denominations.

Luther insisted on the real presence of Jesus at the Eucharist. When the obstinate Wittenberg reformer met Zwingli in October 1529 at Marburg and disputed the question, he pulled out a lump of chalk and scrawled on the

John Calvin, the Genevan reformer.

table, 'This is my body.' For him, that said it all.

A Lutheran creed

In 1530 Charles V, the Holy Roman emperor, called an imperial diet at Augsburg to attempt to unite the empire against the military threat of the Ottoman Turks, who had besieged Vienna the previous autumn. In preparation for this, the emperor wanted to resolve the religious controversies in his realm. The German reformer Philipp Melanchthon (1497–1560) drew up a conciliatory statement of Lutheran beliefs, known as the Augsburg Confession, which he

submitted to the emperor Charles V and other Roman Catholic leaders. Although this document failed in its purpose of reconciling Catholics and Lutherans, it did become the credal basis of the resultant new Lutheran Church.

CALVIN'S GENEVA

An account of the second-generation French reformer John (Jean) Calvin (1509–64) cannot now be separated from his adopted city, Geneva in Switzerland. Yet it was against his will that he ever settled there. In 1536, while passing through the city of Geneva as a fugitive from persecution in his native France, Calvin was virtually terrorized into staying by the fiery local reformer William Farel (1489–1565), at a time when the city was in the midst of the turbulent process of securing political and religious independence. Although Calvin and Farel were both temporarily ousted from Geneva in 1538, Calvin was recalled in 1541 and remained in the city until his death.

Calvin attempted an experiment: to make his new home, Geneva, a model city of God among men. By controlling both church and education, he tried to oversee the morals, ideas and policies of the citizens of Geneva. Naturally, free-minded citizens objected. And the logic of his position led Calvin notoriously to execute the foolhardy visiting Spaniard Michael Servetus for denying the Trinity – though in this he may also have been motivated by a desire to stress his essential orthodoxy to the church at large.

After Calvin's death, Geneva became a haven for fugitive Protestants from many parts of Europe, including Tudor England and Catholic Scotland. John Knox, the Scottish Protestant leader, called Geneva 'the most perfect school of Christ'. Geneva trained and equipped the Protestant asylum-seekers to return home, taking with them the teachings of Calvinism and neo-Calvinism – a logical extension of Calvin's ideas – notably to France, Holland, Hungary and Scotland.

The spread of Calvin's ideas was aided by the new educational system set up in Geneva: primary and secondary schools were created and in 1559 an academy was established which soon became known as the University of Geneva. In 1559 it had 162 students; just five years later it boasted more than 1,500, most of whom intended to become Reformed and proselytizing missionaries in Europe.

The emperor fights back

For some time a series of wars with France and the Ottoman empire prevented the emperor Charles V from turning the full might of his military forces on the Lutherans. However, in 1546, free of international commitments, the emperor, in alliance with the pope and aided by Duke Maurice of Saxony, declared war on the Schmalkaldic League, a defensive association of Protestant princes.

The Roman Catholic forces were at first successful, but Duke Maurice later defected to the Protestants and Charles V was forced to make peace. This religious civil war ended with the Peace of Augsburg (1555), which stipulated that the ruler of every German state – there were about 300 in total at this time – should choose between Roman Catholicism and Lutheranism, and enforce his chosen faith upon his subjects. Each state was to take the religion of its ruler;

John Calvin

A quiet and sensitive man in contrast to the forthright and larger-than-life Luther, John Calvin nonetheless had a profound influence on the progress of the Reformation. John Calvin was twenty-five years younger than Luther and grew up in a world where the new Protestant faith was already becoming established. A Frenchman, he was born in Noyon, Picardy, in 1509, and received a Humanist education at the University of Paris, greatly admiring Erasmus.

At some point between 1528 and 1533, he wrote, 'God subdued my soul to docility by a sudden conversion.' Even as a student, Calvin's asceticism and devotion to learning were clear – and had probably already begun to undermine his health.

In his early twenties, Calvin devoted more and more of his energies to theology as his genius for systematizing ideas was becoming evident. In 1536 he published the first edition of *The Institutes of the Christian Religion*, a systematic exposition of his theology. From this point, his essential ideas did not alter; they were simply elaborated or clarified in the

many subsequent editions of this pivotal work.

In many ways, Calvin echoed Luther. Calvin, like Luther, thought along similar theological lines to Augustine of Hippo, who stated that humans cannot be saved by their own efforts but only by the grace of God. Humans are sinful: left to their own resources, they cannot fulfil God's requirements. They can be righteous – accepted in God's sight – only through faith in Christ. To know God is what humans were created for. God is known as Creator, through his revelation of himself in Scripture, and as Saviour in Christ.

Many have reacted against Calvin's rigorous logic, and particularly to the idea of 'predestination': that 'God has mercy on whom he has mercy; and whom he will he hardens'. Yet, for Calvin, the Bible was the supreme authority; he aimed to present systematically what he saw to be its teachings.

the resulting pattern of Catholic/Protestant areas is still largely visible in Germany and other parts of central Europe today. The longstanding concept of the religious unity of a single Christian community throughout western Europe under the supreme authority of the pope had been destroyed once for all.

AFTER LUTHER

In Germany Protestantism reached its greatest extent under Emperor Maximilian II (reigned 1564–76), when many north German bishoprics converted to Protestantism. Lutheranism was by this time the religion of about half the population. In Saxony, the heartland of Lutheran orthodoxy, Lutheranism became a

Painting depicting the congregation listening to their preacher in the Huguenot 'temple' at Lyon, France. Note the simplicity and the absence of an altar, stained glass and priestly vestments. By Jean Perrissin (1536–1611).

quietistic faith of the ordinary people.

Calvinism developed into a popular movement in Germany only in north-west Rhineland and Westphalia – both neighbouring the Netherlands – with Heidelburg becoming a leading Calvinist intellectual centre. Calvinism also won support from the princes of the Electoral Palatinate. The arrival of Calvinism divided Protestantism itself and helped the Roman Catholic Counter-Reformation to prevail.

Archduke Ferdinand II (reigned 1620–37) led a brutal Catholic reaction in Styria, Carinthia and Carniola, with first the expulsion and then the execution of many Protestants after 1596. Bohemia suffered badly in the devastating Thirty Years' War (1618–48), in which many Protestant nobles either had their property confiscated, or were executed. This laid the foundation for Czech hatred of German domination.

France

In France (where the Calvinists were known as Huguenots) the first Reformed ministers arrived in 1553, and the first Reformed congregation was set up in Paris in 1555. By 1561 there were already 2,150 Huguenot churches in France, and Calvinists were estimated to number about 10 per cent of the population – in total about a million people, including a number of aristocratic families. The Huguenots were concentrated on the Atlantic west coast, around the port of La Rochelle, and in the south-east,

111

The assassination of the Huguenot leader Admiral Gaspard de la Coligny (1519–72), and massacre of other French Huguenots on St Bartholomew's Day, 24 August 1572.

in the Rhone Valley, and worshipped openly in their own churches.

However, between 1562 and 1598 there was continual religious conflict between the Huguenot militants and Catholic hardliners, and a low point was reached on St Bartholomew's Day 1572, when a massacre of Huguenots was ordered in Paris which permanently crippled the French Protestant movement. Peace was restored only when King Henry IV of Bourbon (reigned 1589–1610) converted from Protestantism to Catholicism and effectively partitioned France between the majority Catholics and minority Protestants. The Edict of Nantes (1598) granted Huguenots freedom of worship and political equality, with France thereby officially accepting a Protestant minority.

However, the rise of absolutism in France, with its maxim of 'one king, one faith, one law', led to a renewal of persecution of the Huguenots. In 1628 the last remaining Huguenot stronghold, La Rochelle, was captured. Finally, the Edict of Nantes was revoked by Louis XIV (reigned 1643–1715) in 1685, prompting numerous forced re-conversions and compelling about half a million Huguenots to flee the country. They went mainly to Brandenburg in Germany, the Netherlands and England.

The Netherlands

Reformed ministers from Geneva first arrived in the Netherlands in the 1550s when Lutheranism and the Anabaptists had already taken root, so Calvinism was entering a crowded field. Moreover, Charles V had introduced a Catholic Inquisition to the region in 1524, and with it the stringent persecution of Protestants.

Nevertheless, by 1560 Protestantism accounted for 5 per cent of the population of the Netherlands. The Calvinists were found mostly in Antwerp, Ghent and the areas nearest

RIGHT: Religious divisions of Europe in 1560.

to Germany. Calvinists now formulated a theological defence for the eventually successful rebellion against Spanish rule, which had been extended to the north. After the Council of Dort (1618–19) a strict form of Calvinism became the official creed in the United Provinces, created after the Spanish were driven out of the northern provinces. The Protestants moved into this area from Antwerp and Ghent, which were still under Spanish rule and strongly Catholic.

Poland
Calvinism first reached Poland in 1550. Two leading aristocrats, Prince Radziwill the Black (1515–65) and John (Jan) à Lasco (1499–1560), actively assisted the spread of Calvinism, as did King Stephen II and Stephen Bathory.

Nevertheless, Calvinism did not spread widely. Most Poles did not speak German and most Calvinist preachers did not speak Polish, so language proved a major stumbling-block. In 1573, at the Confederation of Warsaw, Catholics and Protestants agreed to make religious toleration part of the national constitution, to be guaranteed by each king on his succession. But division among the Protestants meant that the Catholic Church still dominated the country, earning it the nickname 'the Spain of the north'.

THE ENGLISH REFORMATION
The course of the Reformation in England was distinctively different from that of much of Europe. There had long been a strong tradition of English anti-clericalism, and the country had

already seen the rise of the medieval Lollard movement, which had in turn inspired the Hussites in Bohemia. By the 1520s, however, the Lollards were barely an active force, and certainly not a mass movement.

The different character of the English Reformation derived from the fact that it was initially driven by the political needs of King Henry VIII (reigned 1509–47), rather than by any theological dispute. In fact, Henry started out a devout Catholic, and in 1521 even wrote a

book attacking Luther's ideas, for which he was awarded the title 'Defender of the Faith' by Pope Leo X (a title, ironically, still boasted by the British monarch, though questioned by her heir).

By the late 1520s, however, Henry wanted to divorce his wife Catherine of Aragon, as she had failed to produce a male heir who survived to reproduce. When the pope refused to annul Henry's marriage, the king decided to get his way by breaking politically with the papacy. In 1533 Henry appointed Thomas Cranmer

The Church of England

Formed as it was in Tudor times in an idiosyncratic mix of political expediency and religious conviction, the Anglican Church entered the seventeenth century with the uneasy Elizabethan Settlement still holding. But during the turbulent early years of the new century, through the reigns of the Stuart monarchs James I (1603–25) and Charles I (1625–49), culminating in the English Civil War and the protectorate of Oliver Cromwell, there were swings back and forth between two factions within Anglicanism. The Puritans and other radicals required more far-reaching reform, while the more conservative churchmen wanted to retain more traditional beliefs and practices. The failure of the king and bishops to submit to Puritan demands for more extensive reform was one of the causes of the ensuing war, casualties of which included King Charles I and Archbishop of Canterbury William Laud (1573–1645), both of whom were beheaded.

During the Commonwealth (1649–60), Anglicanism was disestablished, the Thirty-Nine Articles officially replaced with the Westminster Confession, and the *Book of Common Prayer* supplanted by the *Directory of Public Worship*. Despite this, about a quarter of the English clergy refused to conform, and the period also saw the rapid rise of dissenting sects such as the General and Particular Baptists, Congregationalists and Quakers, as well as more radical millenarian and communitarian groups.

With the restoration of Charles I's son, Charles II, Anglicanism was reimposed in a form close to the

Elizabethan Settlement, and an attempt made to suppress dissent by harsh measures. When Charles' successor James II (reigned 1685–88) seemed intent on reviving Roman Catholicism, he was forced into exile and replaced by the Protestant William of Orange and his wife Mary, James' daughter.

The aim of comprehending all the people in a single church – taken for granted by the Tudor monarchs – now had to be abandoned, and limited toleration granted, including freedom of worship for nonconformist churches such as the Presbyterians, Baptists and Congregationalists – though not the Unitarians. Penal laws restricting English Catholics were not repealed until 1829.

The religious landscape of England now took on something like its present form, with an Anglican established church occupying the middle ground, and those dissenting from the establishment – too strong to be suppressed – continuing outside the national church. Restrictions and official suspicion continued well into the nineteenth century.

Anglicanism outside England
At the time of the English Reformation, the Church of Ireland had also separated from Rome and adopted articles of faith similar to the English church's Thirty-Nine Articles. However, unlike England, the Irish Anglican Church never attracted the loyalty of the majority of the population, who still adhered to Roman Catholicism.

The Scottish Episcopal Church was inaugurated in

(1489–1556) Archbishop of Canterbury. The following year, his new primate granted Henry a divorce, thus freeing the king to marry his lover, Anne Boleyn, who was already pregnant with Henry's child, Elizabeth.

In 1534 an act of the so-called 'Reformation Parliament' made Henry 'Supreme Head' of the Church of England, so separating the Church of England from the Church of Rome. Between 1535 and 1540, under Henry's advisor Thomas Cromwell

(c. 1485–1540), the English monasteries were dissolved after visiting commissioners claimed to have discovered sexual and financial corruption among their monks and nuns. It is estimated that at this date the English church owned between one-fifth and one-third of the country, so dissolution brought huge amounts of land and property into the hands of the crown, who gave much of it in turn to the English aristocracy and gentry. The vested interest Henry created in this way built a

1582, when James VI of Scotland (later also James I of England) attempted to reintroduce bishops after the Church of Scotland became Presbyterian.

The Scottish Episcopal Church helped later in the creation of the Episcopal Church in the USA after the American Revolution, when the first American bishop, Samuel Seabury – refused consecration by English bishops as he could not take the necessary oath of allegiance to the English crown – was consecrated in Aberdeen, Scotland. The organization of both the Scottish and American churches, and consequently of their daughter churches, has differences from that of the English church – as for example in their being led by a presiding bishop rather than an archbishop.

Catholic revival

The Oxford Movement, a Catholic revival movement within nineteenth-century Anglicanism, opposed the growth of liberalism and encouraged a high doctrine of the church and greater ceremonial. It succeeded in transforming the liturgy of the Anglican Church, repositioning the Eucharist as the central act of worship and reintroducing the use of elaborate vestments and ceremonies that had long been banned in the English church. It raised fears among some that Roman Catholic practices were being reintroduced into the Church of England. Among early leaders of the Oxford Movement was John Henry Newman, who in 1845 announced he had moved to the Roman Catholic Church.

Evangelical resurgence

After the Second World War, the emergence of a generation of conservative intellectuals created a new force in American Protestantism, symbolized in 1956 by the founding of the journal *Christianity Today*. These leaders expressed unity as a co-operative effort by like-minded people in areas such as evangelism, education and social action rather than as denominational mergers or worldwide ecumenism.

Within the Church of England, the leader in a similar movement to bring evangelical Christianity back into the mainstream was John Stott. Born in 1921 and educated at Cambridge, he served at All Souls' Church, London, from 1945 to 1975. Through his lecturing and writing he became known throughout the world as an outstanding evangelist, apologist and Bible teacher.

Twentieth century

During the twentieth and early twenty-first centuries, Anglicanism continued its attempt to comprehend a breadth of theological persuasions – evangelical, high church, liberal, charismatic and radical. In the late twentieth century it grappled with the issues of the ordination of women as priests and bishops, and the ordination of gay men. Such issues threatened to split the church nationally and internationally, with more conservative churches in Africa particularly opposing liberal views.

powerful party in support of the monastic dissolution and hence, if only passively, in favour of Henry's reforms.

But many prominent figures opposed Henry's reforms, including Sir Thomas More (1478–1535), Henry's previous Lord Chancellor, and the Bishop of Rochester, John Fisher (1469–1535), both of whom were executed for their pains. In the north of England in late 1536 and early 1537 a series of uprisings by Roman Catholics opposed to the dissolutions broke out, known as the Pilgrimage of Grace, but were soon put down.

There was also a growing party of English Protestants who began to follow the Zwinglian and Calvinist theology now circulating in Europe. In 1539, Henry authorized the publication of the English 'Great Bible', largely based on William Tyndale's English translation of the Hebrew and Greek text. (Tyndale had been burnt at the stake in exile in Belgium just three years earlier, with Henry's approval.)

Portrait of Archbishop Thomas Cranmer by Gerlach Flicke.

furniture and practices were abolished in church buildings, and the requirement that clergy be celibate was lifted. Recent research has shown that, at the local, popular level, such changes were not necessarily welcomed or even implemented. And Edward's Protestant reforms were soon under threat when he died childless in 1553.

Edward VI

When Henry died in 1547, he was succeeded by his nine-year-old Protestant son Edward VI (reigned 1547–53) who, through his advisers, unequivocally established Protestantism – at least theologically – in the English church. Thomas Cranmer's Protestant *Book of Common Prayer* was introduced in 1549, and a second, more radical, edition replaced it in 1552. Stained glass, holy shrines, statues of saints and other Catholic

Reform reversed

Under Henry's daughter, Mary I (reigned 1553–58), the reforming legislation was repealed and England once more became officially Roman Catholic. Mary married the Catholic Philip II of Spain and did all she could to reintroduce Roman Catholicism, but never became pregnant. She had the Protestant Thomas Cranmer burnt at the stake, and appointed the Roman Catholic Cardinal Reginald Pole Archbishop of Canterbury in his

Question: What is the chief end of man?
Answer: Man's chief end is to glorify God and enjoy him forever.

WESTMINSTER CATECHISM

place. In all, 283 Protestants are believed to have been burnt for heresy during Mary's reign (many of them commemorated in John Foxe's best-selling *Book of Martyrs*, first published in 1563) – more than twice as many as had been executed for heresy in the previous century and a half. Many Protestants also fled to the European continent, where in such cities as Geneva and Strasbourg they imbibed Reformed theology and often became further radicalized.

Elizabeth's middle way

When Mary died, Anne Boleyn's daughter Elizabeth I (reigned 1558–1603) inherited the throne, and set about attempting to restore a moderate reformation and religious peace. In 1559, an Act of Supremacy made Elizabeth the 'Supreme Governor' of the Church of England. From being, under Henry VIII, a national Catholic Church without a pope, the English church now moved towards a 'middle way' (*via media*) – originally between the extremes of Roman Catholicism and Puritanism – often said to characterize the Anglican communion ever since. The compromise was at first uneasy and unstable.

An Act of Uniformity (1559) forced people to attend Sunday worship in an Anglican church and the Thirty-Nine Articles established Anglican doctrine. Cranmer's sonorous *Book of Common Prayer* also helped define the national church.

The Puritans

Elizabeth's reign saw too the emergence of Puritanism. Elizabethan Puritans were Protestants who, while agreeing that there should be a single national church, felt that the church had as yet only been partly reformed. They wanted the Church of England to resemble more closely the Protestant churches of Europe, and especially Geneva.

Some Puritans objected to 'Catholic'

passages of the Prayer Book, church ceremonies and vestments, while others wanted church governance radically reformed and 'purified' – hence the name 'Puritan'. By the early 1590s, revolutionary Presbyterian Puritans, who advocated the outright abolition of bishops, had lost their campaign. Reforming Puritanism, and the Puritan mindset, however, survived and went on to influence the English Civil War – and English and American life generally.

The Authorized (King James) Version of the Bible, translated under the sponsorship of Elizabeth's successor, James I (reigned 1603–25), and first published in 1611, helped unite Protestantism and the English nation by providing what was to become the accepted Bible translation for the next 300 years, written in dignified, resonant yet accessible language.

The Reformation tradition

The four most important traditions to emerge directly from the Reformation were the Lutheran, the Reformed/Calvinist/Presbyterian, the Anabaptist (see chapter 9) and the Anglican. Subsequent Protestant denominations and traditions generally trace their roots back to one or other of these four groupings. Almost 70 million Christians belong to Lutheran churches worldwide, while roughly 400 hundred million Protestant Christians trace their origins back to Luther..

CHAPTER 9

Catholic and Radical Reform

THE CATHOLIC REFORMATION

A Roman Catholic Reformation – which was actually under way before Luther ever broke with Rome – continued, and was strengthened by, the conviction that the church had to be reformed from within to avert Protestant criticism and inroads into its adherents. This resulted in a variety of new spiritual movements, the reform of Catholic religious communities, the founding of new Catholic seminaries, the redefining of Catholic theology, and structural changes to the institution of the Roman Catholic Church.

After looking as if it might succumb to Protestantism in the mid-sixteenth century, the Roman Church emerged stronger in 1600 than it had been in 1500. The Protestant Reformation sparked off varied and sometimes far-reaching reactions from a Roman Catholic Church seeking to re-assert its authority.

New piety

An association of priests and lay Christians in Rome called the Oratory of Divine Love, together with several reform-minded popes, led the drive for renewal. The Oratory of Divine Love, formed in Rome in 1517, drew members from all sections of society to unite in Christian service and prayer. Chief among the reformers was a pious cardinal, Gasparo Contarini (1483–1542), one of the few in the Catholic hierarchy who seemed genuinely to understand Protestant concerns, and who reached out to Protestants in an attempted reconciliation at Augsburg in 1530 and on other occasions.

The Council of Trent

Unfortunately, attitudes on both sides hardened after the turbulent events of the 1530s. As Protestantism became more institutionalized, the Roman Inquisition and the Council of Trent, in northern Italy (1545–63), hammered out a hardline response by the Roman Catholic Church to the Protestant challenge.

But the Council of Trent also did much to revitalize the spiritual and ecclesiastical life of the Roman Church, by clarifying doctrines and reforming administrative abuses. The Catholic Reformation re-emphasized the authority of the church, the mysteries of religion and the drama of the mass. These new emphases were also expressed visually in the baroque style of architecture: with their elaborate decoration and dramatic visual effects, baroque churches inspired a sense of awe and wonder in worshippers. A Counter-Reformation seriousness and faithfulness to the biblical narrative is also seen in the work of such fine artists as Ribera, El Greco and Caravaggio.

Depiction of a sitting of the Council of Trent (1545–63). Notice the crucifix at the centre and the dove, representing the Holy Spirit, top centre.

The Society of Jesus

The Society of Jesus (the Jesuits), founded in 1540 by Ignatius Loyola (1491–1556), became another key element in helping to renew the Church of Rome and to deter and defeat Protestantism. The Jesuits, bound by vows of absolute obedience to the pope, particularly emphasized missions, education and counter-reform. It was in missions above all that they excelled, carrying the Christian message to the far corners of the world. The tireless and imaginative work of courageous Jesuit missionaries such as Francis Xavier in India and the Far East, Matteo Ricci (1552–1610) in China and Roberto de Nobili (1577–1656) in India was much admired and emulated.

Ignatius Loyola

Born in 1491 in the Basque region of northern Spain, Inigo (Ignatius) de Loyola's prospects of a military career as a rich knight were shattered at the age of thirty when a cannon ball struck him, wounding one leg and breaking the other. During convalescence at the castle of Loyola, he was converted through reading a life of Christ and a book on the saints, and resolved to become instead a soldier of Christ.

Ignatius now went back to school to study Latin, then on to the University of Paris, where he shared a room with Francis Xavier and Peter Faber. With a few other fellow students, he directed them in what are now known as his *Spiritual Exercises* – a detailed and demanding set of devotions for breaking in new recruits for Jesus, which he later published. Because of his puritanical extremism Loyola more than once came under suspicion from the Inquisition.

In 1539, with the pope's approval, Ignatius and his companions decided to form a community, vowing obedience to a superior who would hold office for life, and offering themselves to the pope to travel wherever he sent them for whatever duties. A vow to this effect was added to the regular vows of poverty, chastity and obedience.

Formal approval for this new order was given by Pope Paul III in 1540. They referred to themselves as the Company, or Society, of Jesus, and its adherents are usually called the Jesuits. Unsurprisingly, Ignatius was elected their first superior.

From his election as 'superior general' until his death, Loyola worked from two small rooms, directing the new society, writing countless letters to every corner of the globe, administering Jesuit affairs and guiding lay men and women in their spiritual life.

During his lifetime, the Society of Jesus expanded from eight to one thousand members, and was soon founding colleges and religious houses all over Europe and as far away as Brazil and Japan.

Education

The Jesuits are well known for their educational work, although initially Loyola had no intention of providing teaching. However, as early as 1548 schools – primarily for the education of the new young Jesuit recruits – had opened in Italy, Portugal, the Netherlands, Spain, Germany and India. In the same year, Ignatius sent five Jesuits to Messina, Sicily, to open a school for lay as well as Jesuit students. Similar projects soon followed, and Ignatius proceeded to set up Jesuit schools and universities all over Europe.

The Jesuits continued to devote themselves to education, reform, spiritual discipline and missions, introducing rigorous educational methods, providing schooling for all ages from primary to university, and specializing in educating the upper classes. Jesuit schools aimed to demonstrate that the Roman Catholic faith fitted into the existing European social order based on privilege, hierarchy and ceremony, helping to strengthen Catholic resistance to Protestantism in such countries as Austria, Bavaria, Poland and parts of the Rhineland.

Teach us, good Lord, to serve thee as thou deservest; to give and not to count the cost; to fight and not to heed the wounds; to toil and not to ask for rest; to labour and not to ask for any reward save knowing that we do thy will.

IGNATIUS LOYOLA

A table-top illustrating the seven deadly sins, with four circular panels depicting the 'four last things', by Hieronymous Bosch (c. 1450–1516).

Spirituality and mysticism

Meanwhile, several Catholic mystics appeared in Spain, among them Teresa of Avila (1515–82), whose spirituality inspired many. Like her contemporary Spaniard John of the Cross (1542–91), her meditations on the life and death of Christ were marked by heights of ecstasy and depths of despair. Ironically, both attracted the attentions of the Inquisition during their lifetime – but both were later canonized by the Roman Catholic Church.

THE RADICAL REFORMATION

The Reformation encouraged radical Protestants to question many areas of Christian teaching and practice. The 'Radical Reformation' – sometimes known as the 'left-wing of the Reformation', or the 'Third Reformation' – was, like the Magisterial Reformation, a response to perceived corruption in the Roman Catholic Church, but also to aspects of the new Protestant movement. Once Protestants had established the

competence of all believers to read and interpret Scripture, increasingly divergent and extreme views became common.

Starting mainly among the peasants of Germany and the Low Countries, the Radical Reformation gave rise in turn to a number of different Anabaptist groups throughout the Christian world. Lutheranism was more attractive to grand, wealthy burghers than to the poor, oppressed and disinherited. Radical

The Jesuits and mission

The Jesuits are known above all for their missions, following the pioneering example of Francis Xavier (1506–52), who became one of Loyola's earliest recruits. Dedicated to the conversion of as much of humankind as possible, in 1542 Xavier sailed to Goa, off the Indian coast, where he baptized thousands of converts before travelling on to Sri Lanka, Malaysia and Japan in 1549. He died while awaiting entry to China.

Xavier has been criticized for adapting the faith, for using the Inquisition and for approving of persecution, yet his proselytizing example encouraged thousands to follow. Jesuit strategy was often to win a ruler's allegiance to the faith, so that he would in turn order the Christianization of his people.

The Jesuit Matteo Ricci worked in China from 1582, initially with success. But the Jesuits were unable to lay any permanent foundations there until a second wave of Catholic missionary activity in the nineteenth century. Although by the end of the sixteenth century many in Japan were converted, vicious persecution eradicated Christianity there in the following decades.

Jesuits in America

In South and Central America, teams of Jesuit missionaries organized mass conversions of the indigenous population. They invented special settlements, known as 'Reductions', where the Christianized people could live isolated from the outside world and directed by European Jesuit priests. Spanish Catholic missionaries learned the languages of the Amerindians and created writing systems for them. Then they preached to the native populations in these languages – for instance Quechua, Guarani and Nahuatl.

A contemporary painting by Narsingh depicting Jesuits at the Fatehpur Sikri court of Akbar the Great (1556–1605), who belonged to the Muslim Mughal dynasty.

Anabaptist preachers protested against landowners who took control of increasingly large areas, kings who centralized control and princes who looked for ever-increasing tax revenues to fund their growing states.

Although the main Anabaptist groups agreed with most of the more important Protestant doctrines, both Catholics and Protestants dubbed them 'heretics', while Luther himself labelled them 'fanatics'.

Invisible church

Unlike both the Catholics and the mainstream Lutheran and Reformed Protestant movements, the Radical Reformation generally rejected the idea of a 'visible church', which they regarded as corrupt and which they contrasted with a pure 'invisible church' – a community of believers who accepted Jesus, and demonstrated this by adult (or 'believer's') baptism. Anabaptists believed infant baptism to be invalid. The term 'anabaptist' ('re-baptizer') was coined as an insult, and tended to be used by opponents of anyone with radical Christian beliefs.

Although most scholars reckon Anabaptists began with the Radical Reformers in the sixteenth century, there were also significant forerunners, such as Peter Chelcicky (c. 1390–1460), a Bohemian reformer influenced by Wycliffe, who taught many of the beliefs considered essential to Anabaptist thinking; and the Waldensians of north-west Italy, who held beliefs

The Lord has more truth yet to break forth out of his holy Word.

JOHN ROBINSON

similar to those of the Anabaptists, and who sustained a Protestant church in Italy down to the twenty-first century. (The Waldensians were named after Peter Waldo, who around 1175 experienced conversion, took up a life of poverty and preaching, and had translations made of the New Testament into the local language.)

Swiss Anabaptists

Anabaptism in Switzerland first developed among some of the Zürich reformer Ulrich Zwingli's early supporters, such as Conrad Grebel, Felix Manz, George Blaurock and Balthasar Hübmaier – scholars who read Hebrew, Greek and Latin. The earliest re-baptisms took place in Zürich in January 1525, but the ideas put forward failed to win over the majority. As a result, there emerged the idea of a church of the separated, persecuted 'remnant'. The Schleitheim Articles of 1527, edited by Michael Sattler, defined Swiss Anabaptism, which set out to separate churches of believers from the world – an essential element in the concept of the 'free church'.

South German Anabaptists

Anabaptism in south Germany was very different, stemming from the re-formulation of the ideas of Thomas Münzer (1490–1525) – the radical attracted to Luther's Wittenberg and who helped foment the Peasants' War – by Hans Hut and Hans Denck.

Münzer, drawing on medieval

mysticism, preached the inner transformation of people by the Holy Spirit, and the consequent transformation of society, as transformed believers acted in a revolutionary way to usher in the kingdom of God. Münzer regarded the Peasants' War as a struggle against all constituted authority, aiming to set up by revolutionary means an ideal Christian commonwealth, based on equality and the community of goods. However, Münzer's revolution died with him in May 1525, in a massacre at Frankenhausen.

Hans Denck (c. 1495–1527) substituted a pacifist *inner* transformation for Münzer's social revolution, focussing on the renewal of individuals rather than of society. He contrasted this inner transformation in Christ with the rival authorities of the Roman Catholic hierarchy and Protestant reformers' scholarly biblical exegesis.

Hans Hut (c.1490–1527), for his part, believed the necessary inner transformation was achieved through both inner and outer struggle and suffering. For him, re-baptism

Separatists and Baptists

In the early sixteenth century, English Congregationalists, part of the Puritan separatist movement, began to found churches that were independent of the state and made up only of believers. Each church was autonomous, though linked in fellowship. The Baptists went further, saying that baptism was only for adults – an expression of their faith in Christ – and not for infants.

The Baptists may have owed something to earlier European Anabaptists. (The Dutch Mennonites, for example, shared with general Baptists believer's baptism, religious liberty, separation of church and state and Arminian views about salvation.)

The earliest known English Baptist church can be traced back to a congregation in Amsterdam, where John Smyth was pastor in 1609. Shortly afterwards, Smyth left and Thomas Helwys took over the leadership, taking the congregation back to England in 1611.

With the victory of Oliver Cromwell's Puritan forces in the English Civil War came a chance to experiment with every shape of Christian grouping, from the violent Fifth Monarchy Men to George Fox's Quakers. Baptist churches spread rapidly.

Toleration
The return of the monarchy in 1660, in the shape of Charles II, brought the re-establishment of the Church of England. For a time dissent was persecuted and oppressed; but it had come to stay, and was first tolerated, then accepted as a British institution. One-

time sects became respectable denominations – Presbyterians, Congregationalists, Baptists and the Society of Friends (Quakers).

The Baptists had a renaissance in the nineteenth century, and were noted for the pulpit oratory of such figures as the London preachers C. H. Spurgeon (1834–92) and John Clifford (1836–1923). They also helped spark the Protestant missionary enterprise that marks the nineteenth century.

To the New World
The Puritans also had great influence in the New World. From the beginning of the seventeenth century, bands of persecuted or pioneering pilgrims set out for America, hoping to find religious freedom and a new life. Famously, the Pilgrim Fathers established a colony with strong Puritan ideas at Plymouth in 1620. And after 1630, Puritans founded a colony at Massachusetts Bay. In contrast, Rhode Island became a colony of religious toleration, and William Penn established Pennsylvania as a refuge for Quakers. Roman Catholics settled in Maryland from 1634.

A more pluralistic pattern emerged in the eighteenth century with the immigration of new denominational groups such as the Baptists, Methodists, Presbyterians, Lutherans and Dutch Reformed.

Independence
After US Independence in 1776, the state churches of the Church of England in the south and

was not intended to form separated congregations, but to mark the elect for end-time judgment. But his movement fizzled out following his death in a prison fire.

Low Countries Anabaptists

Early examples of the Radical Reform were often millenarian in nature, focussing on the belief that the end of the world was imminent. A major Anabaptist movement (the 'Melchiorites') was started in the Low Countries by Melchior Hofmann (c. 1495–1543). A former Lutheran preacher and an eschatology enthusiast, Hofmann was influenced by Hans Denck's ideas into developing his own variety of Anabaptism. Hofmann believed in the imminence of God's kingdom, when the righteous would participate in God's judgment of the world; the purpose of his baptism was to gather the elect to build a new Jerusalem. However, Hofmann died following ten years' imprisonment in Strasbourg for his part in the Münster débâcle (see p. 126).

Congregationalism in the north were disestablished, and all the American churches became free and voluntary bodies.

Issues of social reform came to the fore after 1800, and denominations such as the Presbyterians, Methodists and Baptists became more politically active.

With their militant faith and practical drive, the Puritans helped create a thriving, moralistic society that shaped modern America. The Puritans' trust in the workings of Providence, their strong sense of vocation and their resolve to accomplish their Maker's work all contributed to the American psyche.

US Baptists

The majority of Baptists worldwide today are in the United States, where they form the largest Protestant denomination, trailing only the Roman Catholic Church in numbers. The great majority of Baptists live in the southern states, where the Baptist Church has exerted a powerful influence. Among the main Baptist organizations in the USA are the Southern Baptist Convention, the American Baptist Churches USA and many African-American Baptist groups.

The kingdom of Münster

Revolutionary Melchiorites founded a short-lived and bloody 'kingdom of Münster' (1534–35), first under Jan Matthys, and subsequently under Jan van Leiden. They attempted to inaugurate the millennium by violent means, wreaking bloody vengeance on any who opposed them. Following the crushing of their theocratic city-state by the combined armies of the Catholic Bishop of Münster and the Lutheran Landgrave of Hesse, a few radical groups survived to hold similarly revolutionary beliefs, the largest being the Batenburgers, who lasted into the 1570s.

Melchior Hofmann's pacifism was picked up by Menno Simons (1496–1561), who left the priesthood in 1536, and part of whose name modern 'Mennonites' retain. Following the fall of Münster, Simons rallied peaceful Melchiorites and surviving Münsterites disillusioned with violence, teaching that an era of peace had already begun with Jesus. Menno also taught the transformation of the individual and the gathering of a spotless church – similar to ideas found in Sattler's Schleitheim Articles.

Spiritualizers

Other radical reformers known as 'spiritualizers' played down, or sometimes completely rejected, outward forms of church and rituals, favouring instead inner communion through the Holy Spirit. For instance, the Silesian nobleman Kaspar Schwenckfeld (1489–1561) believed that no baptism had been valid for the previous thousand years, and in 1526 recommended the suspension of the Lord's Supper; while Sebastian Franck (1499–1542) rejected the idea of any external church, regarding ceremonies and rituals as props to support an infant church – which in any case he believed had been taken over by the antichrist immediately after the death of the last apostles. Franck held the true church to be invisible, remaining scattered until Christ gathered his own at his second coming.

Persecution and migration

Roman Catholics and Protestants alike persecuted the Anabaptists, resorting to torture and other forms of physical abuse in an attempt to curb the growth of the movement and to achieve the salvation of the 'heretics' by recanting. Protestants under Zwingli were the first to persecute the Anabaptists, with Felix Manz becoming the first martyr in 1527; while in May 1527, Roman Catholics executed the Anabaptist Michael Sattler. King Ferdinand declared drowning ('the third baptism') 'the best remedy for Anabaptism'.

Thousands of Anabaptists were persecuted and executed in Austria, Germany, the Netherlands, Switzerland and other regions of Europe between 1525 and 1660, and continuing persecution in Europe was largely responsible for mass

Since we are to be conformed to the image of Christ, how can we then fight our enemies with the sword?

MENNO SIMONS

Woodcut of Menno Simons, the Mennonite leader.

immigration to North America by the Amish, Hutterites and Mennonites, where they set up separatist communities, some of which continue today.

Anabaptists are frequently referred to – normally abusively – in sixteenth- and seventeenth-century English history. Many Anabaptists seem to have fled persecution in Germany and the Netherlands only to be subjected to further oppression in England.

Anti-Trinitarians

Yet other radicals gave significant weight to reason as well as to the Bible, and included some reformers who held early forms of Unitarian beliefs (for example Michael Servetus, burned in Calvin's Geneva for his anti-Trinitarian views). Rejection of Trinitarianism attained institutional form in the pacifist 'Polish Brethren', later known as Socinians – after Lelio and Fausto Socino (also known as Sozzini) – and in the Unitarian churches of Lithuania and Transylvania, a remnant of which have survived into the twenty-first century.

Anabaptists today

The successors of the various pioneer

The Quakers

Like many Christian groups, the Quakers never intended to form a new denomination. Their founder, George Fox (1624–91), was born in Leicestershire, England. By the time of his death, the movement already had some 50,000 members.

Fox became a religious activist at the age of nineteen, and was imprisoned eight times for preaching that challenged the religious and political establishment of his time. He once told a magistrate to 'tremble' at the name of God and the name 'Quaker' stuck. (Another suggestion is that the name comes from the shaking that sometimes accompanied Quaker religious experiences.) Fox believed there was something of God in every person, an attack on discrimination by class, wealth, race or gender that cut across contemporary hierarchical social structures. Consequently, Quakers refused to take oaths or remove their hats before a magistrate, and continued to hold banned religious meetings, with the result that many were imprisoned between 1662 and 1670.

Fox believed everyone should attempt to encounter God directly and experience the kingdom of heaven as a present reality. He objected to the rituals of the church: God did not want churches ('steeple-houses'), as believers could relate directly with God.

In 1689 the English Parliament passed the Act of Toleration, which brought acceptance and, in time, respectability. By the nineteenth century, the Society of Friends, as they were now officially called, had become another nonconformist denomination. However, its members continued to be noted for their social concerns and philanthropy. Elizabeth Fry (1780–1845) was a pioneering British prison reformer, and many Quakers took an active role in the Temperance movement in Victorian England. Quakers were also active in ending the slave trade and the opium trade, and in fighting for women's rights, anti-racism and human rights.

Quakers believe that war and conflict are against God's will and are dedicated to pacifism and non-violence. Many conscientious objectors are Quakers.

Quakers in America

Quaker missionaries arrived in the American colonies in 1656, and were immediately persecuted – four were executed. However, the movement appealed to many and grew in strength, most famously in Pennsylvania, which was founded in 1681 by the Quaker William Penn (1621–70), a friend of George Fox, and was based on pacifism and religious tolerance.

Anabaptist groups gradually recognized their common emphases on the Bible, adult (believer's) baptism, pacifism and separation from the state church and the world. They also condemned oaths, and the referring of disputes between believers to secular law courts. Although they never united into a single body, some feeling of unity developed, so that in 1591 fifteen different preachers representing Dutch, High and Low German Mennonites signed the 'Concept of Cologne'. Later Anabaptists were much less militant than such extremists as the Münsterites, but continued to find themselves tarred with that brush.

Several denominations can be seen as successors of the European Anabaptists – for instance the Amish, Brethren, Hutterite, Mennonite and Bruderhof communities and perhaps the Quakers.

CHAPTER 10

Heart and Soul

Over the centuries, there has been a continuing dialogue among Christians about the importance of believing the right doctrines (which has sometimes hardened into a cold intellectualism) as against cultivating a heart-felt devotion. Though Luther attempted to stress both, some of his followers failed to sustain his even-handedness.

Forerunners

The seventeenth-century Lutheran Church in Germany continued with Philipp Melanchthon's efforts to construct a distinctive systematic theology, while retaining many of the liturgical traditions of Roman Catholicism. However, the dogmatic debates often centred on obscure points, and there was a tendency towards sterile debate among the Lutheran theologians.

In the Reformed Church, by contrast, Calvin had influenced not only doctrine, but also a particular way of following a Christian life. The Presbyterian constitution gave the people a share in church life which the Lutherans lacked.

Mere knowledge is by no means sufficient for true Christianity.

PHILIPP JAKOB SPENER

Engraving of Philipp Jakob Spener.

In reaction to the perceived barrenness within Lutheranism, one Lutheran writer, Heinrich Müller, described the font, the pulpit, the confessional and the altar as 'the four dumb idols of the Lutheran Church'. Other forerunners of the Pietists – such as the mystic Jakob Böhme and the author Johann Arndt, whose book *True Christianity* was widely read in Germany – advocated a revival of a more practical, devotional Christianity.

PIETISM

Spener

The founder of Pietism (a term of ridicule given to the movement by its opponents, much as 'Methodism' was in England in the following century) was Philipp Jakob Spener (1635–1705). Born in Alsace, Spener, like Arndt, became convinced of the need for moral and religious reform within Lutheranism. Studying in Strasbourg and Geneva, he believed that true Christian living was being sacrificed to a rigid Lutheran orthodoxy. In 1669 he started to hold religious meetings (*collegia pietatis*) in his home, where he re-ran his sermons, expounded passages from the New Testament and encouraged discussion of religious questions.

In 1675 Spener published his *Pia Desideria* (full name, *Earnest Desires for a Reform of the True Evangelical Church*), in which he proposed six measures to restore life to the church. These suggestions included: holding Bible study meetings; lay involvement in church leadership; greater emphasis

129

on practical Christian living; a more sympathetic hearing for the heterodox and unbelieving; a greater stress on the devotional life in theological training at the universities; and sermons that nourished the soul and bore fruit in changed lives, rather than consisting merely of impressive rhetoric. *Pia Desideria* had considerable impact throughout Germany, and many pastors immediately adopted Spener's practical proposals.

The Age of Reason

The scientific revolution of the seventeenth century paved the way for the eighteenth-century intellectual movement known as the Enlightenment. Beginning with the earth-shifting theory of the Polish astronomer Nicolas Copernicus (1473–1543) in the sixteenth century, and followed by the experiments and observations of Galileo Galilei (1564–1642) in the seventeenth, the scientific community began to raise troubling questions for Christians. Copernicus argued that the movements of the planets were best explained by a heliocentric universe: 'In the middle of all sits the Sun on his throne...' (His views were much more damaging to astrology than to religion – though twenty-first-century astrologers seem still not to have realized this.) Galileo supported Copernicus' views from observations, but was brought to trial by the Inquisition for his pains.

Other thinkers, such as the French philosopher and mathematician René Descartes (1596–1650), raised disturbing questions for Christian thinkers. Descartes' *Discourse of Method* established a process of methodical doubt ('I doubt, therefore I am' – *cogito ergo sum*) to establish to his own satisfaction the existence of God. In the hands of others, such as Baruch Spinoza and G. W. Leibnitz, this became a tool for rationalism and for empiricism in the instance of the English thinker, John Locke. It has been said that the disastrous turn of Descartes' thinking was to retreat into individual self-consciousness as the only sure starting-point for philosophy.

The Enlightenment gave its other name to the era: the 'Age of Reason'. European intellectuals set up reason as the final arbiter in all matters, demoting Scripture and Christian doctrine, unless they were deemed 'reasonable'. Enlightenment authors such as John Locke, Voltaire, Jean-Jacques Rousseau, David Hume, Adam Smith and Immanuel Kant believed that through reason they could understand and master nature and that this would in turn lead to 'progress'.

Men such as Voltaire (1694–1778) became the forerunners of the modern secular intellectual, marginalizing religion as superstitious. They developed the Renaissance notion that humans could do anything if they took control of their own lives: through the critical exercise of reason, humans could arrive at a natural understanding of themselves, religion, philosophy, law and the universe – which was itself governed by natural laws.

Moreover, most Enlightenment thinkers abandoned organized religion and embraced instead Deism – the belief in a God who created the world like a Great Watchmaker, and subsequently relinquished control of it, allowing it to run according to natural laws, without further intervention.

Since this period, dominant Western thinkers have been, if not outright atheists, essentially secularists, for example Marx, Darwin and Einstein; while religious intellectuals have generally been relegated to the sidelines.

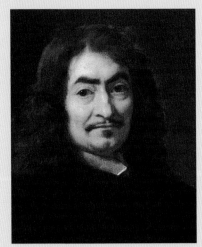

Presumed portrait of René Descartes by Sebastien Bourdon (1616–71).

When a group of theologians at Leipzig, among them August Hermann Francke (1663–1727), started to lecture on practical and devotional Christianity along Spenerian lines, they met opposition from both

Count von Zinzendorf

students and townspeople, and left the city to found the new University of Halle, where every theological professor was in agreement with Spener's ideas. They believed Christianity to consist mainly in a change of heart and consequent holiness of life. Orthodox Lutherans rejected this as over-simplified, and for their part stressed the need for an institutional church and for sound theological foundations.

Spener died in 1705, but the movement, guided by Francke from Halle, spread throughout central and northern Germany. Francke influenced devotion as far east as Moscow, and helped teach Swedish students. Responding to the Pietist call to practical Christianity, Francke also founded a famous orphanage at Halle in 1695.

The Moravian Church

No distinct Pietist church was formed, however, until Count Ludwig von Zinzendorf (1700–60), Spener's godson, founded a colony at Herrnhut on his estates in Saxony in 1722, which became known as the Moravian Brethren. The Moravian Brethren became active and dynamic missionaries in Europe and across the Atlantic. Among their pioneering missionaries were Bartholomaeus Ziegenbalg (1682–1719) and C. F. Schwartz (1726–98) in India and Georg Schmidt (1709–85) in South Africa. Moravian Pietism also deeply influenced the Norwegian Lutheran missionary Hans Egede (1686–1758), who became known as 'the apostle of Greenland'.

Excess

Spener's emphasis on the need for a new birth and separation from the world led to more extreme behaviour among some followers. Many Pietists began to insist that the new birth must always be preceded by agonized repentance, and that only born-again theologians could teach; and Pietists generally avoided 'worldly' entertainments, such as dancing and the theatre.

Pietism reached its greatest strength in the mid-eighteenth century, its individualism ironically helping to prepare the way for secular

Enlightenment thinking. Cutting across class and creed, Pietism contributed significantly to the revival of biblical studies in Germany and to making religion once again a matter of the heart and of daily life, not merely of the intellect; and it gave new import to the role of the laity in the church. The Pietists were also deeply concerned for missions and evangelism, as well as Christian social concern.

Prussian union

Pietism helped bring about the creation of the Evangelical Church of the Union in Prussia in 1817. Affronted that he and his wife, from different church traditions, could not take communion at each other's church, the king of Prussia ordered the Lutheran and Reformed churches in Prussia to unite under the name 'Evangelical' (i.e. 'Protestant'). This union

John Wesley

John Wesley (1703–91) was born in Epworth, Yorkshire, England, the son of an Anglican clergyman. At the age of six he was rescued from the burning rectory; he afterwards described himself as a 'brand plucked from the burning'.

In 1720 Wesley went to Oxford University, and was ordained into the Anglican ministry. In 1729 John's younger brother, Charles Wesley, formed the 'Holy Club' with some fellow Oxford students; they were dubbed 'Methodists' because of their methodical habits – taking communion weekly, fasting often and abstaining from most entertainments and luxuries. They also visited the poor, the sick and prisoners.

When, in 1735, a clergyman was needed in the American colony of Georgia, John Wesley responded,

and remained there for two years. Yet he felt his mission was a failure, and returned to England in 1738, dissatisfied with his mere orthodoxy and uncertain of his salvation.

Strangely warmed

Back in London, while attending a Moravian meeting in Aldersgate Street on 24 May 1738, Wesley listened to a reading from Luther's preface to Paul's letter to the Romans. Describing the experience later he said, 'I felt my heart strangely warmed.' His 'new birth' was the impetus for a new career of gospel preaching.

A breath of fresh air

Wesley's Oxford friend, the evangelist George

John Wesley is attacked by the mob at Wednesbury, in the English Midlands.

I fear, wherever riches have increased, the essence of religion has decreased in the same proportion.

JOHN WESLEY

movement spread to many other German-speaking states in the early nineteenth century. Pietism, with its looser attitude towards confessional theology, had opened churches to the possibility of uniting. A number of stricter Lutherans dissented from this movement, some emigrating to America and forming the Lutheran Church-Missouri Synod, or to Australia where they formed the Lutheran Church of Australia.

Pietism was a major influence on John Wesley and others who began the Methodist movement in eighteenth-century England, and modern American Methodists and members of the Holiness movement continue to be influenced by both Spener and the Moravian legacy. Pietism also inspired Alexander Mack (1679–1735) to begin the New Baptists, or Brethren group, in Germany, today known as the Church of the Brethren.

Whitefield, had been barred from preaching in English parish churches on his own return from America. In February 1739 at Kingswood, near Bristol, he broke with convention and preached in the open air to local miners. Wesley, too, was soon preaching in the open air.

After this, Wesley never hesitated to preach anywhere, even using his father's tombstone as a pulpit. He continued his itinerant ministry for fifty years – entering churches when invited, standing in fields, halls, cottages and chapels when churches were closed to him.

Late in 1739, Wesley decided to form his own followers into a separate society. 'Thus without any previous plan, began the Methodist Society in England,' he wrote.

Portrait of John Wesley by Nathaniel Hone (1703–91).

John Wesley was no systematic theologian. The best popular expression of his theology is in the hymns of his brother, Charles.

Persecution

From 1739 onwards Wesley and the Methodists were persecuted by clergymen and magistrates, and attacked in sermons, in print and by the mob. But Wesley regarded himself as commissioned by God to bring revival to the church, and opposition and persecution did not shake his resolve.

Since John Wesley and the few clergy working with him could not alone accomplish all that they wanted to do, as early as 1739 Wesley approved lay preachers – men and women who had not been ordained by bishops but were permitted to preach.

Controversy

Wesley was also a controversialist. He spoke out strongly against the Calvinist doctrines of election, while Whitefield held with Calvinism. The two separated in 1741 – Whitefield, with others, founding Calvinistic Methodism.

Wesley the man

Wesley travelled continually, generally on horseback, preaching two or three times a day. He rose at four in the morning, lived simply, and was never idle if he could avoid it. He formed Methodist societies, opened chapels, commissioned preachers, organized charities, prescribed medicine and set up schools and orphanages. Wesley died poor, leaving some 135,000 Methodists, 541 itinerant preachers and a set of written sermons that continue to form the basis of the Methodist creed.

METHODISM

Preaching to England's largely unevangelized population, John Wesley, along with his hymn-writing younger brother Charles, soon gained thousands of followers. Some took an evangelical zeal into the Church of England, others joined denominations such as the Baptists and Congregationalists, but most formed the 'societies' which, in 1784, became the Methodist Church.

John Wesley set out on horseback to preach wherever he could gather an audience. 'The world is my parish,' he famously declared. Before his death, it is estimated Wesley travelled some 250,000 miles, spoke to open-air gatherings of up to 30,000 people at one time, and preached more than 40,000 sermons.

Wesley's meetings were often interrupted; the town-crier would shout, horns would be blown or cows driven into the crowd. But frequently he transformed the mob: 'They were amazed, they were ashamed, they were melted down, they devoured my words.'

Charles Wesley

John's brother, Charles Wesley (1707–88), contributed to Methodism through his vast outpouring of hymns, including such lasting favourites as 'Love divine, all loves excelling' and 'Hark, the Herald Angels sing'. Until the Wesleys' time, Anglicans had sung only psalms; Charles wrote countless hymns to celebrate the Christian life.

Late in 1739, John Wesley decided to form his followers into a separate Methodist society. Since these societies needed places to worship, he began to provide chapels, first in Bristol, then in London and elsewhere. As his societies multiplied and Methodism took on the

Hymns

In the early days of Christianity, the word 'hymn' was used to refer to any song of worship; later it was restricted to specially written poems, as distinct from psalms and other arrangements of passages from the Bible.

Christians of the Syrian, Byzantine and Armenian churches used hymns much more than Christians in the West. Their ancient 'Oxyrhynchus Hymn', named after the site of its discovery, dates back as early as around AD 300, and is the earliest known hymn with music notation – and also one of the last known pieces written in an ancient Greek letter notation.

The earliest hymn still in use today is probably 'O gladsome light' (Greek *Phos Hilaron*) credited to Hilary, Bishop of Poitiers (c. AD 315–68). Basil the Great referred to it in the fourth century as already being a very old hymn. Ambrose of Milan followed with a number of popular and simple hymns.

At the conclusion of the Fifth Ecumenical Council, Emperor Justinian I is supposed to have composed a hymn summarizing the council's conclusion, 'Only begotten Son', subsequently incorporated into the liturgy of John Chrysostom and still sung today.

Protestant hymns

Martin Luther, instigator of the German Reformation, wrote many hymns himself and encouraged others to do so too. He wanted to ensure that everybody joined in worship. Many of his hymns were psalms rewritten in rhyme, and set to folk-tunes or old plainsong chants. Luther scandalized some pious Germans by setting new Christian lyrics to popular love songs – for instance the Easter hymn, 'O sacred Head, now wounded'.

These straightforward Lutheran hymns were deliberately contrasted with the complex music of the medieval church. The devout Lutheran composer J. S. Bach utilized 'chorales' from these hymns in his church cantatas, written for soloists, choir and orchestra for performance at specific seasons in the church's calendar. Among at least 295 cantatas he composed, mainly while cantor at Leipzig, is the celebrated 'Jesu, joy of man's desiring'.

By contrast, John Calvin's services were plain and

elements of a church, the breach between Wesley and the Church of England widened. Wesley refused to leave the Church of England; yet neither would he stop field-preaching or lay preaching, nor dissolve his Methodist societies. As the societies increased in number, Wesley could no longer retain personal control over them; so in 1743 he drew up a set of rules to govern them.

As numbers increased, doctrinal and administrative matters also needed resolution; ten leaders met in London in 1744 for what became the first 'Methodist Conference'. British Methodism has no bishops, but has always had a strong central organization, the Connexion, which holds an annual conference. Two years later, Wesley appointed 'helpers' to circuits of Methodist chapels. Wesley believed it was healthy to move preachers from one circuit to another every year or two, and insisted that they follow this 'itinerant' pattern of ministry.

Schism and reunion

Schisms and local revivals in British Methodism led to the formation of a number of separate denominations calling themselves Methodist. The largest of these were the Primitive Methodist Church, arising out of a revival at Mow Cop in Staffordshire, the Bible Christians and the United Methodist Church (itself the result of a union of three smaller denominations). The original Methodist Church became known as the 'Wesleyan Methodist Church', to distinguish it from these other Methodist groups.

Methodism proved particularly strong in Wales and Cornwall, both areas noted for their nonconformity. In 1932 the three major streams in British Methodism united to form the

simple. Though he himself liked music, he mistrusted its use in religious services, believing it distracted people from worship and seeking God.

English hymnwriters

In England, the earliest known writers of hymn-tunes were Thomas Tallis and Orlando Gibbons. Scotland followed the lead of reformers such as Calvin in keeping only to settings of the psalms.

In eighteenth-century England a strong tradition of hymn-writing started, influenced by the Moravians. Isaac Watts wrote such hymns as 'When I survey the wondrous cross', John Newton 'Amazing grace' and above all the Wesley brothers wrote hundreds of hymns, among them 'Love divine, all loves excelling'.

> *Amazing grace! How sweet the sound*
> *That saved a wretch like me!*
> *I once was lost but now am found,*
> *Was blind but now I see.*
>
> JOHN NEWTON

Early English settlers in North America often sang their hymns to English folk tunes – variations on them can still be heard in gospel songs in the south.

The Wesleys and William Booth, founder of the Salvation Army, introduced rousing hymns to express the new joy and assurance of their converts. In the USA too, camp evangelists and campaign revivalists such as Moody and Sankey wrote bouncy new hymns – for example, the frequently reprinted collection of *Sacred Songs and Solos*. In the twentieth century, the charismatic movement particularly created a number of new hymns.

Methodist Church of Great Britain.

The impact of the Wesleyan movement was immense. It affected lives all over the British Isles, on the European continent and in America. It produced a popular style of direct evangelical preaching and emphasized hymn singing, both of which became part of the tradition of evangelical nonconformity.

THE FIRST AWAKENING

The First Great Awakening (c. 1726–70) was an evangelical revival that swept across the American colonies. Begun in the Dutch Reformed Church it was then taken up by Presbyterians and Congregationalists. The revival is most closely associated with Jonathan Edwards (1703–58), 'the greatest philosopher-theologian yet to grace the American scene', and began in New England.

One of Wesley's Oxford associates, George Whitefield (1714–70), visited America in the late 1730s and sparked revivals in several of the coastal areas where he preached. He preached in a new and idiosyncratically dramatic and emotional style. This new type of sermon, coupled with the practical way people practised their faith, breathed new life into religion. As with German Pietism, people became more emotionally involved rather than passively listening to clever sermons, and began to study the Bible at home.

Whitefield's and Edwards' work in turn

Evangelicalism

Two influential revivals occurred in nineteenth-century Anglicanism – Evangelical and Catholic. The Evangelical revival led to a new wave of social activism in Britain. An informal network of Anglican clergy and lay people, which became known as the 'Clapham Sect' because most of them lived near the London suburb of Clapham, strongly affected the course of political and social reform in the late eighteenth and early nineteenth centuries.

Members of the sect included such notable Evangelicals as the Revds John Venn, rector of Clapham, and Charles Simeon, Charles Grant, a director of the East India Company, Lord Teignmouth, a governor-general of India, Zachary Macaulay, governor of Sierra Leone, Granville Sharp, Hannah More, an inveterate tract-writer, and William Wilberforce (1759–1833).

It was Wilberforce who led the successful campaign to abolish first the slave trade (1807) and then slavery itself within the British empire (1833). Wilberforce and his Evangelical colleagues led the way in educational and prison reforms, making education more accessible and prisons more humane. The Clapham Sect was also active in the establishment of the Church Missionary Society (1799) and the British and Foreign Bible Society (1804). Evangelical Anglicans and nonconformists were in addition at the forefront of founding and funding overseas missionary societies.

Later in the century, Evangelicals powered important social and political reform movements such as child protection and welfare legislation, and the development of public health and public education. The Evangelical Conservative politician Lord Shaftesbury (1801–85) worked through parliament to improve working conditions for factory hands and for child and female labourers, for the protection of children from abuse as chimney sweeps, and the protection of milliners and dressmakers. Shaftesbury also set up Ragged Schools for slum children, and introduced schemes of training ships and industrial schools for young workers. Among a host of other societies and organizations – many of which were inter-denominational but led by Evangelical Anglicans – in 1882 Evangelical Anglicans also set up the Church Army, an Evangelical social welfare association.

… the work of conversion was carried out in a most astonishing manner… souls did, as it were, come by flocks to Jesus Christ.

JONATHAN EDWARDS

Jonathan Edwards, whose most famous sermon was entitled 'Sinners in the Hands of an Angry God'.

of the College of New Jersey (now Princeton University). In the end, the pro-revivalists won and 'revivalism' has continued to be a major part of American Christian life.

METHODISM IN AMERICA

Methodist circuit riders, many of them laymen, also arrived in America and started to travel by horseback, preaching the gospel and establishing churches. One of the best-known circuit riders was Robert Strawbridge, who emigrated from Ireland in the early 1760s and settled in Maryland.

American Methodists, lacking an ordained minister, were unable to receive communion in their own churches. When the Bishop of London refused to ordain a minister for them, Wesley lost patience, and in 1784 he himself consecrated Revd Dr Thomas Coke (1714–1814), by the laying on of hands, to be superintendent in America, with orders to ordain Francis Asbury (1745–1816) as a joint superintendent of the new Methodist Episcopal Church in America.

However, at the Baltimore Christmas Conference in 1784, Asbury said he would not accept the position of superintendent unless the Methodist preachers voted for him – which they proceeded to do. Coke, who has been called the 'Father of Methodist Missions', ordained Asbury a deacon, an elder and a bishop on three successive days. Asbury became the leading bishop of early American Methodism.

encouraged Presbyterian and Reformed ministers in the Middle Colonies to preach in similar ways. However, with Edwards in New England, the revival was a spiritual reawakening of major proportions. Coldness and corruption in the orthodox churches provoked many Christians to a desire for greater spiritual warmth and reality. After the awakening in New England, the revival swept up and down the Atlantic seaboard, affecting every denomination. However, it also split nearly every major Christian group into those who opposed such preaching and those who supported it.

Edwards himself was eventually driven out of his pulpit, becoming first a missionary to the Native American Indians and later President

During his time in America, Coke worked vigorously to increase Methodist support of Christian missions and recruit mission workers. After strengthening the infant American Methodist Church, alongside Francis Asbury, Thomas Coke left to work as a missionary and died on a mission trip to India.

Bishops or no bishops?

But the issue of Methodist bishops in America was still unresolved. At the 1792 General Conference, the delegates sided with Francis Asbury, a bishop himself and a firm advocate of episcopacy. However, two groups, the Primitive Methodists and the Republican Methodists, both in the south-east, split away from the Methodist Episcopal Church over the issue.

The Second Awakening

A Second Great Awakening (c. 1787–1825) occurred in North America in the form of a nationwide wave of revivals. In New England, renewed interest in religion inspired a wave of social activism. Methodism grew rapidly and set up a number of colleges, notably Boston University. The revival reached Yale University through the preaching of Timothy Dwight in 1802. Methodism also saw the emergence of a Holiness movement. In the west, especially at Cane Ridge, Kentucky, in 1801 and in Tennessee, the revival strengthened both the Methodists and the Baptists. It is estimated that a camp meeting at Cane Ridge attracted between ten and twenty thousand for six days from as far away as Ohio.

Slavery and Methodism

Disputes over slavery posed problems for the American Methodist Church in the first half of the nineteenth century, with the northern church leaders fearful of a split with the south, and therefore reluctant to take a stand. The Wesleyan Methodists (later the Wesleyan Church) and the Free Methodist Churches were formed of staunch abolitionists, with the latter especially active in the 'Underground Railroad' that helped liberate the slaves.

Finally, in 1845 at Louisville, the churches of the slave-holding states split away from the Methodist Episcopal Church and formed the 'Methodist Episcopal Church, South'. Not until 1939 were the northern and southern branches of Methodism reunited in a merger that also included the Methodist Protestant Church. Even then, some conservative and strongly segregationist southerners opposed the merger, and in 1940 formed the Southern Methodist Church.

The Third Awakening

A Third Awakening (c. 1858–1908) saw a huge growth in Methodist Church membership, and a proliferation of institutions such as colleges. An awakening in many cities in 1858 started the movement, but in the north it was interrupted by the

A revival is nothing else than a new beginning of obedience to God.

CHARLES FINNEY,
PRESBYTERIAN MINISTER
DURING THE SECOND
GREAT AWAKENING

Civil War. In the south, the Civil War stimulated revivals, especially in General Robert Lee's army.

Peace

Between 1914 and 1917 Methodist ministers made strong pleas for world peace. To meet their demands, President Woodrow Wilson (a Presbyterian) promised 'a war to end all wars'. In the 1930s many Methodists favoured isolationism. In 1936, Methodist bishop James Baker released a poll showing that 56 per cent of Methodist ministers opposed warfare.

The Salvation Army

The Salvation Army began as a Christian mission in 1865 when William Booth, a London Methodist minister, gave up his pulpit and decided to take his message to the streets to reach the poor, homeless, hungry and destitute. His original aim had been to send his converts into the churches, but he soon realized they felt neither comfortable nor welcome in most churches and chapels in Victorian England. Churchgoers were appalled when joined by the shabby unwashed.

For this reason Booth decided to found an organization especially for his converts – the East London Christian Mission, which was renamed the Salvation Army in 1878, and adopted the uniforms, ranks and flag of a quasi-military organization.

Catherine, William Booth's wife, also preached, which was scandalous at that time. Together they worked to help others, bringing both a spiritual and a practical message. William said his approach could be summed up as '3 S's': soup, soap and salvation. Much of his teaching was derived from his Methodist origins.

At first, the Army's main converts were alcoholics, drug addicts, prostitutes and other marginal members of society. Booth's pragmatic approach led him not to include baptism and Holy Communion in his services. The Salvation Army also prohibited alcohol, smoking and gambling.

As the Salvation Army grew, it generated fierce opposition. Opponents, who sometimes dubbed themselves 'The Skeleton Army', disrupted meetings, throwing rocks, rats and tar and assaulting members. Much of this violence was led by public houses that were losing business because of the Army's stand on alcohol.

In 1880, Booth sent George Scott Railton and seven women 'soldiers' to New York to set up the Salvation Army there. By the 1900s, the Army had spread around the world and soon had officers and soldiers in thirty-six countries. Its organized but flexible structure inspired many much-needed services: women's social work, food depots, day nurseries and missionary hospitals. The Army has also been noted for its band music. During the Second World War, the Salvation Army operated 3,000 service units for the armed forces.

Today, in over 106 nations around the world, the Salvation Army continues similar work where the need is great. Among modern problems it has responded to are missing persons, AIDS and international disasters.

An early Salvation Army open-air meeting, depicted by Jean François Raffaelli.

United Methodists

The United Methodist Church in America was formed in 1968 as a result of a merger between the Evangelical United Brethren and the Methodist Church. The former church was the result of mergers of several groups with a German Methodist heritage that no longer wished to worship separately in German.

In addition to the United Methodist Church, there are more than forty other denominations that claim direct descent from the Methodist movement, such as the African Methodist Episcopal Church, Free Methodists, Wesleyan Church (formerly Wesleyan Methodist), Congregational Methodist Church and First Congregational Methodist Church.

Others are more indirectly related. The Salvation Army was founded by William Booth, a former Methodist, and derives its theology in part from Methodism. Also related is the Church of the Nazarene. Moreover, the teachings of Wesley served as a basis for the Holiness movement from which Pentecostalism, including the Pentecostal Holiness Church and the Assemblies of God, parts of the Charismatic movement and the Christian and Missionary Alliance are offshoots.

Social concern

From its beginnings in England, Methodism strongly emphasized social service and education. Many Methodist institutions of higher education were founded in the United States in the first half of the nineteenth century, and about twenty Methodist or Wesleyan universities and colleges still survive in America.

METHODISM WORLDWIDE

An estimated 75 million people worldwide belong to the Methodist community, a number that has gone into steady decline, especially in North America, where many people are more inclined to join theologically conservative churches.

Canada

American Methodist Episcopal circuit riders started to arrive from New York State on the north-east shore of Lake Ontario in the early 1790s. In 1817, British Wesleyans also arrived in Canada, but soon agreed with the Episcopal Methodists to confine their work to Quebec, while the latter kept themselves to Ontario. In 1833, the Canadian Conference merged with the British Wesleyans to form the Wesleyan Methodist Church in Canada.

The Methodist Church of Canada was the result of the union of several pioneer Methodist churches in 1884, and in 1925 it merged with the Presbyterians (then by far the largest Protestant church in Canada), most Congregationalists, Union Churches in Western Canada and the American Presbyterian Church in Montreal, to form the United Church of Canada.

The Commonwealth

Missionaries from Britain, North America and Australia founded Methodist churches in many British Commonwealth countries. These are now independent and many of them are stronger than the founding churches. In addition to churches, missionaries often also founded schools to serve the local community. Strong national churches include the Methodist Church Ghana and the Methodist Church Nigeria.

In Australia in 1977 the Methodist Church merged with the majority of the Presbyterian Church of Australia and the Congregational Union of Australia to form the Uniting Church.

Some independent Methodist congregations were established by Tongan immigrants.

A high proportion of the Polynesian people of Fiji are Methodists – the island has the highest proportion of Methodists in the world.

The strongest Methodist Church in the world is probably now in South Korea.

Europe

There are small Methodist Churches in many European countries, the strongest being in Germany. They were mostly founded through links with the American, rather than British, Methodist Church.

PENTECOSTALISM

Pentecostalism, or the 'Charismatic renewal', is a recent movement in Christian churches that teaches that after conversion Christians can experience 'baptism in the Holy Spirit' – a fresh encounter with God. The evidence of this is seen to be speaking in tongues – an ability to speak languages previously unknown to the speaker. According to Pentecostals, baptism in the Holy Spirit is for all Christians, and the teaching of both a first and second baptism is the 'full gospel'.

Beginning in 1901 with a handful of students in a Bible school in Topeka, Kansas, the number of Pentecostals increased steadily worldwide during the twentieth century until by the 1990s they had become the largest grouping of Protestants in the world. They are often described as the 'third force' in Christianity, alongside Roman Catholics and Protestants.

A new movement?

Although the Pentecostal movement began in the United States, it owed much of its theology to earlier British perfectionist and Charismatic movements such as the Methodist Holiness movement, Edward Irving and his followers, and the Keswick 'Higher Life' movement.

The Holiness movement that sprang out of Methodism at the end of the nineteenth century was probably the most important immediate precursor to Pentecostalism. From John Wesley, the Pentecostals inherited the idea of a crisis experience after conversion called the 'second blessing', first outlined by Wesley in his *A Plain Account of Christian Perfection* (1766). Wesley's colleague, John Fletcher, labelled this second blessing 'baptism in the Holy Spirit'. During the nineteenth century, thousands of Methodists claimed to have received this second blessing, though they did not connect this with speaking in tongues.

In the early nineteenth century, Edward Irving, a popular Scottish minister in London, suggested that the gifts of the Spirit or 'charisms' – from the Greek word *charisma* meaning 'gift' – might be restored in the modern church. In 1831 he led the first attempt at 'Charismatic renewal' at his Presbyterian church, when tongues and prophecy were both experienced. Although his movement failed, Irving pointed to tongues (or *glossolalia* from the Greek words 'tongue' and 'speak') as the outward sign of baptism in the Holy Spirit, a major element in later Pentecostal doctrine.

A third contributor to Pentecostalism, named the Keswick (after the town in the English Lake District) 'Higher Life' movement, flourished in Britain after 1875. Led at first by American Holiness speakers such as Hannah Whittall Smith and William E. Boardman, this Holiness group taught that the second blessing gave spiritual 'power' for Christian work. In America, Keswick teachers such as A. B. Simpson and A. J. Gordon introduced a new emphasis on divine healing too.

So by the time of the Pentecostal outbreak in America in 1901 there had been at least a century of movements emphasizing a second blessing or 'baptism in the Holy Spirit'.

National Holiness

Pentecostalism in America was born organizationally out of the Holiness movement and first appeared primarily among American Holiness churches and camp meetings, most of which had Methodist connections and views on the second blessing. American Methodism experienced a major Holiness 'revival' in a crusade that originated in New York, New Jersey and Pennsylvania after the American Civil War. Starting in 1867 in New Jersey as the 'National Camp Meeting Association for the Promotion of Holiness', this movement attracted huge crowds to camp meetings, where thousands claimed to receive a second blessing of holiness.

From 1867 to 1880 the Holiness movement grew strongly within the Methodist churches and other denominations, with the hope that it might bring worldwide revival to the church. After 1875, the American Holiness movement, influenced by ideas from Keswick, also began to stress Pentecostal aspects of the second blessing.

The Holiness movement was

A Methodist 'camp meeting' in nineteenth-century America, engraved from an illustration by Jacques Milbert (1766–1840).

supported by mainstream churches until around 1880, when leaders began to worry about some of its aspects. Among these was a separatist ('come-outer') movement led by radicals who gave up hope of renewing the existing churches. Other radicals began to push novel ideas, such as sinless perfection, strict dress codes, 'marital purity', and a 'third blessing' baptism of fire that followed the Holiness experience.

FIRST PENTECOSTALS

The very first Pentecostal churches were created by the Holiness movement before 1901, and included the mainly African-American Church of God in Christ (1897), the Pentecostal Holiness Church (1898), the Church of God, with headquarters in Cleveland, Tennessee (1906), and other smaller groups.

Most Pentecostals believe the modern Pentecostal tradition began with Charles Parham in Topeka, Kansas, and/or at the Azusa Street revival, Los Angeles, led by William J. Seymour. However, Pentecostalism itself pre-dates both the 'breakthrough' in Topeka and the Azusa phenomenon, which have become a kind of Pentecostal mythology. As the twentieth century approached, there were apparently scattered incidents of people speaking in tongues and physical signs of the Holy Spirit's powers – such as gifts, signs and wonders – all of which seem to have come together at Azusa Street.

Topeka

On New Year's Day 1901, the first 'Pentecostals' in the modern sense are said to have appeared at Bethel Bible College, Topeka, Kansas, which had been set up by Charles Parham (1873–1929), a Holiness teacher and former Methodist pastor. On that day, Agnes Ozman received the baptism of the Holy Spirit and subsequently spoke in tongues. A few days later, the same thing happened to others at the college, including Parham himself. Pentecostal Christians often speak of this as the 'second Pentecost'.

As a result, Parham now started to teach that speaking in tongues was the 'Bible evidence' of baptism in the Holy Spirit, and a supernatural gift of human languages to help in world evangelization. Missionaries no longer needed to study foreign languages, since they would be able to preach in miraculous tongues wherever they went.

Azusa Street

However, it was not till 1906 that Pentecostalism achieved worldwide attention through the Azusa Street revival in Los Angeles, led by the African-American preacher William Joseph Seymour (1870–1922). Seymour had heard about Agnes Ozman, and in 1906 he opened a meeting in a dilapidated former African Methodist Episcopal Church building at 312 Azusa Street, downtown Los Angeles. For more than three years his Apostolic Faith Mission conducted three services a day, seven days a week, where thousands of people claimed to have received the gift of tongues and baptism in the Holy Spirit.

People from every ethnic minority in Los Angeles were represented at Azusa Street, in striking contrast with the racism and segregation of the period. The seemingly chaotic meetings were characterized by dancing, jumping up and down, falling, trances, 'slaying in the Spirit', tongues, jerking, hysteria, strange noises and 'holy laughter'. The seekers would be 'seized with a strange spell and commence a jibberish of sounds'.

The sight of blacks and whites worshipping together under a black pastor seemed in itself incredible to many. Azusa Street seems to have merged white American 'Holiness' Christianity with African-American worship traditions and featured black music, shouting, dancing and tongues, creating a new form of Pentecostalism that was to prove attractive to many disinherited and deprived people in America and in the wider world.

Pentecostalism spreads

Pioneers who had experienced tongues at Azusa Street began to travel across America spreading the new doctrine, in the first instance to Holiness churches, missions and camp meetings. In the early days, it was thought necessary to go to Los Angeles to receive the 'blessing', but before long people were receiving the tongues experience wherever they lived.

New churches

Soon several Holiness denominations had been swept into the new movement, including the Pentecostal Holiness Church, the Fire-Baptized Holiness Church and the Pentecostal Free-Will Baptist Church. Charles Harrison Mason (1866–1961) took the tongues experience back to his Church of God in Christ at Memphis, Tennessee; the denomination mushroomed, and by 1993 it was the largest Pentecostal Church in North America, with some five and a half million members in 15,300 churches.

After receiving a tongues experience at Azusa Street in 1907, William H. Durham returned home to Chicago where he led thousands more into the Pentecostal movement, forming the Assemblies of God denomination in 1914. Largely white, this church introduced racial separation to the Pentecostal movement. In time the Assemblies of God Church became the largest Pentecostal denomination in the world.

PENTECOSTALISM WORLDWIDE

In 1906 a Norwegian Methodist pastor, Thomas Ball Barratt (1862–1940), later known as the 'Pentecostal apostle' in northern and western Europe, claimed to have received the gift of tongues and baptism in the Spirit in New York. Returning to Oslo later the same year, he conducted the first Pentecostal services in Europe. Barratt then travelled to Sweden, Britain and Germany, setting up national Pentecostal movements in each country, led by Lewi Pethrus, Alexander Boddy and Jonathan Paul respectively.

From Chicago, and through the influence of William Durham, the Pentecostal movement spread quickly to other countries and continents. In 1908 two Italian immigrants to Chicago, Luigi Francescon and Giacomo Lombard, took the new experiences to fellow Italians in America, Brazil, Argentina and Italy itself. Two Swedish immigrants, Daniel Berg and Gunnar Vingren, also took Pentecostalism to Brazil in 1910, resulting in the formation of the Brazilian Assemblies of God, which grew to become the world's largest national Pentecostal church, claiming 15 million members in 1993. In 1909 Willis C. Hoover, a Methodist missionary from Chicago, led a Pentecostal revival within the Chilean Methodist Episcopal Church, and subsequently founded the Pentecostal Methodist Church there.

Africa

African Pentecostalism owes its origins to the work of John Graham Lake (1870–1935), who received a Pentecostal experience and spoke in tongues in 1907 after hearing Parham preach.

Members of the Zion Christian Church dance at Moria, Limpopo Province, South Africa, during their Easter service. The church claims some four million members.

Lake abandoned his insurance business and led a group of missionaries to Johannesburg in 1908, where he began to spread the Pentecostal gospel. Lake founded two large and influential Pentecostal churches in South Africa: a white branch – the 'Apostolic Faith Mission' – in 1910, and a black branch later called the 'Zion Christian Church', which by 1993 was the largest church in South Africa.

Pentecostal missionaries from several countries spread the movement to many parts of Africa. The Pentecostal Holiness Church in South Africa was founded in 1913 by J. C. Lehman, who arrived with Lake in 1908; the Assemblies of God was established in 1917, and the Church of God (Cleveland, Tennessee) in 1951.

Eastern Europe
Pentecostalism first reached eastern Europe through a Russian-born Baptist pastor, Ivan Voronaev, who received a Pentecostal experience in New York in 1919. In Odessa, Ukraine, in 1922 he set up the first Pentecostal Church of the Soviet Union. Although arrested, imprisoned and eventually killed in 1943, the churches he founded survived persecution to become a major denomination in Russia.

Neo-Pentecostalism
This first wave of Pentecostal pioneering missionaries set up a multiplicity of churches and denominations worldwide. Typically, the new movement was initially dismissed by existing churches, leading to the setting up of fast-

growing independent missions and indigenous churches.

With the American evangelist Oral Roberts, and Californian dairy farmer Demos Shakarian, who founded the Full Gospel Business Men's Fellowship International in 1951, Pentecostalism moved closer to the mainstream. Shakarian's organization gained converts through special breakfast meetings during which professional people and church leaders were presented with the message of the Charismatic movement. South African-born David J. du Plessis (1905–87), known as 'Mr Pentecost', helped make Pentecostalism into an international and inter-denominational movement.

By the early 1960s so-called 'Charismatic renewal' was growing rapidly. Led by Dennis Bennett,

Rector of St Mark's Episcopal Church, Van Nuys, California, the Protestant 'Neo-Pentecostal' movement started in 1960. Within a decade, it had spread to many major Protestant groupings worldwide, influencing millions of people. In 1962 du Plessis organized the first meeting of Charismatics from non-Pentecostal traditions. The Catholic Charismatic Renewal movement began in Pittsburgh, Pennsylvania in 1967 among students and faculty at DuQuesne University. This renewal spread to the Roman Catholic Church, where the Belgian Joseph Cardinal Suenens became its patron. Several leading American Charismatics had television ministries, including Rex Humbard, Pat Robertson, Paul Crouch, Jimmy Swaggart and Jim Bakker.

The congregation listen to the preacher at Yoido Full Gospel Church, Seoul, South Korea.

There was also a significant spread of Pentecostalism in Asia, the best-known example being David (Paul) Yonggi Cho, an Assemblies of God pastor in Seoul, Korea, who started a tent church in 1958 and built it into the world's largest congregation, the Yoido Full Gospel Church, with a membership of more than half a million. In Latin America, by 1987 it was estimated that between 80 and 85 per cent of Protestants were Pentecostals or Charismatics, most of whom belonged to indigenous independent churches.

A Third Wave

The most recent movement, the so-called 'Third Wave' of the Spirit, originated in 1981 at Fuller Theological Seminary, Los Angeles, in the 'signs and wonders' movement of John Wimber and his Vineyard Fellowship. This group claimed to possess the power to perform miracles to promote 'church growth'. Related to it is the 'Toronto Blessing', characterized by outbreaks of uncontrollable laughter known as 'holy laughing'.

Together these Pentecostal and Charismatic movements came to constitute a 'third' force in world Christianity, with explosive growth rates. Today Pentecostalism is found in almost all churches and denominations. Pentecostalism has promoted ecumenicity, and is trans-denominational and trans-confessional. Members of virtually all churches, Protestant and Roman Catholic, Calvinist and Arminian, Baptist and Covenantal, share one 'Spirit', despite other doctrinal differences.

Many large and growing churches are founded on Pentecostal teachings, while others welcome it among their members. Parts of the Roman Catholic Church have embraced Pentecostalism, while among Protestant churches that have approved of it are Reformed churches and Evangelicals. Pentecostalism has become the largest and fastest growing segment of Christianity in the world.

CHAPTER 11

Post-Reformation Rome

THE COUNCIL OF TRENT

One response of the Roman Catholic Church to the Reformation was to tighten her own organization. A great council met at Trent, in northern Italy, between 1545 and 1563, to redefine and re-emphasize traditional views. The council and its repercussions are discussed in greater detail in chapter 9.

Absolutism

Rome received further shocks with the growth of national consciousness and the rise of the absolute rulers. In the eighteenth century, Catholic monarchs of western Europe whittled away at the papacy's right to intervene in political matters and instead asserted their rule over the church in their respective countries. Pope Benedict XIV (reigned 1740–58) negotiated concordats to preserve some of the church's rights and protect the practice of the faith. But the monarchs persisted.

The Catholic monarchs particularly disliked the Jesuits, who stood up for the pope and criticized the treatment of native peoples in some of the rulers' colonies. In 1773, in response to pressures from the monarchs of France, Portugal and Spain, the weak Pope Clement XIV agreed to dissolve the Society of Jesus.

THE FRENCH REVOLUTION

The Roman Catholic Church reeled with the coming of the French Revolution. Enlightenment thinking, revolutionary politics and the egalitarian atmosphere had all undermined traditional Catholicism.

The French church now suffered greatly. The lower clergy had been hard-working and usually poor, but the bishops were mainly aristocrats, and many monasteries had become extremely wealthy. During the turmoil of the Revolution, resentment towards the church led to the execution of some clergy and the flight of many more. The state confiscated and sold off church property. The revolutionary National Assembly denied the pope's authority and established the Civil Constitution for the clergy, which put them under the control of the state.

Pius VI (reigned 1775–99), too, was an aristocrat, who spent large sums adorning Rome but delayed when the French clergy needed his help. He failed to condemn the Civil Constitution until too late.

Napoleon and the papacy

Although Napoleon restored the church, he cynically used it for his own ends. In 1796 he took the revolution to Italy, 'liberating' parts of the Papal States and occupying Rome. Fearing that the sick pope would become a focus for resistance, the French kidnapped him and took him to France, where he died in 1799.

Pius VII (reigned 1800–23) then made peace with Napoleon and began to restore the church's fortunes in France; but in 1804 Napoleon proclaimed himself emperor and persuaded the pope to come to Paris for his coronation. When Pius refused further demands, in 1809 Napoleon had him arrested and brought to France, where he remained till the emperor fell. At the Congress of Vienna (1815), the victorious nations restored the Papal States, while Pius restored the Society of Jesus in 1814.

Reaction

After the Congress of Vienna, the church identified itself closely with the reactionary regimes of Europe – such as Metternich in Austria and Louis Napoleon in France. The French experience had made the popes wary of revolutionary movements. When Nationalist Catholic Poles revolted against Orthodox Russia (1830–31), Tsar Nicholas I soon restored Russian hegemony. In 1832 the deeply conservative Pope Gregory XVI (reigned 1831–46) reminded the Polish bishops and their churches in an inflammatory brief that their duty was to obey legitimate authority (i.e. Russia). Gregory so feared modern civilization that he would not allow railways – 'roads to hell' (*chemins d'enfer*) in the Papal States. In response, Italian revolutionaries insisted that papal government must be overthrown.

THE AMERICAN REVOLUTION

But while the Catholic Church suffered badly as a result of the French Revolution, the American Revolution of 1776 heralded a new era for Catholics. Many of the English colonies had restricted Catholics. But the American Revolution created a novel form of government that gave preferential status to no religion and freedom to all of them.

Freedom of religion was an Enlightenment concept, pressed by the deist politician Thomas Jefferson, and the Vatican and many European Catholics eyed it suspiciously. However, John Carroll (1735–1815), Bishop of Baltimore from 1789, was a defender of the revolution, and led American Catholics in strong support of freedom of religion. Anti-Catholicism did not disappear in the United States, but Catholics could now practise their faith in peace and take a full part in American life.

America's largest church

When the territories of the Louisiana Purchase fell into his area, John Carroll became bishop of the largest diocese in the world. He persuaded the Vatican to set up new dioceses, allowing for the development of the American Catholic Church.

By 1860, intensive Catholic immigration from Germany, Ireland and southern and eastern Europe made Catholicism America's largest religious body, which it has remained ever since. The immigrants' fears of assimilation – and the Vatican's worries about America's secularism – led to the rapid growth of a Catholic subculture of schools, societies, athletic leagues and publishers, which strengthened the church but fanned Protestant suspicions.

Pius IX

One reaction to liberal and sometimes revolutionary assaults was to make grander and grander claims for the papacy. The most extreme Christian response to the problems of the industrial age was that of Pope Pius IX ('Pio Nono', reigned 1846–78).

Pius started what became in Europe the 'revolutionary year' of 1848 as a moderate liberal. However, the events that followed transformed him into a reactionary who vigorously opposed anything that smacked of modernism, republicanism, liberalism, socialism or nationalism. Although Catholic monarchs advised him to democratize his government, he steadfastly refused. In 1864, Pius IX issued his notorious *Syllabus of Errors*, listing forbidden 'modern' movements – a rag-bag that included democracy, toleration, socialism, Bible societies, pantheism, rationalism and liberalism. This fatal tendency to ally with reactionary political movements damaged loyalty to, and the credibility of, the pope.

In 1854, Pius promulgated the novel dogma of the Immaculate Conception – the belief that Jesus' mother Mary was born free of original sin. He also summoned and presided over the First Vatican Council (1869–70), which claimed for the pope infallibility in matters of faith and doctrine in his official (*ex cathedra*) statements and the pope's immediate jurisdiction in any and every diocese. Although some Catholics objected to this new doctrine, they were simply excommunicated for their pains.

Against Pius' stubborn stance, the Italian movement for unification gained momentum, and in 1870 revolutionaries captured Rome, putting an end to the Papal States. Pius became a 'Prisoner of the Vatican'.

The Industrial Revolution

The churches of late nineteenth-century Europe and the United States could not ignore the sweeping new problems caused by the rapidly spreading Industrial Revolution, and particularly the rapid rise in the numbers of workers crammed into the newly industrialized cities of such countries as Britain, France and Germany.

One major response to these problems was socialism and Marxism, which advocated state control over the means of production to ensure a more equitable distribution of wealth and goods to the people who were creating it by their labour. Karl Marx, in particular, was hostile to the churches, famously branding religion as 'the opium of the people'. His powerful *Communist Manifesto*, co-authored with Friedrich Engels and published in 1848, and his much unread *Das Kapital* of 1867, attracted intellectuals and working people to his movement. Marxism emerged as a kind of socio-religious alternative to the Christian churches of the nineteenth century.

Science and religion seemed to draw further apart with the publication of Charles Darwin's two landmark works, *Origin of Species* in 1859 and *The Descent of Man* in 1871, which divided Christians between those who accepted his views and their implications and those who rejected them. Moreover, the new geology and the wider application of scientific methods to society also created new tensions – especially between Darwinism and evangelical and Roman Catholic Christianity. Clashes between Darwinians and Christian thinkers became more bitter in the twentieth century, as discussed in chapter 2.

Pope Pius IX,
Pio Nono.

'New things'

Yet in 1878, the cardinals chose a different kind of pope. Leo XIII (reigned 1878–1903) was an intellectual who was worried that the church was losing the new urban masses. His encyclical *Rerum Novarum* defended the rights of workers and preached a just economic system, based on Christian values. Leo also attempted to revive the theology of Thomas Aquinas, which still influences much Catholic thought. He showed that the loss of the Papal States did not necessarily also mean the loss of the pope's religious prestige. The papacy seemed to be beginning to come to terms with the modern world.

In Britain, Cardinal John Henry Newman (1801–90) impressed both Catholic and Anglican scholars and lay people with his learned writings, somewhat mitigating the prevalent British anti-Catholicism that dated back to the Reformation period.

But, unlike Leo, Pius X (reigned 1903–14) mistrusted theologians who embraced modern scholarship, and his suspicious attitude weakened Catholic theology for decades. His successor, Benedict XV (reigned 1914–22), tried without success to prevent the First World War, and afterwards the victorious powers shut him out of their discussions.

Pius XI (reigned 1922–39) stood up for the rights of workers, and tried to establish Catholic social principles in an effort to combat the threat of Communism. His fear of the latter, however, prevented him initially from recognizing the equally pressing dangers of fascism in Italy and Germany. His efforts, too, to prevent another war failed. In 1929 he reached an agreement with the Italian government to establish the Vatican City as an independent state.

Pius XII

The controversial Pope Pius XII (reigned 1939–58), who had been Pius XI's secretary of state and his favoured candidate to succeed him, was a lifelong diplomat. During the Second World War, he followed a policy of neutrality similar to that of Benedict XV during the First World War. In the 1960s, a number of critics accused him of anti-Semitism, claiming he did not denounce the Nazis with sufficient harshness. Pius XII ended a previous ban on Catholics joining Action Française, a French anti-Semitic organization; and when asked to condemn the Nazi holocaust, the Vatican replied it was 'unable to denounce publicly particular atrocities'. However, after Germany occupied Rome in 1943, the Vatican City was offered as a refuge and 477 Jews were hidden there, with another 4,238 protected in Roman monasteries and convents.

JOHN XXIII

Stirrings of new spiritual life occurred under the leadership of Pope John XXIII (reigned 1958–63), whom many had expected to be only a caretaker pope. Born Angelo

Giuseppe Roncalli, Pope John feared that the church had lost contact with the modern world, and became the first pope to address an encyclical to all people (*Pacem in Terris*, 1963). But, most importantly, he called the Second Vatican Council (1962–65) for the purpose of *aggiornamento* or 'updating' the church.

Among other things, Vatican II extensively reformed the Catholic Church's structure, attempting to take it firmly into the twentieth century. This included modernizing the liturgy by authorizing celebration of the mass in the vernacular, and placing less emphasis on many Roman feast and fast days.

The council also encouraged closer relations with other Christian churches, and particularly the reduction of tension between Rome and Protestant churches, making it easier in most countries for Roman Catholics to fraternize with other Christians. The council raised issues that had not been broached for centuries in the Roman communion. The 'winds of change' seemed to be blowing through the Christian world, although John, frail as he was, did not live past the first session.

After Vatican II there was a fresh approach in many areas. With new liturgies and the mass in local languages, a new emphasis on Bible reading, a willingness to reconsider issues that had previously been regarded as simply matters of 'authority', and an openness to new ideas and new methods, the Roman

Truth calls for the elimination of every trace of racial discrimination, and the consequent recognition of the inviolable principle that all states are by nature equal in dignity.

JOHN XXIII

Pope John XXIII, whose crucial act was to call the Second Vatican Council.

Catholic Church was again tackling the challenge of being 'the church in the world'.

John XIII's immediate successor, Paul VI (reigned 1963–78), is particularly remembered for his encyclical *Humanae Vitae* (1968), which repudiated artificial contraception. Many Catholics in democracies ignored the encyclical, creating a crisis of authority that continues into the twenty-first century.

John Paul II

John Paul II (reigned 1978–2005), a Pole, became the first non-Italian pope for more than 400 years. A vigorous man, he travelled widely, at risk to his life, striving to align the church with those suffering in the Third World. He created more saints than all his predecessors combined –

Mother Teresa

The work of Mother Teresa (1910–97) among the poverty-stricken in Calcutta paradoxically made her one of the world's most famous people. Born Agnes Gonxha Bojaxhiu in Skopje, Macedonia, she decided to become a missionary nun at the age of eighteen. After teaching in Calcutta for many years, in 1950 Teresa received the Vatican's permission to start her own order, 'The Missionaries of Charity', to care for 'the hungry, the naked, the homeless, the crippled, the blind, the lepers, all those people who feel unwanted, unloved, uncared for throughout society, people that have become a burden to the society and are shunned by everyone'.

In 1952, Teresa opened the first Home for the Dying in Calcutta in an abandoned Hindu temple, and not long afterwards set up an orphanage and a home for those suffering from leprosy. Her order was soon attracting recruits and donations, and by the 1960s had opened hospices, orphanages and homes for leprosy sufferers all over India. Mother Teresa was also among the first to open homes for AIDS sufferers.

Mother Teresa admired Francis of Assisi who, like her, emphasized poverty, chastity, obedience and submission to Christ, and also devoted his life to serving the poor and leprous.

Mother Teresa's organization soon grew rapidly outside India, with early houses in Rome, Venezuela and Tanzania, and later openings in many countries in Asia, Africa and Europe – including the former Soviet Union and eastern European countries and her native Albania. By the early 1970s she had become an international celebrity, largely as a result of Malcolm Muggeridge's 1969 documentary *Something Beautiful for God*, and in 1979 she was awarded the Nobel Peace Prize 'for work undertaken in the struggle to overcome poverty and distress'.

Critics have argued that Mother Teresa's organization provided sub-standard care, and was primarily interested in converting the dying. (Baptism was performed on the dying – most of whom were Hindus and Muslims – to convert them to Catholicism; Teresa called this 'a ticket for St Peter'.)

At her death, Mother Teresa's Missionaries of Charity numbered more than 4,000 sisters, a linked brotherhood of 300, and more than 100,000 lay volunteers, working in 610 missions in 123 countries, including hospices and homes for people with HIV/AIDS, leprosy and tuberculosis, soup kitchens, orphanages and schools. The Roman Catholic Church plans to make her a saint.

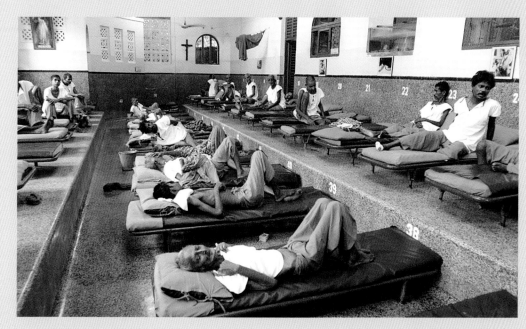

When a poor person dies I want them to die in the arms of someone who loves them.

MOTHER TERESA OF CALCUTTA

Mother Teresa's home for the aged homeless, *Nirmal Hriday* ('pure and soft heart').

many from the Third World – and helped to weaken Communism in eastern Europe.

Personally conservative, John Paul II tried to limit what he regarded as the excesses of Vatican II. He took a strict approach to doctrine, especially concerning marriage, women's ordination and the celibacy of priests. Many Western Catholics disagreed with him, and mass attendance and ordinations declined in some regions. Yet Catholics worldwide admired his work for human rights, and his popularity was demonstrated by the outpouring of grief at his death and the crowds of young people and of foreign dignitaries who attended his funeral.

The twenty-first century

In 2002 American Roman Catholics discovered that hundreds of priests had been abusing children over several decades, and some of the hierarchy had covered up this activity. Some priests were prosecuted, prelates resigned, huge amounts of compensation were paid and American bishops set up a commission to try to ensure this would not occur again.

In April 2005, following the death of John Paul II, Joseph Cardinal Ratzinger of Germany was elected the church's 265th pope, choosing to be called Benedict XVI.

The future

A shortage of priests moved lay people into posts once reserved for clergy. Lay teachers and administrators dominate Catholic education, and parishes have a majority of lay people on their staff – 50 per cent of them women.

The Catholic Church is rapidly expanding into the Third World, particularly Africa. African Catholics' faith is often charismatic and sometimes prophetic.

Only love lasts for ever.

JOHN PAUL II

CHAPTER 12

To the Ends of the Earth

Christian missions

From the outset, as we have seen, Christianity has been a strongly proselytizing faith. It sees itself as being not for one race, age or people group, but for all peoples for all time. Christians also believe they have 'good' news, and have often felt a strong impulse to share it with others near and far. Hence over long periods Christians have engaged in extensive and energetic missionary activity.

PAUL THE MISSIONARY

The first, and still most famous, Christian missionary was the apostle Paul, previously Saul of Tarsus. Apart from his fervour and courage, his achievement was to communicate the gospel to Greek and Roman culture, allowing it to move out of its original Jewish context. We have discussed Paul's significance in more detail in chapter 1.

Do not regard it as your task... to change peoples' manners, customs and uses, unless they are evidently contrary to religion and sound morals.

JESUIT MISSIONARIES' INSTRUCTIONS

Missionary monks

In the early centuries – indeed until the Reformations – most Christian missions were carried out by monks in enterprises such as those described in chapter 5. For example, Celtic and Cistercian monks evangelized much of northern Europe.

Colonizing Christians

As the European powers made territorial advances, such as Spain and Portugal's colonizing conquests in South America, part of the justification for these adventures was the opportunity that they offered to expand the frontiers of Christianity. The pope instructed these colonizing nations to take missionaries with them, to convert the local peoples and to found new bishoprics.

THE JESUITS

After the Protestant Reformation, the Jesuits, founded in 1540 by Ignatius Loyola, were key in helping renew the Church of Rome and deter Protestantism. As described on p. 122, the Jesuits excelled in mission, and carried the Christian gospel to the far corners of the world. The work of courageous Jesuit missionaries such as Francis Xavier in India and the Far East, Matteo Ricci in China and Roberto de Nobili in India became legendary.

One of the aims of the Jesuit order was to evangelize non-Christian peoples; and Jesuits, along with Dominicans, Franciscans, Augustinians and Capuchins, were the main missionary bodies in the Americas during the sixteenth and seventeenth centuries. The Philippines too were colonized by the Spanish in the seventeenth century, after which most Filipinos became Roman Catholic.

In Africa the Jesuits had only a superficial impact at this time, and only in the Congo and Mozambique. Not till the nineteenth century did explorer-missionaries have any lasting effect.

PROTESTANT MISSIONS

For the first century and more after the Reformation, pre-occupied by their struggle with the Roman Catholic Church, Protestant churches did not send out many missionaries to spread the faith. But beginning in the eighteenth century, Protestant churches did begin sending men (and later women) in increasing numbers to take the Christian message to as yet unreached peoples.

Anglicanism spread outside the British Isles both by emigration and by missionary effort. English missionary organizations such as the Society for the Propagation of the Gospel in Foreign Parts and the Society for the Promotion of Christian Knowledge (SPCK) were established to take Anglican Christianity to the British colonies.

In North America, missionaries to the Native Americans included Jonathan Edwards, the renowned preacher of the Great Awakening, who retired from the public preaching of

Francis Xavier ministering to the sick; a hagiographical painting by Jan de Bray (1627–97).

his early years to become a missionary to the Native Americans.

More societies

Following the establishment of Carey's Baptist Missionary Society (see opposite), other missionary societies soon followed. In 1795 Evangelicals from several different Protestant denominations organized the London Missionary Society; and in 1797 Dutch Christians started the Netherlands Missionary Society. In 1799 the Church Missionary Society was founded by Evangelical Anglican churchmen. And in 1810, American Evangelicals started the American Board of Commissioners for Foreign Missions, which was to become a major missionary-sending institution. In 1815 European pietists established a strategic missionary training school in Basel, Switzerland.

Missions to Asia

Often, the cross followed the flag; where European powers colonized, missionary societies preached. The Netherlands Missionary Society, for instance, set to work in the Dutch East Indies.

The earliest missionary to China in this period was the American Robert Morrison (1782–1834), who arrived in Canton in 1807. However, China was not officially open to foreigners until the signing of the Treaty of Nanking in 1842, following the Opium Wars. Five treaty ports – Canton, Xiamen (Amoy), Fuzhou, Ningbo and Shanghai – were designated cities for foreign settlement. British

A Baptist cobbler

On 31 May 1792, a village cobbler in Northamptonshire, England, preached on the theme: 'Expect great things from God; attempt great things for God'. This English Baptist, William Carey (1761–1834), became one of the pioneers of the modern Protestant missionary movement. Around 1780, Carey had read about the English navigator and explorer Captain James Cook's Polynesian voyages. He went on to become a Baptist minister, and eventually to write his famous 1792 tract, *An Enquiry into the Obligation of Christians to use Means for the Conversion of Heathen*, using currently available data to map and count all those who had never heard the gospel.

After years of discouragement, in 1792 Carey persuaded his fellow Baptists to organize the Baptist Missionary Society, only the first of a number of such organizations in a growing missionary enterprise. Then, with Joshua Marshman and William Ward, Carey sailed to India as a missionary himself.

Landing in Calcutta in 1793, Carey set about learning the local languages, translating the Bible, making converts and liberalizing Indian laws and customs. In the Danish trading centre at Serampore, near Calcutta, Carey and his colleagues eventually printed part or all of the Bible in a number of different languages. They also set up a college, which continues today to educate Indian Christian leaders. An indefatigable worker, Carey never returned to Britain. He translated not only from English into Bengali and Sanskrit, but also translated the Hindu *Vedas* into English, producing the first authoritative versions in that language.

Others followed Carey to India. By 1855, missionaries from the Anglican Church Missionary Society had reached Peshawar. More successful were the large numbers of missionaries from both Europe and North America who landed in south India, where they encountered the Catholic Church founded by Francis Xavier and the Malabar Christian communities of Travancore, believed to date from around the sixth century.

It is only by means of native preachers we can hope for the universal spread of the Gospel through this immense Continent.

WILLIAM CAREY

The pioneering Baptist missionary William Carey with his Brahmin pundit (Hindu learned in Sanskrit).

and American missionaries used these ports as springboards for their evangelization of China.

But, following the earlier massacres of Roman Catholic Christians, Japan remained steadfastly hostile to the West, while South Korea received its first missionary only in 1865.

Missions to Africa

Islam still predominated in North Africa, with the exception of the ancient churches of the Copts in Egypt and the Ethiopian Church. By the early nineteenth century, very little remained of the early Roman Catholic missions to Africa.

The first wave of modern missionary activity to achieve success came in the 1830s and 1840s, especially in West Africa. Many West African tribal rulers saw Christianity as a means of gaining prosperity through trade with European missionary-sending countries. Missionaries set up numerous mission stations and schools.

The earliest missions to southern Africa were launched in this period from the Cape of Good Hope, where Europeans had long settled. Dr David Livingstone, the Scottish explorer and missionary, blazed hazardous trails from here which many other missionaries were to follow.

Roman Catholic missions were as active as Protestant missions in Africa in this period, especially the Holy Ghost Fathers (1848) and the White Fathers (1868). Protestant–Catholic rivalry over mission areas intensified and mirrored the political rivalries of the European powers' infamous 'scramble' for African colonies after 1880.

Missions to China

Roman Catholic missions continued to operate in China, despite persecution. With official toleration agreed in a Convention of 1860 between China and France, Catholicism was able to expand faster than Protestantism. There were rapid advances after the setback of the Boxer Rebellion in 1900, with the greatest growth in the Hubei and Guang-Dong provinces.

After the Taiping Rebellion ended in China in 1864, the British Protestant missionary James Hudson Taylor (1832–1905) set up his China Inland Mission. Taylor was a thorough-going nativist, offending many other missionaries by wearing Chinese clothing and speaking Chinese at home. His mission, which made a principle of never requesting funds, was one of the few that had much success in persuading Chinese people to convert to Christianity.

Hudson Taylor's writing, speaking and exemplary lifestyle led to the formation of numerous other missions, and to the setting up of the Student Volunteer Movement. Thousands of volunteer missionaries offered their service, and by 1882 Protestant missionaries were resident in all but three of the Chinese provinces.

Missions to Latin America

During the nineteenth century Protestant missionaries went to Latin America largely from the United States, at a time when Protestant values appeared attractive to the liberal middle classes who had brought independence to the South American republics. Since the ejection of earlier Roman Catholic missions, a shortage of priests had brought a decline in the practice of the Christian faith. Methodists and Baptists came to the Caribbean on the tide of the anti-slavery movement.

By the outbreak of the First World War, all the Latin American republics had established Protestant missions. However, with only half a million Protestant converts in the entire region, they represented only a tiny proportion in comparison with the existing Catholic population.

Missions to Oceania

In the South Seas, missionary activity progressed generally from the east to the west. Hearing favourable reports about Tahiti, Western missionaries journeyed there first, moving on to the more hostile Melanesian Islands in the west. Missionaries from the London Missionary Society were the first to reach the Society Islands; missionaries proceeded from there to the western islands of Polynesia – Tonga, Western Samoa and Fiji – first evangelized by the Methodists. After the American Board converted Hawaii, the huge enterprise of crossing the Pacific was undertaken in 1852 by missions to the Marshall Islands, and to the Caroline and Gilbert Islands.

In the seventeenth century, Spanish Roman Catholics had crossed from the Christianized Philippines to western Micronesia and converted the population of the Marianas Islands; but no further Catholic evangelization occurred until late in the nineteenth century.

The main Catholic missionary bodies in this region were French: in Melanesia, the Congregation of the Sacred Hearts of Jesus and Mary, known as the Pipcus Fathers; and in Polynesia, the Marist Fathers. On these islands the Catholic missionaries' arrival often caused tension and even conflict with the Protestant converts. To avoid such problems, New Guinea was divided by agreement into separate mission fields.

French Catholics established themselves in New Caledonia and in southern New Guinea, as well as on the far eastern islands of Tahiti, the Marquesas Islands, Mangereva and Easter Island.

Australia and New Zealand

The English naval explorer James Cook first charted the coasts of Australia and New Zealand in 1770.

Ruins of a former penal colony on Norfolk Island, in the South Pacific Ocean. The island later became an external territory of Australia.

When Britain decided to set up a penal colony in Australia, an Anglican chaplain, Richard Johnson, went out with the very first convict ship in 1788; Wesleyans followed in 1815, and Presbyterians in 1823. By 1820, Roman Catholic priests were also serving the predominantly Irish Catholic population.

The initially favoured Church of England received government grants of land on which to build churches and schools in New South Wales, though after 1836 these grants were made non-denominational.

The first European settlers went to New Zealand in 1805, and the first missionaries nine years later. Anglicans came to form the majority of the population, but with large minorities of Scottish Presbyterians, Roman Catholics and Methodists.

Missions industry

The nineteenth century became an age of heroic missionary enterprise: the Englishman Henry Martyn, initially a chaplain of the East India Company, went to India, Persia and finally Armenia; the American couple Adoniram and Ann Judson went with the Baptist Triennial Convention to Burma (now Myanmar), where Adoniram was viciously tortured; the German Johann Krapf went with the British Church Missionary Society to India; the Englishman Samuel Marsden to New Zealand; the German Johannes Rebmann with the Church Missionary Society to East Africa; the Belgian Father Damien with the Picpus Fathers to Hawaii to work among those suffering from leprosy; Dr David Livingstone with the London Missionary Society to East Africa; Mary Slessor with the

Charles de Foucauld

Charles de Foucauld (1858–1916) was a man of extremes, an aristocrat whose conversion to Christianity led him into a life of solitude and prayer. Inspired by the 'hidden life' of Jesus in Nazareth, he hoped others would follow his lead.

De Foucauld was born in 1858 in Strasbourg, France. Orphaned at six, he inherited a fortune and followed his grandfather into the army. Excessive in everything he did, as an officer he was best known for his consumption of vintage champagnes. While fighting Arabs in North Africa, he came to respect them, learned Arabic and studied the Qur'an.

Returning to France, he rediscovered his faith in 1886, at the age of twenty-eight. 'As soon as I believed in God, I understood I must live for him alone.' A pilgrimage to the Holy Land in 1889 led to Charles' vocation to emulate the earthly example of Jesus. De Foucauld next spent seven years as a Trappist monk, first in France then at Akbès, Syria. In 1897 he became a servant of the Poor Clares in Nazareth, living in a tool-shed and doing odd jobs while studying the Bible.

In 1901 de Foucauld was ordained a priest and went to the Sahara, living among the Touareg at Tamanrasset in Algeria. He wanted to be with those who were 'most abandoned'. For the next fifteen years he lived as a hermit missionary, preparing the first dictionary of Touareg, and translating the Gospels into that language.

North Africans respected de Foucauld's poverty, prayer and hospitality, yet he made no attempt to convert them. His aim was to 'shout the gospel with his life'. 'I would like to be good enough for people to say, "If that is the servant, what must the Master be like?"'

In 1916 de Foucauld was shot by robbers during an anti-French uprising. Within a decade a biography spread word of him, and his life and writings inspired others to follow his path of prayer and radical simplicity. He had always wanted to found a new religious order, but this only became a reality after his death, in the form of the Little Brothers of Jesus. Today at least nineteen movements worldwide follow de Foucauld's instructions to live simply among the poor, living the gospel more by example than by word.

Calabar Mission to Nigeria; Father Charles Eugene de Foucauld to North Africa; the English test-cricketer C. T. Studd to China, India and Central Africa, where he founded the Heart of Africa Mission, later known as Worldwide Evangelization Crusade; and the Englishman James Hudson Taylor to China. It was also an age of great missionary organizers, such as H. Grattan Guinness; innovative missionary organizations, such as the China Inland Mission and the Mission to Lepers; and great missionary conferences, such as the World Missionary Conference in Edinburgh, Scotland, in 1910.

Problems of expansion

As large numbers of Christian missionaries started to arrive in previously non-Christian countries from western Europe and America, minorities of believers began to appear. These national Christians sometimes suffered reprisals or persecution from their non-Christian neighbours. Such outbursts of oppression and, on occasion, alleged mistreatment of missionaries in some instances led to European intervention in the domestic affairs of non-European powers – for example, in the so-called Boxer Rebellion in China in 1900.

More often, foreign missionaries produced native Christians who took up not only their faith but also their Western culture and habits, making it difficult or impossible for them to continue to live comfortably in their own land. Some countries reacted by shutting their borders to all Christian missions, as for instance in Afghanistan, Nepal and Tibet in 1910. Elsewhere, national Christians emerged to assume leadership positions in their homelands; for instance, Samuel Ajayi Crowther, who became the first African Anglican bishop in 1864.

WINNING THE WORLD

In 1910 the Edinburgh World Missionary Conference was held in Scotland. Presided over by the Student Volunteer Movement leader (and later Nobel Peace Prize winner) John R. Mott, an American Methodist layman, the conference reviewed the state of world evangelism, the number of languages into which the Bible had been translated, the mobilization of church support and the training of indigenous church leaders. Looking to the future, delegates worked on strategies for worldwide evangelism and cooperation. The conference not only established greater ecumenical cooperation in missions, but also helped launched the modern ecumenical movement.

Twentieth-century methods

After the First World War, another wave of missions was started by two influential American missionaries, Cameron Townsend and Donald McGavran, in around 1935. Both men realized that, although missionaries had by this time reached most geographical areas, numerous people

The church has not yet seriously attempted to bring the living Christ to all living men.

JOHN R. MOTT

161

groups remained isolated from the missionaries by language or by class. Townsend founded the Wycliffe Bible Translators, with the aim of translating the Bible into native languages in order to reach these peoples. Meanwhile McGavran concentrated on crossing the class and cultural barriers in countries such as India, which has more than 4,600 different people groups separated by language, culture and caste.

Dr Frank Laubach (1884–1970), an Evangelical missionary and linguist known as 'the apostle to the illiterates', launched the 'Each one, teach one' instructional programme in the Philippines, also in 1935. This quietly revolutionary scheme has since spread around the world, and has brought literacy to the least enabled in many different societies.

An equally important missions strategy was the indigenous method, by which national Christians took the faith to their own people. In Asia this was pioneered by missionary thinkers such as Dr G. D. James of Singapore, Revd Theodore Williams of India and Dr David Cho of Korea. Known as the 'two thirds Missions Movement', this too became a major force in missions.

Missions and culture

As we have seen, in past centuries Christian missionaries often worked very closely with colonial powers; for example, during the European colonization of the Americas, Africa and Asia. Sometimes they damaged local cultures and wiped out traditional religions, discouraging traditional practices that missionaries considered to be backward or pagan, and explicitly or implicitly encouraging instead Western lifestyles. Most modern missionaries and missionary societies have repudiated such cultural imperialism, choosing to stick to spreading the essential Christian message – often by modern means such as radio, television and the internet – and to translating the Bible into the vernacular.

Indeed, missionaries have sometimes helped save cultures from destruction by economic and political forces. Some have even worked to preserve and document the culture of the peoples among whom they live and work. Christian missionaries have also often effected positive cultural change in native societies, striving to stop practices such as torture and ritual human sacrifice in some indigenous cultures, such as that of the ancient Aztecs.

Often, missionaries provide welfare and health services, as a good act in its own right, or to make links with locals. Thousands of schools, orphanages and hospitals have been set up by missions from medieval times down to the present, and many Christian missionaries promote economic development, literacy, education, health care and hospices.

Modern missionaries are no longer based on 'mission stations', which are now often seen to have created converts who were then regarded as outcasts by their own family and culture. 'Mission-station converts' were sometimes so alienated from their surrounding culture that they could get no work outside the mission station, let alone act as ambassadors for the faith.

Instead, most missionaries now tend to live among nationals, if possible with an indigenous family, both to aid language learning and to maintain a relevant link between them and the people among whom the mission is being established.

A TROUBLED CENTURY

At the turn of the twentieth century, many Christians believed that the kingdom of God – or at least a better world – was at hand. Two world wars, followed by fifty years' fearing a third one, buried those hopes of human perfectibility.

The First World War

US President Woodrow Wilson, a committed Presbyterian, viewed the First World War idealistically as a crusade of good against evil and had a vision of a post-war world where nations would live in harmony, resolving their differences through the League of Nations. But the League failed to prevent aggression or preserve peace, and the great 'civil war of the West' – the First World War – undermined Europe's global position.

Dictatorships challenge the church

The great challenge to Christianity in the inter-war period were the dictatorships in Italy, Germany and Russia. As conditions in Germany deteriorated after 1929, many churchmen were attracted to Hitler's nationalist Nazi movement. A pro-Nazi party even arose within the Protestant church, called the 'German Christians'. Meanwhile Hitler signed a treaty with the Vatican guaranteeing German Catholics freedom to practise their religion and independence for the church.

In 1933 Pastor Martin Niemöller (1892–1984) formed the Pastors' Emergency League to combat 'German Christian' ideas. His group set up an alternative church government, known as the Confessing Church, whose theological basis was set out in the Barmen Declaration of May 1934. The Confessing Church was repudiated by many Protestant leaders and harassed by the Gestapo. A few church figures, such as Dietrich Bonhoeffer (1906–45), became involved in the anti-Hitler resistance and even plotted to kill Hitler.

The Second World War

The Second World War had a devastating impact on Christianity. Thousands of churches were destroyed and believers were persecuted or uprooted. The level of violence escalated as a result of the many new weapons, fire-bombing and ultimately the atomic bomb. The deliberate direction of war against civilians, the indifference of leaders in the Christian West to the sufferings of the Jews, and the alliance of Western democracies with the Soviet Union all troubled Christians.

Anti-Nazi Lutheran pastor Martin Niemöller.

A 1931 German cartoon showing the Nazi storm bursting over the church, and scaring the Communists.

The Second World War ended with large parts of Europe and Asia in ruins. West European power had ended, and colonial liberation meant a new world was coming into being. In these de-colonized areas Christianity made enormous strides, and within a few decades the numerical centre of gravity shifted away from Europe and North America to Asia, Africa and Latin America.

The Cold War and the churches

In post-war Germany, the church became part of the Cold War. Konrad Adenauer, first chancellor of West Germany, was an anti-Communist Catholic whose Christian Democratic Union party brought together Catholics and conservative Protestants. The churches were not at first divided by the border imposed across Germany, and their cross-border organization helped sustain the concept of unity. The Protestant *Kirchentag* (Church Assembly), which first met in 1949, attracted huge crowds of lay Christians.

In the Communist bloc, Christians were under intense pressure, varying by country and circumstance. While the Catholic Church in Poland exercised strong influence, Albania banned all religion. Conditions in other Eastern bloc nations ranged between these two extremes. Irreligion was nurtured through the inculcation of Marxist materialism in schools, through atheist organizations and by substituting secular rites for religious ceremonies.

Josef Cardinal Mindszenty (1892–1975) denounced the Hungarian Communist regime and was sentenced to prison after a mock trial in 1949. Released during the 1956 uprising in Budapest, he remained in the American embassy there for years until the pope secured his release.

Racial and ethnic conflict

A serious problem facing the twentieth-century church was ethnic and racial conflict. The most serious example was apartheid in South Africa, which made that country an international outcast and attracted growing internal opposition. Some South African Christians themselves were in the forefront of the struggle: Bishop Desmond Tutu, author Alan Paton, Beyers Naudé of the Christian Institute, Reformed minister Allan Boesak, Michael Cassidy of African Enterprise and Pentecostal minister Frank Chikane.

Christian leaders adopted several statements criticizing the system, such as the Rustenburg Declaration (1990), signed by representatives of every church in South Africa except two Dutch Reformed groups. Finally, the South African regime began to dismantle the apartheid system.

Discrimination against blacks was also a serious problem in the United States, where the struggle for justice was long and hard. The civil rights movement was born and nourished in the black church, and the central figure, Martin Luther King Jr (1929–68), was a Baptist minister. Dr King gave theological direction to the movement and insisted that non-violence and Christian love should always be at the heart of the struggle.

A WORLDWIDE FAITH

In some parts of the world today Christianity is showing tremendous growth; elsewhere it is static or declining, in some places dramatically.

Africa

North Africa was one of the strongholds of early Christianity. But since the early Muslim take-over, the church has been almost non-existent. By contrast, Christianity mushroomed in twentieth-century sub-Saharan Africa. A notable

More than 300,000 people attend a monthly all-night 'revival' at the Lagos, Nigeria, church camp of the Redeemed Church of God.

> *The dividedness of the churches makes it difficult for people to believe in the gospel of Jesus Christ.*
>
> ARCHBISHOP DESMOND TUTU

feature of African Christianity is the huge number of independent churches that exist within it.

Many of the indigenous African churches trace their origins to the mainstream mission churches. Independence has allowed them to synthesize Christian teaching with traditional African ideas and values. Most of these churches are Pentecostal, and stress healing and exorcism.

Several of these indigenous churches have a charismatic prophet as their leader, such as the Kimbanguist Church in Zaire, founded by Simon Kimbangu, and the Harris Church in the Ivory Coast, named after William Harris. Some of the largest and best-known independent churches in Nigeria are the Aladura (or 'praying people') churches. South Africa probably has

the most dynamic independent tradition, with many churches springing up in protest against white control over the existing church.

The Roman Catholic Church is rapidly expanding in the Third World, particularly Africa. African Catholics demonstrate much enthusiasm; like the earliest Christians, their faith is often charismatic and sometimes prophetic.

North America
Church membership in the United States stands at around 60 per cent of the population – higher than in any other Western nation. By contrast, at the beginning of the twentieth century it was only about 20 per cent. Roman Catholicism has become the largest single denomination of American Christianity, making up

about 25 per cent of the population, due largely to immigration. Much of the population is Protestant, of whom the Baptists have replaced the Methodists as the largest denomination, at roughly 15 per cent.

Growth of the traditional Protestant denominations slowed during the 1960s as other non-denominational Evangelical churches became popular. The 'electronic church', in which televangelists command huge audiences, also plays a significant role, and Pentecostals and Charismatics became one of the fastest growing groups within the church, in both the Protestant and Catholic traditions.

In Canada, the Presbyterian and Anglican churches are stronger in the English-speaking provinces of the west, while Catholicism predominates in the French-speaking cities of Quebec province.

South America

In the later twentieth century many of the Roman Catholic clergy in South America were foreigners. Some supported political movements striving for justice and human rights against repressive governments. Foreign clergy were in an easier position to challenge the authorities. Increasingly, the indigenous clergy, and bishops such as Archbishop Romero of Salvador, also denounced their governments from the pulpit. Reactionary persecution of the church followed. Between 1964 and 1978, 260 foreign

Billy Graham

Probably the world's most famous preacher and evangelist, Billy Graham was born in Charlotte, North Carolina. Graham joined an evangelistic organization called Youth for Christ after graduating from Wheaton College, Illinois, and travelled throughout the United States and Europe as an evangelist.

In 1949 Graham held a series of his own missions in Los Angeles, originally scheduled to last only three weeks, but eventually extended to eight. In 1950 he founded the eponymous Billy Graham Evangelistic Association, with headquarters in Minneapolis. US press barons William Randolph Hearst and Henry Luce thought Graham could help promote their anti-Communist platform; so Hearst sent his editors a telegram reading 'Puff Graham', while Luce put Graham's face on the cover of *TIME* in 1954.

In 1957 Graham had successful missions in London and New York, in 1959 in Australia, and countless others elsewhere. Graham gained a reputation for holding crusades in places other evangelists considered impossible: during the Cold War, he spoke to large crowds behind the Iron Curtain. During the apartheid era in South Africa, he refused to speak to segregated crowds. Graham was also one of the few preachers to speak in North Korea.

Billy Graham preached his message to live audiences of more than 210 million people in over 185 countries, and also reached many millions more through television, video, film and webcasts.

Crusades
Billy Graham is best known for his evangelistic crusades. He would preach and then invite people to come forward in response. These 'inquirers' could then speak with a 'counsellor' who answered questions and prayed with them. Graham was apparently always careful to receive only reasonable payment, less than other television evangelists later received.

Graham was a close confidant to US Presidents Lyndon B. Johnson, Bill Clinton, and George and George W. Bush, and was outspoken against Communism. In 2002, declassified Nixon tapes revealed his saying that Jews controlled the American media.

missionaries were expelled from Latin American states, and over 450 priests were arrested.

During the 1960s, Protestant growth escalated, especially in poor urban districts, and most spectacularly among Pentecostal groups – especially in Brazil, Chile, Mexico and Guatemala. Latin America was the most successful region of the world for the Pentecostal churches, the most widespread of which is the Assemblies of God, while the Seventh-day Adventists are the most successful of the denominations.

Christianity in Asia

As a result of China's 1966 Cultural Revolution, Christianity was driven underground. This gave rise to the secret 'house church' movement, which spread rapidly. As government control over religion has relaxed, churches have reopened. However, estimates of numbers of practising Christians are notoriously difficult to assess and hence vary enormously.

In central Asia, Christianity tends to be confined to the Slavic immigrants, who are normally Eastern Orthodox in belief. Islam is very strong in many of these republics. In southern Asia, India has significant Christian communities. Perhaps the most notable are in the enclaves bordering Myanmar – Nagaland and Mizoram – where some 85 per cent of the population are Christian.

Many of the 'boat people' who escaped from Vietnam were Roman Catholic, though a

The evangelist Billy Graham, brandishing his Bible in characteristic fashion, preaches at Griffith Stadium, Washington D.C., USA, in 1960.

I have one message: Jesus Christ came; he died on a cross; he rose again. He asks us to repent of our sins and receive him by faith as Lord and Saviour. And if we do, we have forgiveness of all our sins.

BILLY GRAHAM

significant Christian community remains in the country. Although in Indonesia the church is stronger and officially tolerated, Muslims have reacted to Protestant evangelism, in some instances with persecution.

In South Korea, the government has favoured the growth of the church. Most Christians there are Evangelicals; whereas the Philippines still have one of the densest Roman Catholic populations in Asia.

Oceania

Following the strong Protestant and Roman Catholic missionary influx in the nineteenth century, many of the islands and nations of Oceania have remained strongly Christian. Papua New Guinea, with more than one thousand different tribal groups speaking 816 languages, is the world's most diverse nation; more than 95 per cent of the population consider themselves Christian. Sixty-six languages are spoken in the Solomon Islands and parts of the Bible are being translated into twenty-four of them. Again, more than 95 per cent claim to be Christian. Tuvalu, the 'disappearing island', is also more than 95 per cent Christian, as are Samoa and Tonga. Reportedly half the population of Tonga went on a 'Jesus' march in 1995. Vanuatu, where 109 languages are spoken, is more than 90 per cent Christian; parts of the Bible are being translated into forty-four of those languages.

There is a similarly large proportion of Christians on the Marshall Islands in Micronesia, in the North Pacific. The Cook Islands, Niue, Tokelau and Pitcairn have all been strongly Christian for the last 150 years. At the end of the

Chinese believers celebrate Christmas 1996 at one of the largest 'unregistered' churches, in Guangzhou.

nineteenth century, the British introduced Indians to work on Fiji, in the South Pacific: tensions are high between them and the indigenous Fijians, who have made Christianity a nationalist political issue.

THAT THEY ALL MAY BE ONE
Scandals of division
In 1937 Bishop Azariah of India voiced the feelings of many Christians when he said: 'The problem of union is one of life and death with us.' The scandal of division within the church had become both a growing obstacle to belief and a deepening source of shame. But moves towards unifying the different branches of the Christian faith were in fact already proceeding.

In the late nineteenth century, the American Methodist layman John R. Mott enthused the interdenominational Student Christian Movement with his call to world mission. In 1895 the interdenominational Young Men's Christian Association (founded in 1844 by George Williams, and better known by its initials, YMCA) gave birth to the World Student Christian Federation (founded in 1895) which, with the Student Volunteer Movement, a major mission organization, provided some of the great prophets of Christian unity.

Evangelization in this generation
The 1910 World Missionary Conference, held in Edinburgh and led by Mott under the slogan, 'The Evangelization of the World in this Generation', proved to be a turning point. The largest Protestant gathering up to that time, this conference was called with the express purpose of working across denominational lines for the sake of world missions. The problems of disunity had been brought into focus.

By 1937, in addition to the major Protestant denominations, the Eastern Orthodox Church was also taking part in discussions, as were churches in Africa and Asia. The end of the Second World War spurred the churches to reconvene in 1948 to form the World Council of Churches in Amsterdam. The W. C. C. headquarters were later moved to Geneva, and a series of world assemblies in various continents followed at Amsterdam, Holland; Evanston, USA; New Delhi, India; Uppsala, Finland; and Nairobi, Kenya.

Roman Catholics
But as yet this was not truly a world council: Roman Catholics and Russian Orthodox were notable absentees. Pope John XXIII changed things with his call for 'that unity for which Jesus Christ prayed', and with his summoning of the Second Vatican Council (1962–65) to renew the Roman Catholic Church. A new openness to ecumenical affairs came to the Catholic Church when it was announced that other Christian communions were to be known as 'separated brothers' rather than those outside the church.

In 1999 representatives of the Lutheran World Federation and the Roman Catholic Church signed a joint declaration, apparently resolving the conflict over the nature of justification that had been at the root of the Protestant Reformation more than four centuries earlier.

Eastern Orthodoxy
Eastern and Oriental Orthodox students had been active in the World Student Christian Federation in the late nineteenth century, and some Orthodox patriarchs enlisted as charter members of the World Council of Churches. Yet, for the Eastern Orthodox, Christianity is the church, and the church is Orthodoxy. Therefore, the Eastern Orthodox goal has been

to reconcile all non-Orthodox back into Orthodoxy.

Nevertheless, the anathemas (excommunications) that brought about the Great Schism of 1054 between Catholics and Orthodox were revoked in 1965 by both Pope John XXIII and the Ecumenical Patriarch of Constantinople. But just as the original schism opened up over a long period of time, reconciliation proceeded at a snail's pace too.

Opposition to ecumenism
A number of other Christian groupings oppose ecumenism, particularly those from Evangelical, Pentecostal and Charismatic churches, from conservative sections of mainline Protestant churches and from the Catholic and Orthodox churches. In general, they regard ecumenism as compromising essential doctrine in order to accommodate other Christians, and object to the emphasis on dialogue rather than objective truth.

GRASSROOTS UNITY
Worldwide ecumenism has also been reflected in grass-roots trends towards unity. As early as 1927, five denominations in China gathered in one Church of Christ. Later, and more famously, in 1947 Anglicans, Methodists, Presbyterians, Congregationalists and Reformed joined to form the Church of South India, a model for others elsewhere. The United Church of Canada was created as a merger of several denominations in 1925, and many

smaller denominations combined with one another in the United States. In the 1960s, the English Methodist Church made overtures to the Church of England aimed at church unity; but these were rejected by the Church of England's General Synod.

Another recent trend has been the sporadic sharing of church buildings by two or more denominations, either holding separate services in the same building, or a single service containing elements from all traditions. In North America, many non-denominational churches have been set up, and cooperative non-denominational ventures aimed at helping society, such as in prisons and hospitals, have helped to break down inter-church barriers.

Meanwhile, at a local level many Christians from different traditions take it for granted that they will work, pray and evangelize together. Home Bible study groups, young people's meetings, student groups in colleges and universities, Christian relief work and missions all demonstrate that for many their shared life in Christ is more important to them than their denominational affiliation and tradition.

Further reading

Ahlstrom, S. E., *A Religious History of the American People*, Yale 1972

Bebbington, David W., *Evangelicalism in Modern Britain: A History from the 1730s to the 1980s*, London 1989

Chadwick, Owen, *The Church in the Cold War*, London 1991

Chadwick, Owen, *A History of Christianity*, London 1995

Davidson, Ivor J., *A Public Faith: From Constantine to the Medieval World, AD 312–600* (Monarch History of the Church), Oxford 2005

Davidson, Ivor J., *The Birth of the Church: Jesus to Constantine* (Monarch History of the Church), Oxford 2005

Gray, R., *Black Christians and White Missionaries*, New Haven, Conn. 1990

Green, Vivian, *New History of Christianity*, London, 1997

Heinze, Rudolph W., *Reform and Conflict: From the Medieval World to the Wars of Religion, AD 1350–1648*, (Monarch History of the Church), Oxford 2005

Hill, Jonathan, *The New Lion Handbook: The History of Christianity*, Oxford 2006

MacCulloch, Diarmaid, *Reformation: Europe's House Divided 1490–1700*, London 2004

McManners, John (ed.), *The Oxford Illustrated History of the Church*, Oxford 1990

Moorhouse, Geoffrey, *The Missionaries*, London 1973

Neill, Stephen, *A History of Christian Missions*, 2nd rev. ed., Harmondsworth 1986

Noll, Mark A., *Turning Points: Decisive Moments in the History of Christianity*, Leicester 1997

Pearse, Meic, *The Age of Reason: From the Wars of Religion to the French Revolution*, Oxford 2007

Southern, R. W., *Western Society and the Church in the Middle Ages*, Harmondsworth 1970

Index

A

Abelard, Peter 72
Abu Bakr 79, 92–93
African Methodist Episcopal Church 140, 143
Agape 36
Aladura 165
Alaric 46
Albigensians 54
Alexandria 8, 14–17, 26, 27, 39, 74, 79, 84, 92–93
Alexius IV Angelus 98–99
Alexius I Comnenus 94
Ambrose of Milan 134
American Board of Commissioners for Foreign Missions 156, 159
American Revolution 115, 149
Amsterdam 113, 124, 169
Anabaptists 112, 113, 117, 122–28
Anglo-Saxons 50, 65–67, 68
Anselm of Canterbury 72
Anskar 66
Anti-Catholicism 76, 149, 151
Anticlericalism 76
Antioch 11, 12, 16, 28, 38, 60, 79, 93, 96
Anti-Semitism 98, 107, 151
anti-slavery movement 136, 138, 158
Antony 59–61, 62
Apostolic Faith Mission 143, 145
apostolic succession 38
Aquinas, Thomas 53, 72, 151
Arius 41
Armenia 17, 20, 134, 160
Asbury, Francis 137–38
Asia Minor 8, 11–14, 15, 17, 41, 94
Assemblies of God 140, 144–45, 147, 167

Athanasius 26, 41, 61
Athens 12, 39, 66
Attila 46
Augustine of Canterbury 42
Augustine of Hippo 13, 26, 42–43
Augustinians 69–70, 106, 155
Australia 49, 84, 133, 140, 159–60, 166
Authorized (King James') Version 30, 117
Avignon 55–56, 102
Azusa Street revival 143–44

B

Babylonian Captivity 55, 102
Bach, J. S. 21, 134
Baptism in the Holy Spirit 141–44, 145
Baptist Missionary Society 156–57
Baptists 90, 114, 124–25, 133, 134, 138, 157, 158, 166
Barbarians 17, 46, 47
Barbarossa, Frederick I 98
Barnabas 11, 12, 23, 26
Barratt, Thomas Ball 144
Basil the Great 62, 63, 82, 86, 87
Beatty, Chester 35
Becket, Thomas 53
Bede 65
Benedict of Nursia 62–64, 67
Bennett, Dennis 145–46
Berg, Daniel 144
Bernard of Clairvaux 42, 52, 69, 70, 72, 74, 98
Bible 12, 17, 19–23, 26, 27–36, 38, 40, 42, 44, 48–49, 60, 61, 65, 67, 73, 82, 84, 103–106, 108, 110, 116, 117, 127–29, 134–36, 152, 157, 160–62, 167–68, 170
Billy Graham 166–67
Billy Graham Evangelistic Association 166
Böhme, Jakob 74, 129

Bolsheviks 88
Boniface 65–66
Book of Acts 10, 25, 26, 35
Book of Common Prayer 114, 116, 117
Book of Kells 64
Booth, William 135, 139, 140
Boxer Rebellion 158, 161
Brotherhood of the Common Life 73
Byzantium 16, 78, 79, 92, 94

C

Caecilian 43
Calvin, John (Jean) 13, 42, 104, 109, 110, 134–35
Calvinism 110–13, 133
Canada 49, 140, 166, 170
Cane Ridge, Kentucky 138
Canon 25–26
Capernaum 9
Cappadocia 10, 62
Capuchins 76–77, 155
Carey, William 157
Caribbean 158
Carolingian Renaissance 20, 50
Carroll, John 149
Carthage 16, 26, 39, 42, 43
Carthusian order 68
Cassian, John 59, 62–63
Cassiodorus 62
Catacombs 17, 37
Celibacy 42, 43, 58, 68, 77, 80, 82, 116, 154
Celtic Christianity 20, 49–50, 64, 77, 155
Charismatic renewal 141, 146
Charlemagne 29, 50–51, 93
Charles V 105, 109–110, 112
China 92, 94, 120, 122, 155, 157–58, 161, 167, 170
China Inland Mission 158, 161
Cho, David 162
Christmas 49, 50, 51, 81, 83, 137

Chrysostom, John 78, 82, 134
Church Missionary Society 136, 156, 157, 160
Church of God in Christ 143, 144
Church of Ireland 114
Church of South India 170
Cistercians 68–69, 75, 98, 155
Cîteaux 68, 69
City of God (Augustine) 42
Clapham Sect 136
Clare 71
Clement of Rome 16, 23, 26, 39
Cluny 67–68, 77
Codex Alexandrinus 26, 35
Codex Sinaiticus 26–27, 35
Codex Vaticanus 26, 35
Coke, Thomas 137–38
collegia pietatis 129
Columba 64
Columbanus 64–65
Communist Manifesto 150
Confederation of Warsaw 113
Congo 156
Congregationalists 114, 124, 134, 136, 140, 170
Constantine I 18, 39, 78
Constantinople 41, 45–46, 50, 61, 66, 78, 79, 81–82, 84–87, 93–96, 98–100, 103, 170
Contarini, Gasparo 118
Coptic church 41
Copts 41, 158
Corinth 13, 16, 22, 25
Council of Basel 56
Council of Chalcedon 41, 78, 82
Council of Constance 56, 102, 103, 105
Council of Dort 113
Council of Trent
Councils of Constantinople 41, 46, 79, 82
Councils of Nicea 41, 48, 78–80, 82

Cranmer, Thomas 114–16
Cromwell, Oliver 114, 124
Cromwell, Thomas 73, 75, 115
Crowther, Samuel Ajayi 161
Crusades 55, 69, 72 81, 94–100
Cyprian of Carthage 39, 43
Cyril 31, 67, 84

D

Damascus 11, 12, 13, 16, 92, 93, 98
dark night of the soul 74
Darmstadt Statement 34
Darwin, Charles 32, 130, 150
Dead Sea Scrolls 35
Decius 17, 44
Deism 130, 149
Denck, Hans 123–24, 125
Descartes, René 130
devotio moderna 74
Diet of Speyer 108
Diet of Worms 105, 106, 113
Diocletian 18, 43
Discalced (Barefoot) Carmelites 74, 75
dissolution of the monasteries 73, 75, 76, 115–16
Docetists 23, 38
Dome of the Rock 97
Dominican 53, 72, 73, 155
Domitian 15
Donation of Constantine 81
Donatism 42–43
Donatus 42
Durham, William H. 144
Dutch Reformed 124, 136, 164
Dwight, Timothy 138

E

Easter 8, 48–49, 80, 81, 134
Ebionites 23
Edessa 15, 15, 58, 98
Edict of Milan 44
Edict of Nantes 112
Edinburgh 161, 169

Edwards, Jonathan 136–37, 156
Egede, Hans 131
Egypt 8, 10, 14, 15, 16, 24, 26, 28, 39, 41, 60–61, 71, 74, 79, 84, 92, 158
Elizabeth I 117
Elizabethan Settlement 114
Enlightenment 31–32, 76, 130, 132, 148, 149
Ephesus 13, 16, 20, 22, 25, 41, 82
Episcopal Church 49, 114–15, 137–38, 140, 143–44, 146
Erasmus of Rotterdam 31, 73, 103–104, 110
Essenes 58
Ethiopian Church 158
Eucharist 15, 19, 36, 37, 108, 115
Eusebius of Caesarea 26
Eutyches 41
Evangelical Revivals 136
Evangelicalism 35, 115, 129–32, 134, 136
Evangelism 36, 115, 132, 161, 168

F

Farel, William 109
Fascism 151
Fasting 58, 60, 80, 83, 98, 132
Fiji 141, 159, 169
filioque clause 80
Fire of Rome 13, 44
First Great Awakening 136
First Vatican Council 150
Foucauld, Charles de 77, 160, 161
Fourth Lateran Council 53–54
Foxe, John 109, 117
Francis of Assisi 70–71, 95, 153
Franciscans 71–72, 75, 155–56
Francke, August Hermann 131
Frederick the Wise 106

French Revolution 148–49
Friars 71–72, 73
Full Gospel Business Men's Fellowship International 146
Fundamentalism 33–34

G

Galatia 12, 22
Galatians 12, 22, 25
Galerius 18
Galileo 31, 32, 130
Geneva 109–110, 112, 113, 117, 127, 129, 169
Glasnost 89
Glossolalia 141–44
Gnosis 23, 38
Gnosticism 23, 38
Gospel of Thomas 24
Gospels 9, 22–26, 28, 35, 64, 87, 160
Great Papal Schism 55–56
Great Schism 80–81, 170
Gregorian chant 20
Gregory of Nyssa 40, 82
Gutenberg, Johann 30–31
Guzman, Dominic de 72

H

Harris Church 165
Hawaii 159, 160
Helwys, Thomas 124
Henry Martyn 160
Henry VIII 73, 75, 114, 117
Hermits 59–62, 74, 160
Herrnhut 131
Hijira 92
Hofmann, Melchior 125–26
Holiness movement 133, 138, 140–43
Holy Club 132
Holy Ghost Fathers 158
Holy Land 28, 48, 53, 72, 95, 98, 99
Holy Roman Empire 52, 101, 113
house church movement 167
Huguenots 111–12
Humanae Vitae 152

Humanism 30, 56–57, 73, 103–104, 106, 110
Hus, Jan 105
Hussites 105, 113, 114
Hymn 20, 87, 107, 133–36

I

Icons 30, 79–80
Ignatius of Antioch 38
Ignatius Loyola 74, 120–22, 155
India 14, 71, 120, 131, 136, 138, 153, 155, 157, 160–62, 167, 169, 170
Indulgences 95, 101, 104, 105, 106
Iona 64, 66, 77
Irenaeus of Lyons 25, 38, 44
Irish monasticism 64
Irving, Edward 141
Isaiah 9, 21
Islam 50, 74, 79, 92–94, 97, 98, 100, 158, 167

J

James 23, 26, 49, 58, 81
James I 30, 114, 115, 117
Jamnia 21
Japan 84, 120, 122, 158
Jerome 26, 28–29, 34, 40, 46
Jerusalem 8–13, 16, 19, 39, 48, 58, 72, 79, 81, 84, 92, 93, 95–98, 125
Jesus of Nazareth 8–25, 34, 37–38, 48–49, 52, 58, 77, 79, 81, 92, 94, 108, 120, 123, 126, 148, 150, 160, 167–69
Jihad 91, 98
Jizya 94
John 11, 14, 22, 23, 24, 25–26, 28, 49, 54, 91
John Mark 11–12, 14, 22, 24, 25, 28
John of the Cross 74, 121
John the Baptist 58, 80
John the Divine 14
Joseph of Volokolamsk 87
Justin Martyr 16, 38, 39
Justinian I 46, 47, 78, 134

K

Kempis, Thomas à 73, 74
Keswick 'Higher Life' movement 141
Kimbanguist Church 165
kingdom of God 9, 33, 80, 124, 162
Knights Hospitallers 72
Knights Templar 72
Knox, John 110

L

La Grande Chartreuse 68–69
Lake, John Graham 144–45
Lasco, John (Jan) à 113
Latin America 21, 147, 158, 164, 167
Laubach, Frank 162
Lectionary 49
Leiden, Jan van 126
Lent 48–49, 83
Leo the Great 46
Letter to the Romans 14, 22, 24, 132
Lindisfarne 64, 66
liturgical year 48–49, 81
Livingstone, David 158, 160
Lord's Supper 15, 108, 126
Louis XIV 112
Louvain Bible 30–31
Luke 10, 14, 22, 24, 25, 28
Luther Bible 30, 34, 106
Luther, Martin 30, 35, 42, 49, 101, 104–108, 110, 117, 118, 123, 129, 134
Lutheran Church-Missouri Synod 133
Lutheran World Federation 169
Lutherans 49, 108–110, 129, 131, 133

M

Magnus, Albertus 53
Manichaeanism 42
Marcion 24, 38, 58
Marcionism 38
Marcus Aurelius 15
Mark 11, 12, 14, 22, 24, 25
Martel, Charles 93

Martin of Tours 62
Martyrdom 15, 28, 49, 58, 59, 126
martyrs' relics 17
Marxism 150
Mary I 116
Mass 21, 54, 72, 76
Matthew 21, 22, 24, 25, 28, 44, 60, 70
McGavran, Donald 161–62
Mecca 8, 79, 91–92, 93
Medina 92, 93
Melanchthon, Philipp 109, 129
Mennonites 89, 124, 126–28
Methodism 49, 124, 125, 129, 132–45, 158, 159, 160, 166, 170
Methodist Episcopal Church 137, 138, 140, 143, 144
Methodius 31, 67, 84
Metropolitan Alexis 87
Mission to Lepers 161
Missioners of Charity 77
Monastery of the Holy Trinity 87
Monasticism 29, 58–77, 87, 88–90, 115, 148, 151
Monophysites 41, 79, 94
Montanism 23, 38, 58
Monte Cassino 62
Moravians 131–33, 135
More, Sir Thomas 104, 116
Mother Teresa 77, 153
Mott, John R. 161, 169
Mozambique 156
Muhammad 79, 91–92, 93
Münster 113, 125–26
Münzer, Thomas 108, 123
Music 20–21, 134–35, 139, 144
Mysticism 74, 121, 124

N

Neo-Platonism 74
Nero 13, 15
Nestorian church 94
Nestorius 41
New England 125, 136–38

New Zealand 159–60
Newman, John Henry 21, 33, 115, 151
Nicene Creed 41, 79–80
Nikon (Patriarch) 87
Nilus of Sora 87
Ninety-five Theses 49, 101, 105, 106
Non-Possessors 87
North Africa 16, 39, 42–43, 46, 71, 93–94, 158, 160–61, 164

O

Oceania 159, 168–69
Old Believers 87, 89
Oratorios 21
Oratory of Divine Love 118
Origen 17, 24, 26, 27–29, 39, 74, 94
Orthodox 11, 24, 42, 48, 66, 78–90, 96, 99, 113, 131, 167, 169–70
Otto I 51–52
Ottoman Turks 100, 103, 109
Oxford Movement 115
Oxyrhynchus Hymn 134
Ozman, Agnes 143

P

Pacem in Terris 152
Pachomius 61, 62
Palamas, Gregory 74
Papal States 55, 113, 149, 150, 151
Parham, Charles 143, 144
Passover 9, 10, 48
Patmos 14
Patrick 64
Paul of Tarsus 11–14, 16, 17, 20, 22, 23, 25, 42, 44, 81, 83, 94, 155
Pax Romana 8
Peasants' War 108, 123, 124
Pentateuch 19–20
Pentecost 10, 48, 49, 81, 83, 143, 146
Pentecostalism 140–47
Persia 15, 92, 160
Peter 10–11, 14, 16–17,

25–26, 44–46, 50, 52, 56, 81, 83, 105, 153
Pharisees 9, 11, 13
Philip 11
Philip II Augustus 98
Philippines 156, 159, 162, 168
Photius (Patriarch) 79, 84
Pia Desideria 129–30
Picpus Fathers 160
Pietism 74, 129–33, 136, 156
Pilgrim Fathers 124
Pilgrims 10–11, 48, 72, 73, 91, 95, 98, 99, 124–25
Poland 113, 120, 164
Pole, Reginald 116–17
Polycarp of Smyrna 15–16
Pontius Pilate 9
Poor Clares 71, 77, 160
Pope Alexander VI 56–57
Pope Benedict XIV 148
Pope Benedict XVI 154
Pope Boniface VIII 55
Pope Clement XIV 148
Pope Damasus 28
Pope Gregory I 47
Pope Gregory VII 52
Pope Innocent III 52–54, 99
Pope John Paul II 90, 152, 154
Pope John XXIII 56, 105, 151–52, 169, 170
Pope Leo X 57, 105–106, 114
Pope Nicholas V 56
Pope Pius VII 149
Pope Pius X 33, 151
Pope Pius XI 151
Pope Pius XII 151
Pope Sylvester I 45
Pope Urban II 95
Possessors 87
Predestination 42, 43, 109, 110
Presbyterians 49, 114, 115, 117, 124–25, 129, 136, 140–41, 160, 166, 170
Prussia 132–33
Puritans 114, 117, 124–25

Q

Qumran 35, 58

R

Radical Reformation 121–27
Railton, George Scott 139
Reductions 122
Reformation 29, 30, 57, 71, 73, 75, 101–128, 148, 155, 169
Rerum Novarum 151
Revelation 14, 23, 25, 26, 33, 35
Ricci, Matteo 120, 122, 155
Richard I, Lionheart 98
Roman Empire 8–11, 14–23, 29, 39, 42, 45–46, 52, 78–79, 101, 113
Rome 10, 13–17, 20, 22, 24, 25, 26, 38, 41, 42, 44–57, 62, 64, 66, 76, 78–79, 86, 97, 100–101, 105, 106, 108, 113, 114–15, 118–20, 148–55
Rule of Benedict 62–64, 68
Russian Orthodox Church 84–90, 169

S

Saint Callixtus, Church of 17
Saladin 98–99
Salvation 23, 43, 53, 83, 106, 108, 124, 126, 132, 139
Salvation Army 135, 139–40
Schleiermacher, Friedrich 32
Schmalkaldic League 110
Schütz, Roger 21, 77
Scopes, John T. 33–34
Scopes monkey trial 33–34
Scottish Episcopal Church 114–15
Seabury, Samuel 115
Second Great Awakening 138, 156
Second Vatican Council 84, 152, 169
Secularism 15, 55, 88, 130–32, 149
Separatists 124, 127, 143

Septuagint 27–29
Serampore 156
Sergius of Radonezh 87, 89
Servetus, Michael 109, 127
Seventh-day Adventists 167
Seymour, William J. 143
Shaftesbury, Lord 136
Shepherd of Hermas 23, 26
Silas 12
Simons, Menno 126
Smyth, John 124
Society for the Promotion of Christian Knowledge (SPCK) 156
Society for the Propagation of the Gospel in Foreign Parts 156
Society of Jesus 120, 148, 149
South Africa 131, 145–46, 164–65, 166
South Korea 141, 146, 158, 168
Spanish Inquisition 75
Spener, Philipp Jakob 129
Spiritual Exercises 120
Spurgeon, C. H. 124
St Catherine's Monastery 26, 35, 61
St Fulda 66
St Peter's 45, 51, 105
Stephen 11, 49
Strauss, David Friedrich 33
Studd, C. T. 161
Student Volunteer Movement 158, 161, 169
Stylites, Simeon 60–61
Suleiman the Magnificent 97, 100
Summa Theologiae 53, 72
Syllabus of Errors 150
Synod of Robbers 41
Synod of Whitby 48, 50
Synoptic Gospels 22 *see also* individual gospel writers

T

Taizé 77
Tarsus 11, 13, 155

Taylor, James Hudson 158, 161
Temple Mount 97
Teresa of Avila 74, 75, 121
Tertullian 14, 18, 25, 39, 43
Tetzel, Johannes 106
Thaddaeus 15
The Institutes of the Christian Religion (Calvin) 110
Theodosius 18
Theotokos 79, 81
Third Great Awakening 138, 156
third race 36
Third Reich 34
Third Rome 86
Thirty Years' War 111
Thomas 14, 24
Tikhon (Patriarch) 89
Timothy 12, 22, 25
Tiridates 17
Tischendorf, Konstantin 26, 35
Tonga 141, 159, 168
Tongues *see glossolalia*
Toronto Blessing 147
Townsend, Cameron 161–62
Treaty of Nanking 157
Trinity 39–43, 72, 80, 87, 109
Tyndale, William 30, 116

U

Umar 92–94, 97
Umayyad dynasty 92–94
Unitarians 114, 127
United Methodist Church 135, 140
Uniting Church 49, 140
University of Halle 131

V

Valerian 17
Vatican 26, 90, 149–51, 163
Vatican Council 84, 150, 152, 154, 169
via media 117
Vietnam 167–68
Vincent de Paul 75

Vingren, Gunnar 144
Virgin Mary 9, 10, 49, 50, 79–81, 150
Visigoths 46–48
Vladimir I of Kiev 84–86
Voltaire 130
Voronaev, Ivan 145
Vulgate 29–30, 34–35

W

Waldensians 123
'Way, the' 11, 12, 36
Waldo, Peter 123
Wesley, Charles 132–34
Wesley, John 132–34, 141
Western Samoa 159
White Fathers 158
Whitefield, George 132–33, 136–37
Wilberforce, William 136
Wittenberg 30, 101, 106–108, 113, 123
World Council of Churches 169–70
World Missionary Conference 161, 169
World War II 34, 62, 72, 89, 115, 139, 151, 163–64, 169
Worldwide Evangelization Crusade 161
Worship 8, 10–11, 13, 20, 36, 49, 61, 63, 67, 78–80, 83, 91–92, 101, 112, 114–15, 117, 134–35, 140, 144
Wycliffe Bible Translators 162
Wycliffe, John 104–105, 123

X

Xavier, Francis 120, 122, 155, 156, 157

Y

Young Men's Christian Association 169

Z

Zion Christian Church 145
Zinzendorf, Count Ludwig von 131
Zurich 108, 113, 123
Zwingli, Huldrych (Ulrich) 108, 123, 126

Picture acknowledgments

Picture research by Zooid Pictures Ltd and Lion Hudson plc.

p. 2 David Reed/Alamy; p. 4 Keith Bedford/Reuters/ Corbis UK Ltd; p. 10 British Library/AKG; p. 12 Araldo de Luca/Corbis UK Ltd; p. 14 Walters Art Museum, Baltimore, USA/Bridgeman Art Library; p. 18 Ron Sanford/Corbis UK Ltd; p. 19 Hanan Isachar/ Holylandimages.com; p. 24 Zev Radovan, Jerusalem; p. 27 British Museum; pp. 28–29 Sandro Vannini/Corbis UK Ltd; p. 31 Annebicque Bernard/Corbis Sygma; p. 32 Visual Arts Library (London)/Alamy; p. 37 Lion Hudson; p. 40 Rabatti – Dominige/AKG; p. 42 Visual Arts Library (London)/Alamy; p. 45 Elio Ciol/Corbis UK Ltd; p. 47 Archivo Iconografico, S.A./Corbis UK Ltd (top); p. 47 Ali Meyer/Corbis UK Ltd (bottom); p. 51 Krause Johansen/Archivio Iconografico, Sa/Corbis UK Ltd; p. 52 Visual Arts Library (London)/Alamy; p. 54 Sandro Vannini/Corbis Uk Ltd; p. 55 Werner Dieterich/Getty Images; p. 56 TopFoto; p. 59 Joseph Martin/AKG; p. 63 Musee Conde, Chantilly, France/Bridgeman Art Library; p. 64 David Ball/Alamy; p. 65 AKG; p. 69 Visual Arts Library (London)/Alamy; p. 70 AKG; p. 71 Fabian Cevallos/Sygma/Corbis UK Ltd; p. 75 POPPERFOTO/ Alamy; p. 80 AKG; p. 82 Visual Arts Library (London)/Alamy; p. 85 Erich Lessing/AKG; p. 86 Robert Harding Picture Library Ltd/Alamy; p. 88 RIA Novosti/ RIA-Novosti; p. 89 TopFoto; p. 91 Kazuyoshi Nomachi/ Corbis UK Ltd; p. 95 Archivo Iconografico, S.A./Corbis UK Ltd; p. 96 Sonia Halliday Photographs; p. 97 Hanan Isachar/Holylandimages.com; p. 99 Pharaonic Village Cairo/Dagli Orti/Art Archive; p. 102 TopFoto; p. 103 Visual Arts Library (London)/Alamy; p. 104 Bradford Art Galleries and Museums, West Yorskshire, UK/Bridgeman Art Library; p. 106 Bettmann/Corbis UK Ltd; p. 107 Visual Arts Library (London)/Alamy; p. 109 AKG; p. 111 University Library Geneva/Dagli Orti/Art Archive; p. 112 University Library Geneva/Dagli Orti/Art Archive; p. 116 Visual Arts Library (London)/Alamy; p. 119 AKG; p. 121 Visual Arts Library (London)/Alamy; p. 122 The Trustees of the Chester Beatty Library, Dublin; p. 125 Collection of the New York Historical Society, USA/Bridgeman Art Library; p. 126 AKG; p. 129 Interfoto Pressebildagentur/Alamy; p. 130 Visual Arts Library (London)/Alamy; p. 131 The Print Collector/Alamy; p. 132 Private Collection/Bridgeman Art Library; p. 133 National Portrait Gallery, London, UK/Bridgeman Art Library; p. 137 Mary Evans Picture Library/Alamy; p. 139 Fine Art Photographic Library/Corbis UK Ltd; p. 142 Visual Arts Library (London)/Alamy; p. 145 Getty Images; p. 146 Ray Chiang; p. 151 Mary Evans Picture Library/Alamy; p. 152 Erich Lessing/AKG; p. 153 Baldev/Corbis UK Ltd; p. 156 AKG; p. 157 Bettmann/Corbis UK Ltd; p. 159 Christine Osborne/Corbis Uk Ltd; p. 163 Hulton Archive/Getty Images; p. 163 Mary Evans Picture Library/Mary Evans Picture Library (top); p. 165 Associated Press/PA Photos(bottom); p. 167 Bettmann/Corbis UK Ltd; p. 168 Rex Features.